INTERNATIONAL DEVELOPMENT AND HUMAN AID

This series publishes ground-breaking work on key topics in the area of global justice and human rights including democracy, gender, poverty, the environment, and just war. Books in the series are of broad interest to theorists working in politics, international relations, philosophy, and related disciplines.

Studies in Global Justice and Human Rights
Series Editor: Thom Brooks

www.euppublishing.com/series/sgjhr

INTERNATIONAL DEVELOPMENT AND HUMAN AID

PRINCIPLES, NORMS AND INSTITUTIONS FOR THE GLOBAL SPHERE

Edited by Paulo Barcelos and
Gabriele De Angelis

EDINBURGH
University Press

Edinburgh University Press is one of the leading university presses in the UK. We publish academic books and journals in our selected subject areas across the humanities and social sciences, combining cutting-edge scholarship with high editorial and production values to produce academic works of lasting importance. For more information visit our website: www.edinburghuniversitypress.com

Edinburgh University Press Ltd
The Tun – Holyrood Road
12(2f) Jackson's Entry
Edinburgh EH8 8PJ

Typeset in 11/13 Sabon by
Servis Filmsetting Ltd, Stockport, Cheshire

A CIP record for this book is available from the British Library

ISBN 978 1 4744 1447 0 (hardback)
ISBN 978 1 4744 1448 7 (webready PDF)
ISBN 978 1 4744 1449 4 (epub)

CONTENTS

Part III   Justice and International Institutions

CONTRIBUTORS

Gabriele De Angelis, Instituto de Filosofia da Nova, Universidade Nova de Lisboa

Paulo Barcelos, Instituto de Filosofia da Nova, Universidade Nova de Lisboa

Alexander Brown, University of East Anglia

Julian Culp, University of Frankfurt

George F. DeMartino, University of Denver

Nicole Hassoun, Binghamton University

Sylvie Loriaux, Université Laval

Jonathan D. Moyer, University of Denver

Philippe Van Parijs, Université de Louvain

Peter G. N. West-Oram, Christian-Albrechts-Universität zu Kiel

ACKNOWLEDGEMENTS

This book collects the extended versions of some of the papers that were presented at the 2nd Lisbon Conference on Global Justice (2011). Further contributions were invited. The editors would like to thank the participants in the conference and all their colleagues at the Nova Institute of Philosophy who made the event possible. We also thank the Portuguese Foundation for Science and Technology for supporting the conference as well as our research in global justice.

We are indebted to Thom Brooks, the editor of the series in which this book is being published, for encouraging our proposal. His useful critical remarks helped us to improve the collection consistently. We also would like to thank three anonymous reviewers for their constructive comments and criticisms. Last, not least, this book was also made possible by the patient and expedient help of Edinburgh University Press's editorial team. Our special thanks go to Jenny Daly, Michelle Houston and Ersev Ersoy.

Chapter 1

JUSTICE IN A COMPLEX WORLD: AN INTRODUCTION[1]

Paulo Barcelos

Da nossa própria fome – respondeu o Padre de Varzim – podemos dizer que é um problema material e prático. A fome dos outros é um problema moral.

[Of our own hunger – answered the Priest of Varzim – we can say it is a material and practical problem. The hunger of others is a moral problem.]

Sophia de Mello Breyner Andresen, *O Jantar do Bispo*

Tortilla prices are high these days in Guatemala. They have doubled in the last three years, as a reaction to the steep rise in the prices of corn that the country needs to import to meet internal consumption. The explanation for the price fluctuation works as a fable of the effects of globalisation and the interconnectedness of markets on the poor segments of the world population, especially in countries which are more vulnerable to the changing patterns of world economy and the actions of its leading agents.

Guatemala, in fact, suffered twice the pressures of globalisation related to corn. At one time the country was nearly self-sufficient in its production of the cereal. In the 1990s, however, its producers were no longer able to compete with the exports of American corn, whose production was subsidised by the US government. The result was a production drop of over 30 per cent over the span of a decade. In recent years however, the availability of cheap corn imports has been dramatically reduced, mainly due to changes to agricultural and economic policy in the Western affluent countries on the use of corn and other food crops. To illustrate, recent laws in the United States and Europe,

1

driven by the ecological imperative of progressively reducing carbon dioxide emissions to the atmosphere, mandated an increase in the supply of greener propellants such as biofuel, to be blended with the regular vehicle fuel supplies. Approximately 40 per cent of American corn production is now directed towards the production of biofuels.[2]

Emphasis on the use of corn for biofuel production in wealthy countries has led to two significant consequences for Guatemala. First, a reduction in availability of foreign corn has meant that import prices have risen dramatically, with a similar rise in prices also affecting sugar-cane imports. Second, biofuel producers in wealthy countries have sought to minimise production costs by shifting the production of raw materials (corn, sugarcane and palm oil) to poorer countries, where production costs are lower. Guatemala is an ideal location for cheap agricultural production of these raw materials. Consequently, a very significant share of the Guatemalan land formerly used for agriculture, previously leased to subsistence farmers, is now being employed to extensively cultivate these raw materials. Needless to say, Guatemala exports the vast majority of the biofuel raw materials it produces, which are transformed elsewhere, and consumes extremely small quantities of this greener propellant.

The majority of families in Guatemala spend over two thirds of their income on food. In light of this, it is unsurprising that there is a link between the trends noted above and the perpetuation of children's malnutrition and stunting rate in Guatemala. According to the World Food Programme, it is the highest in Latin America and the Caribbean, and is especially prevalent in rural areas and among indigenous populations.

The Guatemalan narrative not only exemplifies the pervasive, and potentially highly damaging, effects of an increasingly globalised world economy, it also highlights the pattern of inequity characteristic of the global order, and can be used to call for a moral response. In fact, this is the type of story often used by the proponents of global distributive justice to empirically sustain their contentions. It serves to illustrate the following reasoning: if the living conditions and the welfare opportunities of citizens have ceased to be determined primarily by the shape of the internal institutions and practices of the state but are dependent to a large extent on a number of international or transnational actors, institutions and practices, then the very concept of moral community must be rethought. If the relations of mutual interference, cooperation and coercion that establish a given population and institutional unit as a 'basic structure'[3] have expanded in such a way that they engulf the entire globe, then there are no material reasons disallowing the necessary supranational extension of the net of protection and assistance that is usually considered as valid for the domestic sphere. This was the thesis presented by Charles Beitz in his seminal work, *Political Theory and International Relations*:

> [I]f evidence of global economic and political interdependence shows the existence of a global scheme of social cooperation, we should not view national boundaries as having fundamental moral significance. Since boundaries are not coextensive with the scope of social cooperation, they do not mark the limits of social obligations. (Beitz 1979: 151)

JUSTICE: IF NATIONAL, WHY NOT GLOBAL?

As articulated by Beitz, reasoning in terms of global justice – which, we might say, had its first explicit contemporary affirmation in the work just quoted – has as its starting premise the mistrust of the overlap, undisputed throughout modernity, between the political form of the nation-state and the idea of the 'moral community' to which a given citizen belongs. Theorising about global justice starts, therefore, by questioning the symbolic role classically attributed to national borders as not only physical and administrative circumscriptions but also frontiers demarcating the contours of the groups of people that are included and excluded from a scheme of distributive justice, that is, from a system of rules and institutions designed to regulate the distribution of the benefits and burdens originated from social cooperation between the individuals that compose a given community's *basic structure*.[4]

Many global justice theorists have specifically departed from a particular conception of distributive justice, a particular way of designing criteria to judge the moral validity of existing distributive schemes and of modelling ideal ones: liberal egalitarianism.[5] They start by identifying a paradox at the heart not only of that conception of justice but of the liberal creed in general. First, one of liberalism's foundational assertions is the moral equality of each person – with the accompanying assignation of a uniform and universal sphere of inalienable rights to everyone – derived from the simple fact of each person's humanity.

As Rawls has emphasised in *A Theory of Justice*, no morally arbitrary features of a certain individual, acquired through genetic inheritance (or, in Rawls's words, 'natural lottery'), may be established as reasons determining a differential distribution of the 'social primary goods'. That is, characteristics such as one's sex, race, social class, or even natural talents cannot be factors diminishing the possibilities of a certain segment of a society's population of acceding in equitable terms to basic rights, liberties and economic freedoms, income and wealth, public offices, or the 'social bases of self-respect' (Rawls [1971] 1999a: 15, 74–5, 311; 2001: 58–9).[6]

Paradoxically however, the validity of this basic assertion has seemed to be confined to the limits of domestic societies. While themes such as the stability of the international system, rules of conduct between states and the conditions for just wars were prevalent topics of modern thought on the morality of international relations, until the second half of the twentieth century there were no influential accounts concerning principles of economic justice between states, or between peoples of different citizenships and nationalities. That is, liberal theories of justice have tended not to consider the scope of social and economic justice obligations as extending to the entire universe of 'moral persons'. This category of 'moral persons' would comprise, to use again a concept of the Rawlsian lexicon, all those who possess the two 'moral powers': first, the ability to form and revise an individual *conception of the good*; second, the capacity for a *sense of justice*, that is, to follow reasonable precepts of justice and abide by fair terms of cooperation ruling inter-individual life (Rawls [1993] 2005: 19–20).

Were liberal theories of justice to adopt this, or a similar, conception of moral person to its fullest extent, proponents of such theories would have to acknowledge the totality of the world's population as the focus of the precepts of justice. That would seem the natural corollary of the second half of the expression *liberal egalitarianism*. Nevertheless, if we consider what Rawls has written about international justice before he published *The Law of Peoples* (1999b), we can observe that he has asserted early on that the problem of justice between nations was to be treated separately from the topic of justice for a domestic society. First of all, for him, the construction of a conception of justice must depart from the assumption of the basic structure of a society as a 'closed background system', that is, as a self-sufficient and self-contained system without communication with other societies and whose members 'enter it only by birth and leave it only by death' (Rawls [1993] 2005: 12, 272). For Rawls, the question of international justice is secondary to that of domestic justice, considered only after the conception of justice for a domestic society is formulated in its entirety.

However, Rawls's secondary treatment of international justice is not merely sequential, but also substantive, and indicative of the asymmetry between his views of the domestic and international spheres – there is no natural and unmediated extension of the principles of the domestic sphere to that of international or global justice; they are constituted as two very distinct moral universes. Even if the procedure of construction designed to attain those principles is analogous in both spheres, Rawls does not contend that the representatives of different nation-states would choose the same ground rules as representatives of a sole nation determining how to govern the internal life of their state. In *A Theory of Justice* Rawls contends that the principles arrived at for international justice would be the 'familiar ones', those that were inscribed in the classic modern codes of international law, while there is no mention of the 'difference principle' (Rawls [1971] 1999a: 331–3).[7]

In *The Law of Peoples* this dichotomy is clarified. Rawls argues that the difference principle may indeed be selected to apply to the basic structure of each domestic state individually, but not to evaluate the global scheme of trade, income and wealth. In this way, Rawls's principle of economic justice for the international sphere is not directed at an evaluation and correction of the global norms, practices and institutions shaping trade relations among countries, or the world distribution of income. Instead, it focuses only on the assistance of those persons that, for reasons of economic frailty, are unable to achieve the institutional conditions allowing their regime to join the club of those meeting the threshold of *decency*.[8] The economic assistance ceases once that desideratum has been attained – that constitutes its *cut-off point*.

The paradox alluded some paragraphs ago now becomes explicit. What is paradoxical about liberal egalitarianism is the fact that this theory of justice, devoted to the elimination of those arbitrary discrepancies among individuals which perpetuate asymmetric access to social goods, is also anchored on statist principles of domestic justice that perpetuate those same discrepancies. If features like race and gender are deemed morally irrelevant in determining one's desert, it is unclear why seemingly irrelevant factors, like nationality or place of birth, should be given any serious consideration in deciding on questions of justice. Nationality, as Pogge claims, would be 'just one further deep contingency (like genetic endowment, race, gender, and social class), one more potential basis of institutional inequalities that are inescapable and present from birth' (Pogge 1989: 247). Indeed, in our highly unequal world, one's place of birth can be highly determinative of not only one's ability to formulate a viable plan of life but even one's very prospect of survival.

To illustrate, according to the most recent United Nations *Report on the World Social Situation*, while global income inequality has been reduced since the year 2000, international inequality still remains very high. According to the report:

> In 2010, high-income countries – that accounted for only 16 per cent of the world's population – were estimated to generate 55 per cent of global income. Low-income countries created just above one per cent of global income even though they contained 72 per cent of global population. (UNDESA 2013: 25)

The empirical conclusion to be extracted from these data is the same arrived at by global egalitarians: 'the country where a person was born, or where they live, is an important determinant of their expected income, given the enduring, large disparities in national income per capita' (ibid.: 27).

Based on similar findings, Joseph Carens argued that the effects of the modern notion of citizenship are analogous to the impacts of feudal-era social stratification and its notions of individual status, and social standing could be equated with the status of the individual and the social stratification in the feudal era. Then as now, each person's social role, status, prospects and entitlements were strictly determined by their circumstances of birth. In Carens's words,

> To be born a citizen of an affluent country like Canada is like being born into the nobility (even though many belong to the lesser nobility). To be born a citizen of a poor country like Bangladesh is (for most) like being born into the peasantry in the Middle Ages. (Carens 1992: 26)

To summarise, defenders of global liberal conceptions of justice employ two types of argument to justify the inclusion of all persons worldwide within the web of normative ties between persons that create duties of moral assistance. First, global obligations and the ideal of a human moral community are grounded in institutional considerations – the arbitrariness of state borders and of the place where one is born, and the factual existence of commercial norms, practices and institutions interconnecting the world and having a pervasive impact on the lives of everyone from A to Z, from Afghanistan to Zimbabwe. The nexus between one's welfare and the other's misery that characterises the existence of a social basic structure also exists at the global level – national autarchy is a vanished Westphalian belief.

Second, the existence of a global moral community may be defended not just via examination of the empirical conditions of globalisation, but also from an ontological analysis of the bonds uniting humans qua humans. As we have seen, all persons, by the fact of their humanity, possess the two moral powers that make them worthy of respect and protection.[9] Everyone, irrespective of his or her national origin or their sharing with others a structure of global rules and institutions, has the capacity to abide by fair terms of cooperation with others and the capacity to pursue and revise a plan of life. Every human inhabitant of this world, then, notwithstanding the cultural instantiations through which he or she materializes and to which he or she gives expression, shares not only these morally relevant properties but the needs and capacities (or *capabilities*) associated with the moral powers (Beitz 1983: 595; Caney 2005: 36–7).

To find these universal human traits, according to Martha Nussbaum, one just has to ask the *Aristotelian question*: 'What activities characteristically performed by human beings are so central that they seem definitive of the life that is truly human?' Her answer is a list of basic capabilities. These comprise human goods such as *life* (being able to live the expected human life); *bodily health and integrity* (comprising health, nourishment, shelter, freedom of movement, sex and reproduction); *senses, imagination and thought* (the capabilities to develop and express freely the capacities for reasoning and imagination); *emotions* (opportunities to create bonds with people and things); *practical reason* (being able to form and revise a life plan and a conception of the good); *affiliation* (engaging in social interaction under the aegis of friendship and respect); caring for other *species*; being able to *play*; and the capacity to have *control over one's environment*, in terms of both 'political' participation and 'material' ability to have access to social goods (Nussbaum 1999: 41–2).

COSMOPOLITANISM: OLD, NEW AND NEWEST

Based on these two grounds of justifications globalist authors defend a universalist moral system. More specifically, they advocate for the need to extend the 'appeal to universal principles that are to hold for all lives and across all situations' (O'Neill 1996: 11) to the sphere of social and economic inequalities worldwide. In doing so, these theorists engineer an encounter between cosmopolitanism, which might be succinctly described as the claim that the existence of moral principles holding for all individuals, irrespective of their contingent specificities, derives from an ideal of individual ethical identity whose 'primary allegiance is to the community of human beings in the entire world' (Nussbaum 1994), and one of the major spheres of application of duties of assistance – social justice. This was not originally an obvious association, since, from its classical original, and throughout modernity, cosmopolitan thought was disconnected from considerations of economic justice.

In the Greek world, philosophers such as Diogenes and Zeno employed the idea of a *kosmopolis* to criticise conventional morality and the positivist legal systems of political units from the perspective of a world community, guided by the precepts implicit in nature. 'The only true commonwealth was [. . .] that which is as wide as the universe', claimed Diogenes of Sinope (Diogenes Laertius 1995: 72). He did not mean by that, however, the necessity of forging a global polis, or any other explicitly political proposal. For the Greek Cynicism and Stoicism, the *kosmopolis* corresponded more to a mental sphere than to a territorial space, more to a set of immutable principles to be followed by the virtuous – the true *citizens of the world* – in their conduct and assessment of man-made institutions than to the keystone holding a desirable world state (see, for this and the next paragraph, Douzinas 2007; Long 2008; Brown 2006).

Roman thinkers such as Cicero have also united the idea of the onto-logical sameness of every individual as endowed with rationality to the political prospect of making all communities obey the single *recta ratio*, the eternal and unchanging natural law. '[T]here will not be different laws at Rome and at Athens, or different laws now and in the future, but one eternal and unchangeable law will be valid for all nations and all times [. . .].' This assertion by Cicero (*De re publica*, III, 33) backed the project of submitting the domestic law of every city to a first order international legal system (the *ius gentium*), which in turn would be the positivation of that universal *ius naturale*, authored by God.[10]

Even here, nonetheless, the ideal conception of the world as a kind of civil union is dissociated from explicit references to matters of economic assistance and redistribution among peoples. The same happened throughout modernity. This conspicuous absence is noted, to take another illustrious example, in the writings of Kant on perpetual peace and cosmopolitan universal history.

Kant had the crucial role of giving a political shape to the ideal of *citizen of the world*. He achieved it by, first, integrating the creation of a *ius cosmopoliticum* between states as a final stage of the predetermined and cumulative process of historical progression of societies from the anarchic plan of the *state of nature* to the establishment of a *perfect civil constitution*. Men are naturally led to fulfil their human essence, to transpose all the steps mediating between animality and rationality, in a cumulative process that can only be undertaken collectively, through the – mostly unconscious – work of generations. That is the 'hidden plan of nature': to bring about, both in the domestic and international spheres, a system of rule of law in which individuals' conduct is framed by a set of external norms enhancing human agency and autonomy (Kant [1784] 1991: 50–1).

Kant backed his teleological vision of history and human progress by devising an ideal of institutional and juridical structure that could accomplish the notion of world citizenship. On the one hand, he anchored his project of *perpetual peace* in a federal contract among peoples, which was itself intended as the basis for the subsequent pacification of the globe. In response to the assumed impossibility of an integral transfer of sovereignty from the existing states to a world government, Kant proposed the *negative substitute* of a voluntary league of (republican) states. This voluntary league was proposed as being even more robust than a classic international pact since it sought to end not merely a particular hostility but, instead, the very possibility of the use of armed conflict to settle disputes between states (Kant [1795] 1996). For Kant, this *foedus pacificum* would be the achievement of History's cosmopolitan purpose, that of constituting 'a civil society which can administer justice universally' (Kant [1784] 1991: 45).

Kant's cosmopolitanism has not just an institutional facet but also a juridical one. To the two traditional areas – civil and international – of public law Kant adds the creation of a layer of protection of citizens' fundamental rights transcending the nation-state. *Cosmopolitan law* indicates citizens as the prime units of moral concern and juridical protection, creating the idea of a universal moral community whose subjects are every human individual and not the communities that subsume them.

Despite this, Kant's cosmopolitanism does not contemplate, in its institutional or juridical aspects, a preoccupation with economic justice beyond national borders. As noted above, this is a common trait of modern cosmopolitanisms, from approaches such as Grotius's norms-based conception of international society or Erasmus's Christian pacifism, to Anacharsis Cloots's robust model of world state or 'universal republic'. Similarly, modern natural law theories of international morality revolve around the cessation of war, or political unification, rather than global redistribution of individual welfare or social goods. They justify schemes of universal protection of citizens' political rights, and rarely comment specifically on economic rights. In the case of Kant, the cosmopolitan morality is restricted to the 'conditions of universal hospitality', that is, the right of everyone to freedom of movement and to be treated fairly in any foreign territory in which one travels. He does not, however, acknowledge a universal right of permanent migration (Kant [1795] 1996: 328–31).

While economic justice has not typically been considered in international distributive justice theory historically, there is one sentence in 'Toward Perpetual Peace' that could be employed by contemporary defenders of principles of global economic justice as justification for the global reach of what was traditionally confined to the domestic sphere. Towards the end of the paragraphs clarifying the 'Third Definitive Article for Perpetual Peace', Kant writes:

> Since the (narrower or wider) community of the nations of the earth has now gone so far that a violation of right on *one* place of the earth is felt in *all*, the idea of a cosmopolitan right is no fantastic and exaggerated way of representing right. (Kant [1795] 1996: 330)

This affirmation suggests that there are in fact moral consequences which should be extracted from empirical factors of the globalised world. Given that the globe is increasingly unified and interconnected, it can be argued that a violation of a right in a given place not only echoes around the world, but may even be produced or supported by the consequences of the interconnection of all political and economic systems, as is often the case in violations of social and economic human rights. Consequently, it can be argued that this has to lead to the extension of moral principles, originally designed to frame the lives of people who live in close proximity to one another, to apply to all persons worldwide.

Indeed, as noted above, the two main concepts employed to justify the existence of global principles of economic justice depart from the moral repercussion of the conditions of proximity and connection among human beings. It might be ontological interconnectedness, in the case of authors defending cosmopolitan principles of distributive justice as being conceived in terms of human rights, that is, deriving from our common human nature and requiring the minimisation of the inequalities between subjects perpetuated by 'morally arbitrary characteristics' such as nationality and the place of birth (Jones 1999; Caney 2005). It may also be material interconnectedness, in the case of those defending a parallel between the existence of a *global basic structure* – of a global system of distribution of advantages and burdens derived from the existing norms, practices and structures giving shape to the mutual interdependence and coercion between peoples – and that of the need for global principles to assess the fairness of such institutions (Beitz 1979; Pogge 1989, 2002).[11]

From these two ideas evolved a multitude of global conceptions of justice. The role of this text is not to describe or assess them, but we note some among the most prominent. We have, first and foremost, the conception departing from a globalisation of Rawls's *justice as fairness* and of the procedure of justification – the *original position* – he employs to arrive at the principles of justice. Some authors defend that if that deliberative situation were replicated at the international level, the procedure would mirror the normative conclusions arrived at in the domestic stage of deliberation (Pogge 1989, 2002; Beitz 1979; Moellendorf 2002).

An alternative conception, departing from a 'humanity-centered' cosmopolitanism, derives from it a principle of *global equality of opportunity* allowing the implementation of Article 23(2) of the Universal Declaration of Human Rights – 'equal pay for equal work' – and the right to attain an equal number of positions of a commensurate standard of living (Caney 2001, 2005).

Peter Singer (1972), in an already classic article, departs from a utilitarian calculus to defend that a stringent obligation of international aid is derived from our general duty to help others in distressful situations (such as a child drowning in a pond), as long as we do not sacrifice anything of comparable importance.

The proponents of the 'capabilities approach' advance, first of all, the idea that the metric of justice must not be strictly monetary (or made out of Rawlsian *primary goods*), since what must be distributed is what makes possible to very different individuals with very different social, bodily and cognitive capacities to take advantage of the largest possible range of freedoms. A conception of social justice extended to the globe must, therefore, assure and maximise a bundle of human *capabilities*, of those functions – some examples of which were set out earlier in this text – common to every individual since they are definitive of a life that is truly human (Nussbaum 1999; Sen 1999).

There is also a group of conceptions, usually amalgamated in the catalogue of 'hybrid views', that do not necessarily choose one of the sides in the dichotomy opposing statism to cosmopolitanism, recognising instead the coexistence of multiple *grounds of justice* – which can range from the sharing of common humanity to the membership in a state or the subjection to the global rules of trade – corresponding to different levels of stringency of global principles of economic assistance. This is the position of Mathias Risse (2012), but many other authors, with the natural degree of variation, also develop pluralist accounts of the relation between domestic and global justice, arguing that the state is a paramount instrument for the realisation of global principles of justice (for instance, Valentini 2011; Ypi 2012).[12]

These modulations of cosmopolitanism are not, certainly, confined to theoretical explorations concerning the existence of duties of assistance binding each individual to (all) others. A significant amount of work in cosmopolitan theory focuses on applied questions pertaining to the development of operative principles to be applied to specific areas of moral and ethical consideration. There is now a growing body of literature dedicated to a number of important dilemmas originated from the current global institutional system and the way we face sovereignty and the relations among states. Classic among these problems, and the one that inaugurated this discipline of international moral theory, is the debate concerning the kind and amount of economic assistance that should be devoted to developing countries and the globally least well-off people. Correlatively, there is a significant literature on the extent of any changes that should be produced in the field of world trade, and in the relations between debtor and creditor countries in order to orient them towards an ideal of fairness (Pogge 2002; Moellendorf 2002). While this is, of course, an issue which receives a great deal of theoretical attention, there are many more examples.

To illustrate, a significant early question of global justice theorising focused on the implications of a cosmopolitan perspective on the rights of states to hold exclusive control over their borders, and to grant (or refuse) entry to non-citizens. Other noteworthy examples include debates concerning principles for the external policy of democratic states (what stance should they adopt in their relation towards non-liberal and non-democratic cultures?, what principles for legitimate humanitarian intervention should be followed?), environmental justice (who should be liable for the costs of climate change?, what should be the volume of compensation for inducing it?), global health (is the current regime of intellectual property rights fair?, should we establish principles directing pharmaceutical research to the needs of the poor populations?) or proposals to revise the global institutional scheme in terms either of specific sector reforms or of new models of multilevel and post-sovereign cosmopolitan democracy.[13]

VOLUME OVERVIEW

It could be argued that this growing body of literature is directly connected, in a reactive way, to the deepening of the globalisation process: as individuals and states become more intertwined and as the global connections become stronger and more numerous, more and more spheres of life and human activity fall inside the *global basic structure*. This kind of approach, which bridges the gap between the normative and the empirical arena, and between ideal and non-ideal theory, might plausibly be seen as the way forward for the study of global justice. It seems so not only in terms of philosophical depth but also in what concerns the possibility of dialogue with those that do not dwell in ivory towers, of engaging with public opinion and political actors. Consequently, it also enables theorists to effect real changes in public policies with a global reach. This dual focus on the empirical and the theoretical is central, I believe, to the chapters of this volume.

The authors' contributions reflect a double task. First, some assess the very plausibility of asserting conceptions of justice for the global sphere. As Rawls's rejection to globally extend his justice as fairness has shown, one of the main challenges that a conception of global justice needs to address pertains to the justification of a universalistic conception of rights and duties applied to a sphere characterised by a radical plurality of cultures and conceptions of the good. The challenge is to propose a conception of justice that is expected to have a transversal application without its being accused of ethnocentrism or parochialism. That challenge led Rawls to construe a very low threshold for the catalogue of human rights (Rawls 1999b: 64–8), much narrower in terms of protection of individual rights than the various declarations that integrate international law. This does not seem robust enough to be considered as a conception of global justice, as opposed to strict humanitarian assistance. The challenge for cosmopolitans is therefore to devise an axiological lingua franca that might legitimise a robust conception of global rights and obligations. The texts belonging to Part I of the book address these challenges.

The second and third parts of the book, which deal with empirical questions, explore the ramifications of theories of global justice in terms of their application to the political realm. The texts in Part II of the book investigate principles of global justice applied to some of the most pressing issues of public policy at the global level, such as humanitarian and development aid, health care assistance and reparations for historical injustices. The final set of chapters, in Part III, deals with the criteria of evaluating current international humanitarian schemes and international organisations, such as the United Nations Central Emergency Response Fund and the European Union as an avant-garde international regime.

The two chapters composing Part I address a basic problem in every account of global justice: the difficulty of extending the outlook and the scope of justice, *mutatis mutandis*, from the domestic to the global sphere. The purpose of Sylvie Loriaux's text is, particularly, to highlight the difficulty of this challenge and to point to the unsatisfactory character of two common modes of conceiving the universality of human rights.

Indeed, the profusion of human rights declarations over the years and the continuing definition of people's needs and liberties as having that kind of fundamentality did not necessarily lead to a more general acceptance of the transcultural validity of the contemporary human rights catalogue. The critiques of the historically and culturally contingent character of human rights – or, more specifically, of their Western parochialism – are well known. This is especially visible in those rights that are at the centre of the global justice debates. It does not seem, in fact, unreasonable to ask if rights such as that to 'periodic holidays with pay', to 'equal pay for equal work' or to 'the highest attainable standard of physical and mental health' have the same scope and level of stringency as the right to live or the rights not to be held as a slave and not to be subjected to torture, and if they are therefore justified to bind all states, irrespective of social structure and customs, to guaranteeing the enjoyment of such rights. This questioning seems especially relevant when the fulfilment of some economic, social and cultural rights presupposes the institutions and social practices that are present solely in some parts of the world. If we do not find fine-grained criteria to distinguish human rights from other human aspirations, Loriaux warns, the efficacy of the former – resting on their character as a special class of stringent claims with a universal scope – might be lost amidst the current plurality of rights.

Loriaux assesses two main approaches – moral and political – in asserting what is a universal human right. The first develops a criterion from the universal and ahistorical human needs derived from our common humanity and common need to develop our potential for agency and personhood. Loriaux objects that this proposition rests on a univocal ontology. In particular, it does not consider how different social and historical conditions mould what people consider as the conditions for attaining a worthwhile life and, therefore, the very catalogue and description of fundamental rights.

The second approach is more pragmatic in its view of human rights, setting them as the sole rights that can serve as curbs to state sovereignty, leading to an obligation of external interference in case a government violates them in dealing with its citizens. This solution, however, Loriaux claims, by placing the responsibility to determine what constitutes a human right violation in the hands of states, underestimates the consequences of the asymmetrical distribution of power in the global sphere. It entails the risk of laying the visibility of some human rights violations to the detriment of others in the hands of powerful states' interests and agendas.

Nicole Hassoun's chapter approaches what she believes to be a possible solution for the problems raised by Loriaux. This involves a shift of focus towards the currency of economic justice, that is, the way of measuring what kind of things must be guaranteed by human rights and, consequently, of defining what a decent society must enable its members to secure. The need for indexes pertaining to that kind of measurement derive, therefore, from the fact that they can provide the necessary mediation between the human rights as codified in law and their application in public policy programmes and action, and serving as guidelines for decision-makers and standards to assess the progress of a given society in securing their citizens' human rights. Furthermore, and importantly, the consensus around an index, by being based on objective measurement of human basic needs, might overcome the lack of agreement around the metaphysical foundations and length of the human rights list.

To be able to achieve that sort of consensus, according to Hassoun, one needs to define an essential account on the features of a (minimally) good life that need to be secured by the governments of decent societies independently of their cultural background. The centrepiece of Hassoun's conception of a minimally good life is the notion of autonomy as a distinctively human feature, that which separates humans from the other biological species. To be autonomous means, in short, to have the ability to plan the course of one's daily life and to pursue one's plans with a measure of reasonable liberty. The advantages of focusing on autonomy are twofold. First, that concept comprises nearly all the things that, in most cases, are needed for someone to lead a minimally good life: from physical and environmental requirements to social, cognitive and emotional goods. Second, the definition of autonomy is sufficiently basic to be accepted by a wide range of cultures.[14]

Hassoun defends her theory of the currency of human needs as the more fine-grained measurement account that is available. The second part of her chapter is dedicated to exploring two groups of alternative accounts of needs – harm based accounts and social role accounts – concluding that in some instances they are too broad in defining what people's basic needs are, and in others they allow leaving important needs unmet.

Julian Culp, in his chapter, considers the ways in which the discourse and practice of the economic and social rights as the basis of official development assistance might enable global acceptance of human rights doctrine. He tries to refocus the global justice debate away from a top-down inquiry to a more inclusive methodology focused on the deliberation among peoples. That is the gist of his proposition of an 'internationalist account of global discursive justice'.

Culp claims that distributive accounts of global justice, if they allow us to grasp the global duties of assistance in a clearer way than the humanitarian supererogatory conceptions, have repeatedly overlooked issues of power relations and humanitarian agenda-setting in the national and global sphere. More than giving to each his or her share, one needs to ascertain if the reasons for maintaining a social and political structure sanctioning a particular mode of production and distribution of its resulting benefits are morally justified. The only way to do it is by subjecting the features of the society's basic norms and institutions to popular deliberation.

In Culp's text, the paramount function of justice is therefore regarded as the granting to citizens of the institutional means to debate and refine the justifications for the current basic structure of their society and, on a broader scale, for the financial and commercial rules and practices embodying the global basic structure. Instead of defining, through an abstract procedure, a set of principles of justice that would extend to everyone through a top-down logic, reducing the world's social complexity to a one-size-fits-all distributive scheme, the discursive model sustained by Culp would allow a certain level of discretion concerning the distributive norms that would be the outcome of each society's deliberation. This fact renders the 'Discourse-Theoretic Rationale' less prone than distributivist theories of justice to charges of ethnocentrism and of misrepresentation of the basic goods needed by the globally least well-off.

Peter G. N. West-Oram's chapter is focused on health care. When analysing it from a global justice perspective, one has necessarily to ascertain both the existence (or non-existence) of duties of assistance that go beyond the ethical individual, hence voluntary, duty to help and the interpretation of what having a duty to assist entails. West-Oram focuses on the second question by evaluating three of the major cosmopolitan accounts of global duties of assistance: Thomas Pogge's account, focused on negative duties, Gillian Brock's minimal needs view, and Henry Shue's model of basic rights.

West-Oram favours the third account since Shue, by rejecting the misleading dichotomy of negative and positive rights – and therefore by supplementing the duty to avoid harming with duties to protect from deprivation and to help the deprived – can overcome the inconsistencies inherent in the other two models. Specifically, Pogge's view, according to West-Oram's interpretation, neglects the crucial role of positive duties to aid the least well-off. Correlatively, Brock's conception makes it difficult to attribute to given agents the responsibility to achieve her sufficientarian threshold. Shue, by employing the lexicon of rights – and not of needs, such as Brock does – and by combining a positive and a negative charge to his tripartite model, is able to propose a more complete and consistent model.

Accepting Shue's account as the most appropriate to interpret the duties correlating to basic rights, according to West-Oram, would have important implications for the assessment of the current assistance of the rich countries to the poor in terms of nutrition, health care, and sanitation and sewerage and, importantly, would imply a revision of the Trade Related Aspects of Intellectual Property Rights (TRIPS) regime. The monopolistic use of patents by their owners, in order to control the prices of medicines needed to reduce mortality in developing countries, would not be consistent with Shue's model. According to West-Oram, the current intellectual property rights regime fails to fulfil the principles of justice advanced by Shue and must therefore be revised, because it excludes a vast number of the people who need those pharmaceuticals the most from access to essential medicines.

George F. DeMartino and Jonathan D. Moyer's chapter addresses the theme of historical injustice. This is not only a major issue in the relations among nations but also one that any theory of global justice must tackle. Any such account must clarify the role it attributes to the backward-looking assessment of possible historical injustices that might have contributed to the crystallisation of current positions of individuals and nations as more or less well-off.

Most theories will admit that a continued history of exploitation of some societies by others implies the obligation to rehabilitate the wronged society through economic compensation. Knowing exactly what sort of compensation is fair in each case implies the development of very troublesome historical conjectures seeking to ascertain the degree of wrong one society has perpetrated on another, the level of deprivation on the wronged society it has helped to perpetuate and the translation of that injustice in terms of a material sum that would be fair to attribute at present.

DeMartino and Moyer stress that such debate concerning restitution must be preceded by a normative choice. We need criteria to ascertain what types of practice entice an obligation to rehabilitate a society or a group of individuals; that is, what kind of past acts which influence the agents' present situation may be considered moral wrongs and, consequently, give rise to legitimate claims for restitution. They proceed, therefore, to analyse three prominent theories of justice (libertarianism, liberal contractarianism and the capabilities approach), distinguishing their different accounts of the situations warranting restitution. The conclusion reached is that, although they all regard some instances of wealth and development differentiation between societies as involving restitutive correction, what might be considered a past injustice according to each is subject to a degree of variation, with important public policy repercussions.

Nozick's libertarianism, if it contemplates a principle of rectification, does it by restricting its scope to situations of extra-market appropriation (such as slavery or other coerced appropriations). What derives from the mutually consensual interaction of agents in the global market, even if it leads to oligopolistic tendencies and wide disparities of wealth, should not be subject to corrective interference. Rawls's liberal egalitarianism and Sen's capabilities approach, on the contrary, would regard instances of market-based appropriation – such as concerted action to take advantage of a frail minority in labour or commercial relations – as liable to restitution, since they configure unfair practices. What might differentiate the latter approaches is their standing towards differential gains between communities stemming from historical injustices but that have benefited both of them, though at uneven levels. DeMartino and Moyer point to the fact that both the criteria to define past acts liable to restitution and the amount of compensation that will need to be transferred to the wronged people or group will depend on a previous assignation of a particular theory of justice that is considered as the most fit to apply to this particular problem.

The last two chapters, as stated, make use of principles of global justice to evaluate two important features of the current international system. Alexander Brown's chapter deals with international humanitarian funding mechanisms, which have the crucial task of providing assistance to alleviate catastrophes of sudden development and ongoing humanitarian emergencies. The importance of this role should therefore lead to a careful choice of the imperatives and standards that direct the dispensation of aid.

The main agents of the global management of relief efforts – senior figures at the states' bureaucracies, the United Nations and (international) non-governmental organisations – mostly justify their actions

and priorities through 'formal' principles of effectiveness in the regulation of crisis. Brown's text alerts us to the insufficiency of such a
'narrow' justification of the workings of humanitarian aid devices. He
argues, instead, that a comprehensive justification is due to the people
under distress. If we take decisions that advantage some peoples over
others similarly distressed, we are required not only to enunciate the
principles of regulation employed in the decision to distribute the available funds, but to justify them in more substantial terms. This implies,
according to Brown, appealing to fundamental principles of global
morality and assessing the adequacy between them and the chosen
principles of regulation. Only in that case is it possible to verify if these
measures are indeed the most adequate to direct a given institution.

Brown supplements his argumentation with an institutional
case study, focusing on the working of the United Nations Central
Emergency Response Fund (CERF). Defining the three main regulative
principles that guide the institution's channelling of assistance – timeliness, predictability, and evenness in geographical distribution of aid
– and finding them wanting in terms of the comprehensiveness of their
justification, he then proceeds in three stages. The first is to translate
them in terms of moral principles: correspondingly, the principles of
aid, impartiality and equity. Second, he proposes a general principle of
global justice that can encompass the three specified moral principles.
Brown names it the *Principle of Global Equal Concern and Respect*, and
describes it in contrast to the less demanding *Principle of Global Minimal
Concern*. The former, contrarily to the latter, imposes a consideration of
every individual's interests in terms of strict equality, disallowing any
(politically or emotionally driven) partiality towards one group to the
detriment of another.

Only after having defined which principle of global justice has
authority over the existing humanitarian funding mechanisms it is possible to assess their current procedures. Thus, concluding the chapter,
Brown proposes three guidelines to amend instances of unfairness in
the CERF's criteria on what concerns the distinctions between its two
distinct funding channels ('Underfunded Emergencies Grants' and
'Rapid Response Grants') and in its relation towards NGOs.

The European Union (EU) is widely regarded to be the transnational
experiment that most resembles a polity of its own: it has, for the first
time in world politics, even though with some well-known frailties,
detached the democratic regime from the bounds of the nation-state,

de-territorialising the notion of citizenship and giving shape to a working supranational community of creation and enforcement of fundamental rights.

In his chapter, Philippe Van Parijs extends the view that he has previously outlined in his famous correspondence with John Rawls (Rawls and Van Parijs [1998] 2003), when he defended the federalisation of the Union, accompanied by the development of a European demos, as a path for the 'erection of a genuine European polity'. In the account he presents here, the EU is conceived as playing a vital role in the cosmopolitan extension of principles of justice. What is required of the Union to continue performing that role is to proceed with the expansion of the integration experience and to embrace the natural consequences of building a supranational 'compound polity', to borrow an expression from Sergio Fabbrini (2010). Consequently, Van Parijs argues that there is a political and moral consequence involved in the increasing replication by the EU – in terms of the creation of coercive transnational institutions and of the deepening of the bonds between peoples in the direction of a sense of post-national attachment – of the institutional conditions of a domestic polity. It is a twofold corollary: the Union both sets the blueprint for future development of international regimes and already stands as a living proof of the need to globalise accounts of social justice.

This peculiar nature of the EU and the continuing pursuance of an 'ever closer union' suggests the possibility, even if not necessarily attainable in the short term, of the creation of a Euro-wide system of social policy and redistribution – an 'inter-personal transfer system at a supra-national level'. In considering its political feasibility, Van Parijs assesses three proposals that are likely to implement his claim of balancing the imperative of fairness with the respect for the principle of subsidiarity and the granting of a degree of autonomy for EU member states. The model he proposes is the same he has been defending in other publications – that of a basic income for all the legal residents of the community – a universal euro-dividend. The last part of his chapter is devoted to an analysis of some features concerning the functioning of this social assistance scheme and of the prior cultural and institutional conditions that need to be established for it to be put into practice.

Notes

1. I am grateful to Gabriele De Angelis and Peter West-Oram for their comments and revision of this chapter. I am also indebted to Thom Brooks and the anonymous reviewers of Edinburgh University Press.
2. This information was obtained through an article in the *New York Times* and the sources quoted there. See Rosenthal (2013).
3. This is a concept coined by John Rawls. He conceives the *basic structure* of a society as 'the primary subject of justice' and has therefore coined the term to express 'the way in which the major social institutions distribute fundamental rights and duties and determine the division of advantages from social cooperation'. By major institutions he understands 'the political constitution and the principal economic and social arrangements. [. . .] Taken together as one scheme, the major institutions define human beings' rights and duties and influence their life prospects, what they can expect to be and how well they can hope to do. The basic structure is the primary subject of justice because its effects are so profound and present from the start' (Rawls 1999a: 6–7).
4. Distributive justice might, indeed, be very succinctly portrayed as the field of morality that tries to define 'how a society or group should allocate its scarce resources or product among individuals with competing needs or claims' (Roemer [1996] 1998: 1).
5. I am relying, in this exposition, on the works of philosophers such as Brian Barry, Charles Beitz, Simon Caney, Kok-Chor Tan or Thomas Pogge.
6. It is precisely the inadmissibility of a basic structure stratifying the division of goods among citizens by means of a criterion based on the fortuity of circumstance that leads Rawls to create the *original position* as a 'procedure of construction'. The original position is therefore intended as a hypothetical deliberative situation in which the parties, representing the citizens of any given liberal democratic society, can decide on principles of justice in conditions of strict equality. That is achieved by modelling the original position in such a way – through requiring that the deliberating parties establish principles behind a 'veil of ignorance' – that renders the parties ignorant of the particularities of their biological and social conditions. It is, in fact, the equitable character of the original position that allows Rawls calling his own conception 'justice as fairness' (Rawls 1999a: 12).
7. If I am using Rawls as the prime example of a liberal – and especially of a liberal egalitarian – conception of justice, it is not just because of his obvious and paramount importance for contemporary liberalism but also, and more specifically, since some of the most influential proponents of global justice conceptions – most notably Beitz and Pogge – have departed from the postulates of *justice as fairness*, claiming that Rawls, to remain

true and coherent towards his own theory of justice, should have extended its principles globally.

8. Textually, the eighth principle of international justice is the following: 'Peoples have a duty to assist other peoples living under unfavorable conditions that prevent their having a just or decent political and social regime' (Rawls 1999b: 37). The conditions of decency of a political regime, in turn, depend on a state's not having an aggressive foreign policy and respecting a – rather minimal, at least in comparison with the articles of the Universal Declaration of Human Rights – list of human rights (ibid.: 64–7).

9. I leave aside, for it is not the focus of this short introduction, the important question of how a contractarian theory of justice such as Rawls's should integrate the questions of (severe) disabilities, those preventing an individual from exercising the two moral powers in the way Rawls envisages them. Rawls himself points to the legislative phase, after the determination of the principles of justice (in which the parties at the *original position* represent the interests of only those citizens having a full capacity to be cooperative members of society), as the moment to deal with the rights of the disabled persons (Rawls 2005: 184). One thing is for certain: since the disabled persons have the same human rights as every other individual, an extension of Rawls's conception of justice will have to be designed to accommodate this special condition. In his words, 'I take it as obvious, and accepted by common sense, that we have a duty towards all human beings, however severely handicapped. The question concerns the weight of these duties when they conflict with other basic claims. At some point, then, we must see whether justice as fairness can be extended to provide guidelines for these cases; and if not, whether it must be rejected rather than supplemented by some other conception' (Rawls 2001: 176).

10. We could also quote Marcus Aurelius as another example of an author sharing Cicero's vision both of the different legal strata governing human beings and of the ontological justification for the universal scope of transcendental natural law. In his words, 'If mind is common to us all, then so is the reason which makes us rational beings; and if that be so, then so is the reason which prescribes what we should do or not do. If that be so, there is a common law also; if that be so, we are fellow-citizens; and if that be so, the world is a kind of state. For in what other common constitution can we claim that the whole human race participates? And it is from there, from this constitution, that our intelligence and sense of law derive; or else, where could they derive from?' (*Meditations*, 4.4).

11. We might say, as well, that critics of social justice cosmopolitanism counter the vision of a globalised justice by employing these same concepts of ontological and material connection among humans, but weighting their

consequences in a diametrically opposed way, as if by a mirror effect. In this way, a proponent of communitarian or nationalist theses might regard the prime connection among humans not as that which abstractly gathers the entire species but instead as that which unites a group of people sharing the same traditions, history, language and other cultural traits. If both personal identity and group morality are culturally embedded, then we have to recognise that the duties we owe to our fellow nationals are 'thicker' than those owed to everyone else (Walzer 1994; Miller 1995; Tamir 1995). Proponents of a statist ethic, on the other hand, might say that if it is true that the root of the need for principles of social justice lies in the existence of schemes of mutual cooperation and coercion, the material connectedness that we experience in the domestic sphere of the state is not compared to the much more tenuous linkage binding people from different societies. One must not overlook the effects of globalisation. If there is still a gap between the domestic and the global spheres in terms of the conditions making up a basic structure, than we cannot postulate the necessity of a unified conception of justice for the entire globe (Nagel 2005; Blake 2001; Sangiovanni 2007).

12. The existence of this hybrid set of theories of justice does not mean that cosmopolitanism conceptions cannot accommodate a pluralistic method of conceiving the robustness of social and global obligations, one that is reactive to the kind of recipients considered. There are, indeed, more univocal cosmopolitan conceptions, defending an integral identity between the obligations that we have towards our compatriots and those that must be established between us and everyone else present in the world. But there are also milder ones, structuring our obligations through a model of concentric circles that mirror our priorities: first and foremost towards those that are affectively and politically closer and only then, at the subsequent levels, towards others. What must not vary – since that constitutes the core of all cosmopolitan conceptions – is the commitment to guaranteeing a certain threshold of well-being for all the people taking part in the global basic structure, based on taking every human being as the primary unit of moral consideration and placing a certain responsibility directly upon every individual on the attainment of the defined threshold by every moral agent at the global sphere (Pogge 2002). On the distinction between *weak* and *strong* versions of cosmopolitanism see Miller (2007).

13. For literature concerning these questions see, for instance, Carens 1992 and Risse 2008 on migration, Rawls 1999b and Tan 2000 on toleration and external policy, Gardiner et al. 2010 on environmental justice, Pogge 2005 and Daniels 2007 on the ethics of global health, and Held 2006 and Brock 2009 for cosmopolitan institutional reforms.

14. One could dispute this claim as subject to Loriaux's criticism of abstracting

from human nature a quality – the drive towards autonomy, with everything it entails – that cannot be universalisable, since different cultures will have very different understandings of autonomy and of what spheres of human action must be protected to secure it. Hassoun, nevertheless, asserts that her (minimal) version of the traits of a minimally good life does not include a notion of – Western liberal – personhood and agency.

References

Beitz, Charles (1979), *Political Theory and International Relations*, Princeton, NJ: Princeton University Press.

Beitz, Charles (1983), 'Cosmopolitan Ideals and National Sentiment', *The Journal of Philosophy*, vol. 80, no. 10, pp. 591–600.

Blake, Michael (2001), 'Distributive Justice, State Coercion, and Autonomy', *Philosophy and Public Affairs*, vol. 30, no. 3, pp. 257–96.

Brock, Gillian (2009), *Global Justice: A Cosmopolitan Account*, Oxford: Oxford University Press.

Brown, Eric (2006), 'Hellenistic Cosmopolitanism', in Mary Louise Gill and Pierre Pellegrin (eds), *A Companion to Ancient Philosophy*, Oxford: Blackwell.

Caney, Simon (2001), 'Cosmopolitan Justice and Equalizing Opportunities', *Metaphilosophy*, vol. 32, no. 1–2, pp. 113–34.

Caney, Simon (2005), *Justice Beyond Borders: A Global Political Theory*, Oxford: Oxford University Press.

Carens, Joseph (1992), 'Migration and Morality: A Liberal Egalitarian Perspective', in B. Barry and R. Goodin (eds), *Free Movement*, London: Harvester Wheatsheaf, pp. 25–47.

Cicero (1999), *On the Commonwealth and On the Laws*, Cambridge: Cambridge University Press.

Daniels, Norman (2007), *Just Health Meeting Health Needs Fairly*, Cambridge: Cambridge University Press.

Diogenes Laertius (1995), *Lives of Eminent Philosophers*, vol. II, Cambridge, MA: Harvard University Press.

Douzinas, Costas (2007), *Human Rights and Empire: The Political Philosophy of Cosmopolitanism*, Abingdon: Routledge-Cavendish.

Fabbrini, Sergio (2010), *Compound Democracies: Why the United States and Europe Are Becoming Similar*, Oxford: Oxford University Press.

Gardiner, Stephen, Simon Caney, Dale Jamieson and Henry Shue (eds) (2010), *Climate Ethics: Essential Readings*, Oxford: Oxford University Press.

Held, David (2006), *Models of Democracy*, London: Polity Press.

Jones, Charles (1999), *Global Justice: Defending Cosmopolitanism*, Oxford: Oxford University Press.

Kant, Immanuel [1784] (1991), 'Idea for a Universal History with a Cosmopolitan Purpose', in *Political Writings*, ed. H. Reiss, Cambridge: Cambridge University Press, pp. 41–53.

Kant, Immanuel [1795] (1996), 'Toward perpetual peace', in *The Cambridge Edition of the Works of Immanuel Kant: Practical Philosophy*, ed. Mary J. Gregor, Cambridge: Cambridge University Press, pp. 317–51.

Long, Anthony A. (2008), 'The Concept of the Cosmopolitan in Greek & Roman Thought', *Daedalus*, vol. 137, no. 3, pp. 50–8.

Marcus Aurelius (1997), *Meditations*, Ware: Wordsworth Editions.

Miller, David (1995), *On Nationality*, Oxford: Clarendon Press.

Miller, David (2007), *National Responsibility and Global Justice*, Oxford: Oxford University Press.

Moellendorf, Darrel (2002), *Cosmopolitan Justice*, Boulder, CO: Westview Press.

Nagel, Thomas (2005), 'The Problem of Global Justice', *Philosophy and Public Affairs*, vol. 33, no. 2, 113–47.

Nussbaum, Martha (1994), 'Patriotism and Cosmopolitanism', *The Boston Review*, vol. 19, no. 5, pp. 3–16.

Nussbaum, Martha (1999), *Sex and Social Justice*, Oxford: Oxford University Press.

O'Neill, Onora (1996), *Towards Justice and Virtue: A Constructive Account of Practical Reasoning*, Cambridge: Cambridge University Press.

Pogge, Thomas (1989), *Realizing Rawls*, New York: Cornell University Press.

Pogge, Thomas (2002), *World Poverty and Human Rights: Cosmopolitan Responsibilities and Reforms*, London: Polity Press.

Pogge, Thomas (2005), 'Human Rights and Global Health: A Research Program', *Metaphilosophy*, vol. 36, no. 1–2, pp. 182–209.

Rawls, John [1971] (1999a), *A Theory of Justice: Revised Edition*, Oxford: Oxford University Press.

Rawls, John (1999b), *The Law of Peoples*, Cambridge, MA: Harvard University Press.

Rawls, John (2001), *Justice as Fairness: A Restatement*, Cambridge, MA: Harvard University Press.

Rawls, John [1993] (2005), *Political Liberalism*, New York: Columbia University Press.

Rawls, John and Philippe Van Parijs [1998] (2003), 'Three Letters on the Law of Peoples and the European Union', *Revue de philosophie économique*, vol. 7, no. 3, pp. 7–20.

Risse, Mathias (2008), 'On the Morality of Immigration', *Ethics & International Affairs*, vol. 22, no. 1, pp. 25–33.

Risse, Mathias (2012), *On Global Justice*, Princeton, NJ: Princeton University Press.

Roemer, John [1996] (1998), *Theories of Distributive Justice*, Cambridge, MA: Harvard University Press.

Rosenthal, Elisabeth (2013), 'As Biofuel Demand Grows, So Do Guatemala's Hunger Pangs', *New York Times*, 5 January 2013.

Sangiovanni, Andrea (2007), 'Global Justice, Reciprocity, and the State', *Philosophy and Public Affairs*, vol. 35, no. 1, pp. 3–39.

Sen, Amartya (1999), *Development as Freedom*, New York: Knopf.

Singer, Peter (1972), 'Famine, Affluence, and Morality', *Philosophy and Public Affairs*, vol. 1, no. 3, pp. 229–43.

Tamir, Yael (1995), *Liberal Nationalism*, Princeton, NJ: Princeton University Press.

Tan, Kok-Chor (2000), *Toleration, Diversity, and Global Justice*, University Park, PA: Pennsylvania State University Press.

United Nations Department of Economic and Social Affairs (UNDESA) (2013), *Inequality Matters: The Report on the World Social Situation 2013*, New York: United Nations.

Valentini, Laura (2011), *Justice in a Globalized World: A Normative Framework*, Oxford: Oxford University Press.

Walzer, Michael (1994), *Thick and Thin: Moral Argument at Home and Abroad*, Notre Dame, IN: University of Notre Dame Press.

Ypi, Lea (2012), *Global Justice and Avant-Garde Political Agency*, Oxford: Oxford University Press.

Part I

Human Rights and the World Economy: Questions of Scope

Chapter 2

THE (DIFFICULT) UNIVERSALITY OF
ECONOMIC AND SOCIAL RIGHTS

Sylvie Loriaux

INTRODUCTION

A notable feature of recent work on global economic justice is its increasing resort to the idea of 'human rights'. As some have pointed out, 'human rights discussions have largely replaced earlier proposals for globalised difference principles' (Flikschuh 2011: 17). Thinkers who have long advocated global principles of distributive justice (such as Charles Beitz, Allen Buchanan and Thomas Pogge) now appear to focus their attention on the presumably more modest task of specifying the content and extent of our human rights responsibilities in the face of severe world poverty. Central points of reference in their undertaking are the economic and social rights proclaimed in Article 25(1) and Article 26(1) of the 1948 Universal Declaration of Human Rights (UDHR):

> Everyone has the right to a standard of living adequate for the health and well-being of himself and of his family, including food, clothing, housing and medical care and necessary social services, and the right to security in the event of unemployment, sickness, disability, widowhood, old age or other lack of livelihood in circumstances beyond his control.

And:

> Everyone has the right to education. Education shall be free, at least in the elementary and fundamental stages. Elementary education shall be compulsory. Technical and professional education shall be made generally available and higher education shall be equally accessible to all on the basis of merit.[1]

The attractiveness of human rights language can in large part be explained by the interplay of three commonly held assumptions about the meaning of human rights. First, human rights are often taken to be 'moral rights': as *rights*, they are assumed to set limits on the freedom of others and, correlatively, to confer to their holders standing to press for their recognition and to complain when they are violated; as *moral* rights, they are given an existence that is prior to and independent of their recognition by positive law. Second, human rights are usually regarded as 'high priority' rights, that is, as protecting a sphere of pre-eminent moral importance (such as the 'minimum' conditions for a dignified life) and as therefore providing reasons for action which, though not absolute, are sufficiently weighty to outweigh other reasons for action most of the time. And third, human rights are generally identified with 'universal' rights or rights that are equally possessed and claimable by all human beings. Taken together, these three assumptions tend to promote an image of human rights language as a useful and powerful discursive tool, one which is susceptible to make the broad public more responsive to issues of global economic justice. As far as economic and social rights are concerned, they indeed convey the idea that all human beings everywhere have urgent welfare interests, that these interests impose particularly strong duties on others, and that those who disregard these duties are not simply behaving badly, but are doing a grave wrong to others. The discourse of human rights seems therefore particularly well suited to mobilise ordinary people across the world, to give legitimacy to individual economic and social claims against such powerful agents as states, business and international organisations, and to encourage substantial institutional changes. Importantly, it seems particularly well suited to 'empowering the powerless' and to 'giving voice to the voiceless' (Ignatieff 2001: 70).

Yet, when we turn to the details of international human rights documents, it appears that many of the rights they include, especially economic and social rights, do not seem to serve truly 'urgent' human interests or to represent truly 'minimum' moral standards. Some refer, for instance, to the idea of a 'standard of living *adequate* for [. . .] well-being' (Art. 25(1) of the UDHR; my emphasis) or of '*the highest attainable* standard of physical and mental health' (Art. 12(1) of the ICESCR; my emphasis), or even approach requirements of social justice by asserting, for instance, that 'higher education shall be equally accessible to all on the basis of merit' (Art. 26(1) of the UDHR) or that all have a right to 'equal pay for equal work' (Art. 23(2) of the UDHR) and to 'just and favorable remuneration' (Art. 23(2) of the UDHR). This observation raises the question of whether human rights are properly regarded as protecting a sphere of pre-eminent moral importance, and if not, whether this does not undermine their alleged high priority.[2]

Difficulties also arise with regard to the status of proclaimed human rights as rights. Must we not follow Raymond Geuss and Onora O'Neill in refraining from asserting the existence of rights unless these are effectively enforceable (Geuss 2001: 138–46) or at least claimable (O'Neill 2005)? According to these authors, until institutions are there that specify the content and bearers of their corresponding duties, or even enforce these duties, the economic and social human rights asserted in international declarations and covenants cannot be seen as real rights; they are merely political aspirations that must be aimed at, but that cannot be realised here and now.

A final issue concerns the universality of human rights. It seems to be definitive of human rights that they are held by all human beings irrespective of the social, economic or political situation in which they happen to find themselves. And a usual way to account for this feature has been to ground human rights in some highly valuable characteristic(s) that all human beings would necessarily and equally have in common. On this interpretation, the reason why all human beings can be said to possess the same human rights is that they possess these rights 'by nature' or 'merely in virtue of their humanity'. To some extent, this is in accordance with the way in which human rights are conceptualised in the UDHR and in the ICESCR, and in particular, with the assertion that 'Everyone is entitled to all the rights and freedoms set forth in this Declaration, without distinction of any kind, such as race, color, sex, language, religion, political or other opinion, national or social origin, property, birth or other status' (Art. 2 of the UDHR),[3] the 'recognition of the inherent dignity and of the equal and inalienable rights of all members of the human family' (Preamble to the UDHR and to the ICESCR), and the claim – at least in the Preamble to the ICESCR – that 'these rights derive from the inherent dignity of the human person'. At the same time, however, it is a fact that many of the rights proclaimed in these documents have institutional implications in the sense that they require or presuppose the existence of particular institutions. So Article 25(1) of the UDHR refers to 'medical care', 'necessary social services' and 'unemployment'; Article 26(1) talks of 'free' and 'compulsory' education, and distinguishes between 'elementary and fundamental stages', 'technical and professional education' and higher education'. These articles make sense only against the assumption that certain types of problems ought to be addressed and that certain types of institutions do exist or can be brought into existence. And the trouble is not only that the problems and institutions to which they refer have not always been conceivable throughout history, but also that they may not be conceivable in all parts of the world today. If so, the objection goes, the rights they assert could not possibly be held merely in virtue of humanity, be possessed by all human beings, and hence be human rights.

It goes without saying that the more contested the status of economic and social rights as human rights, the smaller the impact of human rights discourse on global economic justice issues. To some extent, it might be wondered whether this discourse is not falling victim to its own success (Ingram 2008: 401; Raz 2010a: 321–2; Tasioulas 2007: 75). The growing acceptance of human rights, as witnessed by the multiplication of human rights legal instruments and by the increase in the number and types of human rights invocations, can too easily lead to, but also be threatened by, a proliferation of human rights. The temptation is great to make the object of a human right any concern we believe is important enough to be placed on the agenda. But when expanding the reach of human rights norms, we are also inevitably undermining their distinctiveness and force. Much of the criticism raised against the human rights doctrine can be understood in this light. It is a commonplace objection that many of the rights it asserts fail to satisfy the requirements of claimability (or enforceability), pre-eminent moral importance and/or universality, and can therefore not be seen as authentic human rights. If this holds for economic and social rights, then the rhetoric of human rights might turn out to be an inadequate and counterproductive way to conceptualise our global economic responsibilities.

This chapter will focus on the question of universality: in what sense must human rights be universal rights, and do rights with institutional implications necessarily violate the requirement of universality? We can distinguish between two senses in which economic and social rights can be said to have institutional implications: (1) their existence can call for the establishment, reform or dissolution of certain institutions, or (2) their existence can (at least in part) be determined by existing institutional facts. While in the latter sense their existence depends on the prior existence of certain institutions (that is, certain institutions must already exist for people to *possess* these rights), in the former sense it can be established independently on the basis of moral reasoning alone (and certain institutions must be brought into existence for people to *enjoy* these rights).

As we shall see, both kinds of institutional dependency pose a challenge to the requirement of universality. The general aim of this chapter is to examine two possible ways of accounting for the existence of institutionally dependent human rights – namely, by endorsing a 'political' or a 'humanist' approach to human rights – and to highlight their respective weaknesses in doing so. It will start by presenting the basic tenets of each approach and by showing that none of them does *in principle* exclude the existence of institutionally dependent human rights. It will then consider the implications of both approaches for economic and social rights. Against humanist approaches, it will argue that the notion of 'abstract human rights' on which they rely is problematic, as neither the content of a human right nor the content of its correlative duties can be determined without reference to particular times, places and concerns. Against political approaches, it will argue that by tying the nature of human rights to the political role these rights are intended to play within the existing human rights practice, they arbitrarily make the existence of human rights depend on existing power relationships.

POLITICAL APPROACHES

According to so-called political approaches to human rights,[4] the claim that institutionally dependent rights cannot be genuine human rights and that the human rights doctrine should *therefore* get rid of economic and social rights rests on a misunderstanding of what human rights really are. Before being able to decide about the existence and content of particular human rights, we first need to have a good sense of the 'nature' of human rights and this can best be done by examining how the expression 'human rights' is used within the existing human rights practice.

Now, political approaches are not alone in emphasising the need to consult the actual social use of the concept of human rights. As we will see later, humanist approaches may also take the ongoing practice of human rights as the starting point and subject matter of their reflection.

But what distinguishes political approaches is the emphasis they place on the specific *political* purpose for which the human rights doctrine has been developed. They purport to characterise the 'nature' of human rights by referring to the role these rights play (or, at least, are intended to play) in political life. And according to them, this role consists essentially in justifying outside interference in the internal affairs of states. So, human rights are said to be first and foremost 'limits to the sovereignty of states' (Raz 2010a: 328) or 'triggers of international concern' (Beitz 2009: 65). More particularly, they are said to function as a set of norms which states are bound to observe in their treatment of their members and whose non-observance or threat of non-observance by a state is a *pro tanto* reason for taking transnational action against it – be it remedially or preventively.[5]

It is important to note that political approaches do not and need not tie the concept of human rights to a particular form of remedial or preventive action. The basic idea is that, when violated, human rights can justify transnational actions that state sovereignty would in normal circumstances condemn (Raz 2010a: 328, fn. 21). But among these rights, a distinction can be made between those (presumably few) whose violation could justify serious consideration of coercive interference such as economic sanctions or armed intervention and those that could only justify softer forms of interference such as diplomatic or economic incentives (for example, the making of compliance with human rights a condition of admission to international organisations or a condition of qualification for loans), assistance in institutional capacity-building, or public criticism (Buchanan 2006: 166).[6]

The central question to be addressed, then, concerns the kinds of considerations that can justify regarding a particular right as being suited to play the political role assigned to human rights within the contemporary practice of human rights. The most elaborated political accounts of human rights identify three criteria establishing the existence of a human right (Beitz 2009: 109; Raz 2010a: 336). *First*, a human right protects an important individual interest.[7] *Second*, a human right applies primarily to states, which have first-level responsibilities to protect that interest. *Third*, a human right may justify action by eligible (second-level) outside agents when a state fails to fulfil its first-level responsibilities. Importantly, political approaches further emphasise that each justificatory level comprises a dimension of contingency. So, in order for a human right to X (say, to free elementary education) to exist, *the (social, economic or political) circumstances* must be such that: *first*, X must be secured in order for an important individual interest to be met; *second*, it is appropriate to hold states responsible for securing X; and *third*, it is inappropriate to grant states immunity from external interference should they fail to secure X.

The meaning of these contingencies will be considered later. For the moment, it suffices to point out that if this is how the concept of human right is to be understood, then existing human rights treaties and declarations can hardly be criticised on the ground that some of the rights they include cannot be possessed by individuals 'merely in virtue of their humanity'. As the right to free elementary education illustrates, there is no *principled* reason to exclude the existence of institutionally dependent human rights since there is no *principled* reason to believe that these rights could not pass the three-level justificatory test.

HUMANIST APPROACHES

An alternative way of accounting for the existence of institutionally dependent human rights is to start by identifying a set of 'abstract' human rights that would be possessed by all persons 'merely in virtue of their being human' (and so at all times and in all places) and to then apply these rights to the circumstances of the present world to arrive at 'concrete' human rights of the sort proclaimed in contemporary international documents.

A fully fledged version of this approach – which I will call the 'humanist' approach[8] – has been offered by James Griffin (2008). According to him, human rights depend for their existence on two kinds of considerations. The first are considerations of 'personhood'. Human rights are grounded in a highly valuable feature shared by all human beings, namely, their capacity to form and pursue their own conception of a worthwhile life. They protect the necessary conditions for 'normative agency', and more particularly, (1) the capacity to choose one's conception of a worthwhile life (*autonomy*); (2) the capacity to make 'real' choices and to act on these choices (*minimum provision of resources*, including a certain minimum of education); and (3) the capacity to pursue one's conception of a worthwhile life without being forcibly prevented by others (*liberty*). But, Griffin adds, the content of these personhood considerations is often not determinate enough to generate 'effective, socially manageable claim[s] on others' and therefore genuine 'human rights' (Griffin 2008: 38). They show, for instance, that a minimum provision of resources is necessary to function as a normative agent, but they cannot by themselves set limits on the demands that this may impose on others. Assuming, for instance, that we all have a right to life, does this entail that others are required to give us one of their kidneys if they can thereby save our life without risk for their own capacity for normative agency? Or that we all have to give our money to the starving poor until the point at which giving more would prevent us from functioning as normative agents? To solve such questions, Griffin argues, we need to introduce a second kind of considerations: practical considerations ('practicalities'), and more specifically, empirical information about human nature and the nature of human society. The universal (including ahistorical) character of these practicalities is crucial for Griffin. If we want to remain true to the idea of human rights as it has lived through the ages – and which, according to Griffin, is that of *'right[s] that we have simply in virtue of being human'* (ibid.: 2) – then the only considerations that may be consulted in order to establish the existence of human rights are considerations that are not tied to particular times and places.[9]

This does not mean, however, that a same abstract or basic (universal) human right cannot be applied to particular circumstances and produce different concrete or derived human rights whose content will reflect 'particular practicalities', that is, empirical information reflecting particular times, places and concerns. Although a derived human right (for example, freedom of the press) may have no relevance in certain settings (for example, in settings where the concept of press is absent) and so lack universality, it is nevertheless an authentic human right because it is grounded in a basic and truly universal human right (namely, freedom of expression). As Griffin puts it, a same human right 'can be expressed at different levels of abstraction' and '[w]e should claim only that universality is there at the higher levels' (ibid.: 50). Still, particular practicalities differ from universal practicalities in that they do not have the slightest impact on the existence of human rights: they cannot generate any new human rights, but can only concretise those rights whose existence has already been established on the basis of purely universal (personhood and practical) considerations.

On this account too, then, there seems to be no *principled* reason for criticising existing international human rights documents on the ground that some of the rights they include have institutional implications. There seems to be no *principled* reason for excluding the possibility of institutionally dependent human rights since these rights can perfectly derive from basic universal human rights held merely in virtue of humanity, and therefore be genuine human rights.

IMPLICATIONS FOR ECONOMIC AND SOCIAL RIGHTS

From the foregoing it appears that the main points of contention between political and humanist approaches are twofold. The first is that the former deny, and the latter affirm, that the 'nature' of human rights can be grasped without reference to the role they are assumed to play in global political life (humanist approaches do not deny that human rights will have political implications, but they define their nature without reference to their political role as 'rights that persons have merely in virtue of their humanity'). The second is that the former deny, and the latter affirm, that the existence of human rights can be determined without reference to 'particular' contingent empirical considerations (the only empirical considerations that humanist approaches allow to figure in the existence conditions of human rights are ahistorical considerations relating to human nature and the nature of human society).

In this section, I would like to examine what the implications of these approaches are for economic and social rights. Can these rights qualify as human rights? Which ones? And what about their universality?

Let us start with humanist approaches. Griffin specifies that insofar as human rights have to do with the conditions necessary for normative agency, we are provided with a criterion that is at the same time higher than mere subsistence (understood as the resources needed for mere physical survival) and lower than 'a standard of living adequate for the health and well-being of [oneself] and of [one's] family' (ibid.: 183, 186). In other words, the rights included in Article 25(1) of the UDHR are too demanding. They cannot be seen as concretisations of the abstract right to a 'minimum material provision', and hence as (derived) human rights, because their requirements exceed the 'minimal' requirements of normative agency. Another problem with the idea of an 'adequate' or 'satisfactory' standard of living, according to Griffin, is its incapacity to provide us with a 'stable, non-arbitrary normatively-based criterion', the reason being that its content is likely to vary from society to society according to their wealth (ibid.: 183).

It might, however, be doubted whether Griffin's personhood account does better in these respects. By excluding non-universal considerations from the set of existence conditions of human rights, Griffin assumes that both the content of a human right and the content of its correlative duties can be determined without reference to particular times and places. Yet, this twofold assumption is questionable. As already indicated, human rights for Griffin have to do with what is necessary to choose and pursue one's own conception of a worthwhile life, rather than with bare survival. But the kind and extent of resources that a person will need in order to make 'real' choices and to act on her choices (not to talk of the very 'conception of a worthwhile life' she will choose) will inevitably be a function of the kind of society to which she belongs. In a modern knowledge-based society, the necessary conditions for normative agency will include an array of capacities that are not only more demanding than, but also different from those that would suffice in a medieval rural society. It does not help to point out that the personhood account has to do with a 'minimal' rather than with an 'adequate' standard for any conception of the minimal conditions for normative agency will be socially determined. The point is not simply that different societies will satisfy this minimum differently, but also and more fundamentally, that they will have a different understanding of what it means to be able to make 'real' choices and to act on these choices, and presumably also disagree on the very importance of being so able. It seems therefore that the content of the right to minimum material provision – that is, what material resources are necessary to function as a normative agent – cannot be defined *in abstracto* or that there can be no such 'abstract' right.

In addition, even if a 'stable' idea could be formed of the 'minimum' material conditions for normative agency, it remains that protecting this minimum might still be very demanding. Griffin acknowledges that there is no human right without correlative duties. He also acknowledges that human rights are not properly seen as unrestricted protections of personhood values against all imaginable threats and at all bearable costs. A human right, he insists, must be an 'effective, socially manageable claim on others' or provide an 'effective guide to behaviour' (ibid.: 37). His proposal is to appeal to ahistorical practicalities, and more specifically, to the fact that 'human beings' have special commitments and limited understanding and motivation. Yet, it is doubtful that this kind of practicalities can make it clear enough what the idea of a 'minimum provision of resources' requires from others. It rather seems that the 'domain of permitted partiality' – and so the kind of considerations that will be allowed to delimit the content of our duties, as well as the extent to which they will be so allowed – cannot but reflect contingent features of our lives such as the values that are predominant in our culture or the level of technological development reached by our society. What ahistorical practicalities can show is only *that* there are limits on what can be demanded of people, not *what* these limits should be. Again, it seems that the only rights that can exist are 'concrete' rights.

It might even be wondered whether the concretisation of abstract human rights does in Griffin not in fact generate new human rights. Griffin focuses on abstract universal rights, but one could as well point out that people have, as a matter of fact, different derived human rights and that whether or not they have a particular derived human right in part depends on the contingent situation in which they find themselves. Griffin's strategy is to say that any derived human right applies without discrimination to all those who find themselves in a situation in which the right has relevance. So when asserting the human right of AIDS patients to anti-retroviral drugs, he argues that this right is nothing else but the concrete application of the abstract right to a minimum material provision to particular circumstances, and further specifies that even if it applies only in certain circumstances, it is possessed merely in virtue of universal (personhood and practical) considerations, not in virtue of the particular situation in which people happen to find themselves (ibid.: 51, 108). The underlying idea is that particular practicalities allow us only to further specify the content of human rights, a content that is assumed to already have tolerable determinacy. Yet, insofar as particular practicalities not merely make human rights 'enjoyable', but also, and more fundamentally, shape their very content, it might be wondered whether they do not by the same token give rise to different human rights. In practice, the fact indeed remains that on Griffin's account, most of the rights included in human rights documents cannot be seen as 'claim[s] of all human agents against all other human agents' and hence as universal rights (ibid.: 177).

It seems, then, that we face a dilemma: either we preserve the 'universality' of human rights and we lose any 'effective guide to behaviour', or we introduce contingent factors into the existence conditions of human rights and concede that human beings who do not share the same conditions of life may not share the same set of human rights.

A possible way out of this dilemma would be to qualify the requirement of universality in a temporal way and to allow general facts about the conditions of life within some specific period to play a role in determining the existence of human rights.[10] Human rights could, for instance, be understood as protections of important individual interests, but only against threats that are reasonably predictable and that can effectively be protected against at reasonable costs within a well-defined timeframe – under the conditions of modernity, for instance.[11] Human rights would then depend for their existence not on ahistorical practicalities, nor on practicalities tied to particular times and places, but on practicalities that are universal within a particular timeframe.

But the difficulty with what Tasioulas calls a 'temporally-constrained form of universality' (Tasioulas 2002: 87–8; 2010: 671–2) is that it rests on the assumption that all people who share a same historical timeframe also share conditions of life that are sufficiently similar to justify their possessing a same set of human rights. If the fact that, say, medieval and contemporary societies suppose drastically different conditions of life makes it inappropriate to impose on them the same human rights, why would it be appropriate to impose the same human rights on all contemporary societies irrespective of their cultural, social or economic particularities? Given their different social, economic and technological environment, not all people living today are to the same extent subject to the same 'inexorable forces of modernity' – that is, not all are vulnerable to the same predictable threats or live under institutions that have the same capacities. What about societies whose economy includes only marginal forms of wage labour for only a small proportion of workers, with no significant participation in the global cultural and economic life, and having a weak public capacity to raise taxes and provide essential collective goods? (See Beitz 2009: 58.) The danger is that by grounding human rights in empirical generalisations about current domestic and international (economic, legal, cultural) developments, one might also impose on all societies human rights (and, by the same token, values and institutions) that are appropriate only for some types of societies (in the present case, societies that have the features of modernity) and to pressure the yet lacking conditions of life, threats and institutions into existence.

Interestingly, Joseph Raz suggests a *pragmatic* (instead of a *prin-*

cipled) reason for identifying human rights with 'temporally constrained' or 'synchronically' universal rights – a reason that refers to
the interference-justifying role of human rights (Raz 2010b: 42). The
point is not that all human beings alive today *have* the same human
rights because human rights are those rights that people possess both
in virtue of their being human and in virtue of their sharing the same
conditions of life (an empirical premise whose truth is highly questionable), but that they *must have* the same human rights because human
rights are those rights whose role is to constrain state sovereignty. If
human rights are to fulfil their role and to set limits to sovereignty, then
external demands to respect them or complaints about their violation
must be able to block the response that outsiders have no knowledge of
the domestic circumstances of a society and therefore of the rights that
members of this society have. And this is unlikely to be the case unless
human rights are identified with those rights that all people living
today have in virtue of the common conditions of life.

Raz's position has the advantage of, first, not having to establish the
existence of 'abstract human rights', and second, being less prone to
making dubious empirical generalisations about people's conditions of
life. Indeed, it speaks for caution in establishing the existence of (economic and social) human rights, since it requires us to show that (1) all
human beings share *social conditions* which make it appropriate to hold
others to be under a duty to protect a certain individual interest in a
certain way (for example, to provide them with 'formal instruction' as
a way to meet their interest in having the knowledge and skills needed
to be able to have a rewarding life); (2) all human beings share *political
conditions* which make it appropriate for their states to have the duty to
protect that interest in that way (which presupposes that their societies
are organised in states and that all states have the capacity to effectively
enforce the right by law); and (3) that the *international situation* is such
that states are not to be granted immunity from external interference
should they fail to protect that interest in that way (which presupposes
that the right is important enough to call for an international response
and that a fair, effective and reliable interference by international
organisations and/or other states is possible).

But Raz's account faces other difficulties. One of them concerns
the enforceability of human rights. Raz contends that when it is not
appropriate to hold states responsible for enforcing a right and/or to
permit external interference when they fail to do so, then the right is

not a human right. The idea behind this is honourable: a right that cannot be fairly, effectively and reliably enforced by law should not be enforced because its enforcement risks causing more harm than good. This is especially true in the current system of states, where transnational actions to protect human rights depend on decisions by economically and militarily powerful states, and where the human rights discourse risks being used to further empower the already powerful.[12] But the price to pay is that human rights may also lose their empowering potential regarding the powerless. If the actual non-enforceability of a right entails that this right is not a human right, then the weaker a state's institutional capacities or the more vulnerable it is to unfair treatment by other states, the less its members can claim human rights. Why would the fact that a state is incapable of enforcing a human right by law imply that its members do not 'have' that right, and not only that they cannot 'enjoy' that right (Donnelly 1982: 394–5)? Raz's answer is that 'the contemporary practice of human rights identifies as human rights only those that should [and therefore also could] be enforced by law' (Raz 2010b: 44). But the human rights practice is subject to rival interpretations: why not instead favour an alternative ongoing understanding of human rights, namely, as morally justified claims against all others that they work toward securing the enjoyment of their object, be it through legal enactment or through alternate, non-legal ways?

On this understanding, a state's lack of the resources or capacities to enforce economic and social rights could preclude actual enjoyment of the right without implying that there is no right in the first place. Similarly, the question arises of whether one should not be more critical of the interference-justifying role assigned to human rights within the contemporary practice of human rights. Why take it as distinctive of human rights that they are rights whose violation may justify external interference in the internal affairs of states and not focus instead on their role in constraining the global behaviour of institutions in which one directly or indirectly participates (for example, one's own state's foreign policy, international organisations)?[13] On the latter understanding, the likelihood of partial, unfair or ineffective interference in the internal affairs of other states would no longer be a reason to deny the existence of economic and social human rights, and hence that members of vulnerable states have strong welfare claims against us.

On these points, Charles Beitz's political approach looks more promising: not only does it not require that states carry their responsibility by incorporating human rights protection in municipal law (it may sometimes be enough to adopt specific policy measures) (Beitz 2009: 114), but it also broadens the concept of human rights from 'limits to the sovereignty of states' to 'triggers of international concern', making room for duties of 'external assistance' and 'external adaptation' (such as duties to reform international rules and structures) when a state's failure to respect human rights results not from a lack of will but from a lack of capacity or from the conduct of other international actors.

But it still involves another, stronger kind of institutional dependency, peculiar to all political conceptions of human rights. As we have seen, it is definitive of these conceptions that they establish a conceptual link between the nature – and by the same token, the existence – of human rights and existing practices (for example, the fact that human rights are frequently invoked to justify interference in the internal affairs of states). Yet, it is a fact that the shape of these practices is itself largely determined by the existing distribution of power. Certainly, political approaches do leave room for criticising the current practice of human rights: proclaimed human rights that do not pass the three-level justificatory test are not to be considered authentic human rights. But it is important to note that any criticism must be made in the light of the political role that the existing practice assigns to human rights, a role whose specification is not itself critically questioned.

Against this, it could be argued that just as the mere proclamation of a human right does not entail that this right is an authentic human right, so too does the mere use of human rights as triggers of interference in other states not entail that it belongs to the nature of human rights to be such triggers. In this respect, it is important to bear in mind that only those actors that have the power to interfere in other states will invoke human rights violations to justify such interference, and that they will refrain from doing so whenever interference is unlikely to serve their interest (such as in poor and economically insignificant countries). What if they invoke human rights mainly as triggers of military intervention, but seldom as triggers of external adaptation? And what if, as a result, developing countries' persistent call for the recognition of welfare rights remains unheeded in favour of property, civil and political rights – as witnessed by the little reaction aroused by their various proposals for a 'new world economic order', for global taxation schemes or for a revision of the TRIPS agreements? In their own way, political approaches then also pose a challenge to the requirement of universality: for by determining the political role that human rights are to play, powerful actors are inevitably and arbitrarily also determining what rights are to be recognised as human rights, and this, possibly to the detriment of the rights that are most valued by states that are too weak to affect the practice of human rights.

CONCLUSION

In this chapter, I have argued that there are strong reasons to be concerned with the universality of economic and social rights. The main reasons are that (1) the existence of human rights – whether they are understood as 'effective, socially manageable claims on others that we have simply in virtue of being human' (Griffin) or as 'limits to the sovereignty of states' (Raz) – cannot be determined without reference to concrete conditions of life, and that (2) concrete conditions of life are today not sufficiently similar across the world to justify all human beings possessing the economic and social rights asserted in human rights doctrine.

I have also raised some concerns about the emphasis placed by political approaches on the role that human rights are intended to play in global political life. Underlying this emphasis is the idea that universality is a necessary but not a sufficient existence condition for human rights: in order for a right to qualify as a human right, it must not only be universal, but it must also be important enough to justify an international response. But the trouble is that the interpretation of this response (for example, in the narrow sense of military intervention or in the broad sense of international concern), and by the same token the determination of what universal rights are susceptible to be considered human rights, is usually a function of the interests of powerful international actors. What this means concretely is that the existence of economic and social rights is made conditional on existing power relationships.

Whether these difficulties take on a particular significance in the case of economic and social rights (as opposed to civil and political rights), whether they are serious enough to undermine the impact of human rights discourse on world poverty issues, and whether they could be addressed by alternative approaches to human rights are questions that require further investigation. My purpose here has been the modest one of showing the seriousness and inescapability of these questions.

Notes

1. Other important points of reference include Articles 11(1), 12(1) and 13(1) of the 1966 International Covenant on Economic, Social and Cultural Rights (ICESCR): 'The States Parties to the present Covenant recognize the right of everyone to an adequate standard of living for himself and his family, including adequate food, clothing and housing, and to the continuous improvement of living conditions' (Art. 11(1)); 'The States Parties to the present Covenant recognize the right of everyone to the enjoyment of the highest attainable standard of physical and mental health' (Art. 12(1)); and 'States Parties to the present Covenant recognize the right of everyone to education. They agree that education shall be directed to the full development of the human personality and the sense of its dignity, and shall strengthen the respect for human rights and fundamental freedoms. They further agree that education shall enable all persons to participate effectively in a free society, promote understanding, tolerance and friendship among all nations and all racial, ethnic or religious groups, and further the activities of the United Nations for the maintenance of peace' (Art. 13(1)).
2. For a rejection of the claim that human rights must in some way be 'minimalist', see Beitz (2009: 141–4).
3. In the same vein, Article 2(2) of the ICESCR holds that 'The States Parties to the present Covenant undertake to guarantee that the rights enunciated in the present Covenant will be exercised without discrimination of any kind as to race, color, sex, language, religion, political or other opinion, national or social origin, property, birth or other status.'
4. Proponents of a 'political' conception of human rights include among others Charles Beitz (2009), Kenneth Baynes (2009), Jean Cohen (2008), Joshua Cohen (2004), John Rawls (1999), Joseph Raz (2010a, 2010b) and David Reidy (2005).
5. This does not mean that human rights cannot also constrain the behaviour of agents other than states (such as international organisations, corporations, domestic institutions, or individuals), but only that it is *distinctive* of human rights (as identified by the contemporary human rights practice) that they constrain state sovereignty. Nor does it mean that the human rights practice, and with it the political role of human rights, cannot evolve over time and that the primary responsibility for human rights protection, which falls today on states, could not fall on non-state actors in the future (Raz 2010a: 336; Beitz 2009: 124). But it must be noted that in this case, political approaches would need drastic revision, since the nature of human rights would no longer be conceptually tied to the idea of potentially justifiable interference in the internal affairs of a state (Tasioulas 2009: 946).

6. As Beitz puts it: 'The contestable issue is [. . .] not whether infringements of human rights generate reasons for outside agents to act, but what forms of action by which agents would be permissible for various types of violations' (Beitz 2009: 125).
7. Beitz further specifies that this protection is 'against certain predictable dangers ("standard threats") to which they are vulnerable under typical circumstances of life in a modern world order composed of states' (Beitz 2009: 109).
8. I borrow this term from Gilabert (2011). See p. 462, fn. 14.
9. Notice also the order of his inference: his claim is not that it is definitive of human rights that they are universal and that human rights must therefore be held merely in virtue of humanity, but that it is definitive of human rights that they are held merely in virtue of humanity and that human rights must therefore be grounded in universal considerations (which, for Griffin, does not entail that all human rights must themselves be universal).
10. Cf. Allen Buchanan (2008), Jack Donnelly (2003, 2007: 287), James Nickel (2007) and John Tasioulas (2002, 2007, 2010).
11. Such an account of human rights can no longer be labelled as 'humanist' since it does not posit the existence of 'abstract human rights', but grounds human rights in both a conception of human dignity (for example, basic human interests) and empirical premises about contemporaneous conditions of life (Buchanan 2008: 57).
12. On the problems that arise when universal human rights norms are combined with a statist conception of politics, see for instance Chandler (2002: 111, 2005: 171) and Ignatieff (2001: 47).
13. I believe this would get us closer to Thomas Pogge's institutional understanding of human rights. See Pogge (2002).

References

Baynes, Kenneth (2009), 'Toward a Political Conception of Human Rights', *Philosophy & Social Criticism*, vol. 35, no. 4, pp. 371–90.
Beitz, Charles (2009), *The Idea of Human Rights*, Oxford: Oxford University Press.
Buchanan, Allen (2006), 'Taking the Human Out of Human Rights', in R. Martin and D. Reidy (eds), *Rawls's Law of Peoples: A Realistic Utopia?*, Oxford: Blackwell, pp. 151–68.
Buchanan, Allen (2008), 'Human Rights and the Legitimacy of the International Order', *Legal Theory*, vol. 14, no. 1, pp. 39–70.
Chandler, David (2002), *From Kosovo to Kabul: Human Rights and International Intervention*, London: Pluto Press.

Chandler, David (2005), *Constructing Global Civil Society: Morality and Power in International Relations*, London: Palgrave Macmillan.

Cohen, Jean (2008), 'Rethinking Human Rights, Democracy, and Sovereignty in the Age of Globalization', *Political Theory*, vol. 36, no. 4, pp. 578–606.

Cohen, Joshua (2004), 'Minimalism About Human Rights: The Most We Can Hope For?', *Journal of Political Philosophy*, vol. 12, no. 2, pp. 190–213.

Donnelly, Jack (1982), 'Human Rights as Natural Rights', *Human Rights Quarterly*, vol. 4, no. 3, pp. 391–405.

Donnelly, Jack (2003), *Universal Human Rights in Theory and Practice*, 2nd edn, Ithaca, NY: Cornell University Press.

Donnelly, Jack (2007), 'The Relative Universality of Human Rights', *Human Rights Quarterly*, vol. 29, no. 2, pp. 391–405.

Flikschuh, Katrin (2011), 'On the Cogency of Human Rights', *Jurisprudence*, vol. 2, no. 1, pp. 17–36.

Geuss, Raymond (2001), *History and Illusion in Politics*, Cambridge: Cambridge University Press.

Gilabert, Pablo (2011), 'Humanist and Political Perspectives on Human Rights', *Political Theory*, vol. 39, no. 4, pp. 439–67.

Griffin, James (2008), *On Human Rights*, Oxford: Oxford University Press.

Ignatieff, Michael (2001), *Human Rights as Politics and Idolatry*, ed. Amy Gutmann, Princeton, NJ: Princeton University Press.

Ingram, James (2008), 'What Is a "Right to Have Rights"? Three Images of the Politics of Human Rights', *American Political Science Review*, vol. 102, no. 4, pp. 401–16.

Nickel, James (2007), *Making Sense of Human Rights*, Oxford: Blackwell.

O'Neill, Onora (2005), 'The Dark Side of Human Rights', *International Affairs*, vol. 81, no. 2, pp. 427–39.

Pogge, Thomas (2002), *World Poverty and Human Rights*, Cambridge: Polity Press.

Rawls, John (1999), *The Law of Peoples*, Cambridge, MA: Harvard University Press.

Raz, Joseph (2010a), 'Human Rights Without Foundations', in S. Besson and J. Tasioulas (eds), *The Philosophy of International Law*, Oxford: Oxford University Press, pp. 321–37.

Raz, Joseph (2010b), 'Human Rights in the Emerging World Order', *Transnational Legal Theory*, vol. 1, no. 1, pp. 31–47.

Reidy, David (2005), 'An Internationalist Conception of Human Rights', *The Philosophical Forum*, vol. 36, no. 4, pp. 367–97.

Tasioulas, John (2002), 'Human Rights, Universality and the Values of Personhood: Retracing Griffin's Steps', *European Journal of Philosophy*, vol. 10, no. 1, pp. 79–100.

Tasioulas, John (2007), 'The Moral Reality of Human Rights', in T. Pogge (ed.),

Freedom from Poverty as a Human Right: Who Owes What to the Very Poor?,
     Oxford: Oxford University Press, pp. 75–101.
Tasioulas, John (2009), 'Are Human Rights Essentially Triggers for
     Intervention?', *Philosophy Compass*, vol. 4, no. 6, pp. 938–50.
Tasioulas, John (2010), 'Taking Rights Out of Human Rights', *Ethics*, vol. 120,
     no. 4, pp. 647–78.

Chapter 3

ECONOMIC JUSTICE AND THE MINIMALLY GOOD HUMAN LIFE ACCOUNT OF NEEDS

Nicole Hassoun

INTRODUCTION

There are many reasons why one might want an account of what people need.[1] One reason is that, on some accounts, a decent society must enable its members to secure what they need. Needs compete with welfare, opportunity, resource, and capability accounts of the currency of economic justice and there are many compelling arguments that a decent society must enable its members to secure what they need (Pogge 2002; Hassoun 2012; Vallentyne 2005; Alkire 2002; Reader 2006; Copp 1998; Brock 1998; Braybrooke 1998; Buchanan 2004). So, it is important to have an account of needs that might play the requisite role in answering the question "What must a good society enable its members to secure?" After all, if no account can play this role then we should presumably answer this question by referencing a different (that is, welfare, opportunity, resource, or capability) alternative.

Some suggest that a needs account might have an advantage over at least the resourcist alternative, because a decent society might have to enable different people to secure different things (Reader 2006).[2] Some people need only a little food and water. Others (for example, pregnant women) need much more. Some do not need expensive medicines or health care. Others (for example, AIDS victims) require a lot of medical aid. So, any good account of needs must accommodate differences in individuals' needs (Brock 1998; Frankfurt 1988). Ideally, a good account should capture all of the things each person needs without including anything someone does not need.

This chapter will provide an account of needs that (1) can accommodate individual differences in need that (2) decent societies might, plausibly, have to enable their members to fulfill. It will not argue that

51

its account of needs is better than welfare, opportunity, resource, and capability accounts of the currency of economic justice.[3] Rather, this chapter just aims to provide a new competitor worth further consideration. In doing so, this chapter will link discussions about the nature of needs to those about economic justice. It will also critically review several accounts of need in the literature arguing that none can fulfill the above desiderata. More precisely, the second section sketches what this chapter will call the *minimally good human life* account of needs. It argues that autonomy, for instance, is characteristic of, and often necessary for, a minimally good human life. The third section considers the practical implications of the minimally good human life account of needs and shows how it fulfills the above desiderata for a good account. The fourth section argues that some of the best alternative accounts have unintuitive consequences. They either (1) cannot accommodate individual differences in need or (2) are not plausible accounts of what decent societies must enable their members to secure.

THE MINIMALLY GOOD HUMAN LIFE ACCOUNT OF NEEDS

On the minimally good human life account, people need whatever enables them to live minimally good human lives.[4] Although a few theorists have suggested something along these lines, none has said much about what exactly a minimally good life requires (Anscombe 1958; Hassoun 2009a). This chapter will begin this project.

It is possible to provide a perfectionist account of the minimally good life. Most perfectionists are concerned with what it is for a human life to be *good* as opposed to *minimally good*. One can, however, imagine a perfectionist theory intended to explicate the notion of a minimally good human life as one that develops the features that constitute or are central to human nature (Arneson 1999: 120). Such a theory might be developed via a two-stage process. First, sketch a broad account of what a minimally good life would be for animals as well as humans, if not all living things. Then, arrive at an account of the minimally good *human* life by considering "the peculiarities of the human situation" (Kraut 1994: 48).

Perfectionist theories are usually objective list theories and are distinguished from desire-, or preference-, based accounts of what a good life requires. It is reasonable to think that an adequate account of the minimally good human life will be objective in this way: Any conception of a minimally good human life must be sensitive to what people think they need, though it cannot be completely determined by the whimsy and occasional delusion of human desire. Before cashing out such a perfectionist account of the minimally good human life, however, it is important to get clear on the kind of minimalism at issue.

Because the idea would be to explicate a conception of a *minimally* good human life, it is unfortunate that perfectionist theories have their name. The minimally good human life need not be perfect. I think my life would be better if I did something that merited a Nobel Peace Prize. But I do not need to do any such thing to live a minimally good human life.

On the other hand, a human life may not be *minimally* good and yet have some significant and valuable things in it. It is easy to imagine someone with a great career, for instance, living a miserable life, devoid of basic human attachment, completely isolated from the rest of world.

Nevertheless, even *minimally* good lives should have some things of value or pleasure or have some significance. A human life completely devoid of pleasure, significance, and value is not even minimally good.

What exactly is necessary for a *minimally* good human life will probably vary between contexts. In Finland, where the winter is quite cold, heat may be necessary, even for survival. In Hawaii, people can live minimally good lives without heat. Some people need a lot of nutrients just to survive, never mind flourish.

In every context, a minimally good human life for humans cannot just be a life that is worth living. Lives may be worth living even if they are thwarted in significant respects (and contain significant pain and suffering). On balance it may be better to have such a life than to have no life at all. But those whose lives are just barely worth living do not live minimally *good* lives. The threshold for a minimally *good* human life falls between the threshold for a life worth living and a just plain good life.

Consider how a perfectionist account of the minimally good human life might look. Following Richard Arneson, for instance, it is possible to fruitfully (mis)interpret Thomas Hurka's perfectionism as providing an account of the minimally good human life (Arneson 1999). On this account, the minimally good human life includes the things "essential to humans and conditioned on their being living" (Hurka 1993: 16).[5] Following Hurka, one might suggest that practical reason is often essential to a minimally good human life.[6]

Or consider a different perfectionist theory. In "Desire and the Human Good," Richard Kraut might be (mis-)interpreted as suggesting that, to live a minimally good human life, "one must love something, what one loves must be worth loving, and one must be related in the right way to what one loves" (Kraut 1994: 44).[7] Alternately, Martha Nussbaum's list of basic capabilities might be fruitfully (mis-)interpreted as providing a characterization of the minimally good human life.[8]

It may be impossible to provide necessary and sufficient conditions for a minimally good human life, but reflection can help us isolate some characteristic features of such a life. There are common threats to individuals' ability to live minimally good lives—disease, hunger, and complete isolation pose such threats, for instance. Similarly, minimally good lives often share some basic characteristics—some degree of satisfaction with one's lot in life and connection with others in one's community, and so on. Many accounts of human rights help to specify common features of a minimally good life under the guise of establishing that certain interests are truly important (Nickel 2006).

To further illustrate the basic argumentative strategy and add some content to an account of the minimally good human life, this chapter will argue that, because humans are distinctively autonomous creatures, autonomy is characteristic of a minimally good human life. That is, it will suggest that whether or not one lives a minimally good human life is not a completely subjective matter. Rather, a minimally good human life is characteristically choice-worthy and a life in which one can make some significant choices.[9] In making such choices one must be free to shape one's own life (Nussbaum 2000: 72).[10]

Most perfectionist theories embrace the idea that a minimally good human life usually contains at least some autonomy. On Arneson's suggested adaptation of Hurka's theory, for instance, the minimally good human life includes the kind of practical and theoretical reason that this chapter will suggest is essential to autonomy. As Arneson points out, humans are not only physical objects but, more remarkably, living rational animals.[11] Similarly, on Kraut's theory, the minimally good human life requires making appropriate autonomous choices. We need to be able to reflect and evaluate to be related in the right way to the valuable things we love; our good is grounded "in our capacity for rational choice" (Kraut 1994: 48). Some minimal conditions for autonomy are also central to Nussbaum's account (Nussbaum 2007). Before arguing, however, that *any* plausible perfectionist theory should support the conclusion that autonomy is characteristic of a minimally good human life, let us say a bit about the kind of autonomy at issue.

AUTONOMY

To secure autonomy, to shape one's life, one needs to have some freedom from both internal and external constraint (Christman 1989). *Internal freedom* is roughly the capacity to decide "for oneself what is worth doing," one must be able to make "the decisions of a normative agent"—to recognize and respond to value as one sees it (Griffin 2006). One must be able to reason about and make some plans on the basis of one's beliefs, values, desires, and goals (henceforth *commitments*). *External freedom*, or liberty, is roughly freedom from interference to pursue a "worthwhile life" (Raz 1998; Griffin 2006). One must have some freedom from coercion and constraint; one must be able to carry out some plans.

The key difference between internal and external freedom is that the former is freedom from self-constraint, the latter freedom from environmental or other-imposed constraints. So a woman who can think for herself may have internal freedom even if she lacks external freedom because she is imprisoned. To live an autonomous life, however, more is required. One must actually exercise one's freedom—making both some simple and significant choices. And one must have at least some good options from which to choose. Let us consider each of these conditions for autonomy in turn.

First, what does it mean to say that one must be able to reason on the basis of one's commitments? The idea is just this: Autonomous people must have some instrumental reasoning ability. Some hold demanding conceptions of rationality on which saying that autonomy requires the ability to reason would be controversial. Kant, for instance, thinks that (practical) reason requires each of us to acknowledge the categorical imperative as unconditionally required (see Hill 1989; O'Neill 1986). The reasoning at issue does not require this much, however. People must have only some instrumental reasoning ability.

Next, consider what it means to say that one must be able to make some plans on the basis of one's commitments (see Bratman 2005). First, one must be able to make both some simple plans and some significant ones. To make significant plans one need not plan one's whole life or every detail of one's day. Rather, one must be able to navigate through one's day without too much difficulty and make general plans for the future. One must not be constrained to making plans only about how to meet one's needs like Joseph Raz's proverbial man in a pit (Raz 1998). Though one might not choose to exercise this ability, one must have the planning ability necessary to pursue the projects one values— to pursue a good life as one sees it. This ability requires a kind of internal freedom one can have even if subject to external constraint. One must be able to form some plans that would work if implemented. One must be able to make some plans that one could carry through if free from external constraint. There are many ways of making sense of this idea. One might, for instance, analyze the ability to make some plans on the basis of one's commitments in terms of the ability to make one's motivating commitments generally coherent. Alternately, one might give a decision-theoretic analysis of planning in terms of a consistent preference ordering. Yet another option is to explain the ability to make some plans on the basis of one's commitments in terms of ordering one's ends, perhaps by drawing on John Rawls's (1971) work on plans of life.

Consider what is required to carry out some plans. This ability requires both some internal and external freedom. One must be able to decide for oneself what is worth pursuing and be able to carry out those actions necessary to bring some valuable plans to fruition. The importance of the qualifier *some* is just this: One need not be able to carry out every valuable plan that one might want to carry out to have this component of autonomy. Still, the ability to carry out *some* valuable plans is a necessary component of this kind of autonomy. The idea that people must be able to reason about, make, and carry out both some simple and some significant plans is tied to the idea that people must have good options. Good options are not only a matter of what one desires or avoiding harm. One must be able to secure food, for instance, to live a minimally good human life whether or not one wants to do so. One cannot be like Raz's (1998) hounded woman fleeing forever from one tragedy or another.

The kind of options matters as well as numbers. People must be able to "exercise all the capacities human beings have an innate drive to exercise, as well as to decline to develop any of them" (ibid.: 375). People must be able to move their bodies, sense the world, use their imagination, express affection, and occupy their minds. A person needs options that are significant for that person. People lack good options if all of their choices are dictated by others or circumstances. They must not be paralyzed or chained. Their every decision must not be deter- mined beforehand by the dictate to maintain their life. A singer threat- ened with the loss of her voice if she does anything another person dislikes, for instance, is not autonomous. All of a person's options cannot have horrendous effects. On the other hand, if a person acts on his or her options, that must at least sometimes have significant effects. Though, to be autonomous, people need not fully realize their valu- able capacities, they must be able to choose or reject self-realization (ibid.).

What options people need may be relative to the socio-economic- political conditions in which they live. Where participation in the life of the community is necessary for a minimally good life, what is required will be different in different circumstances. There are certain basic options—for example, to be able to secure food, water, and shelter— that everyone needs to secure autonomy. In different circumstances (or cultures), however, different kinds of food, water, and shelter may be necessary. One might worry that the conception of autonomy at issue is objectionably Western, but people in all cultures value the ability to reason and plan and need at least some of the same things to do so. Even to follow the rules of a monastic order or extremely hierarchical community, one must be able to (and actually) decide to do so and, to do that, everyone needs at least enough food, water, and shelter to survive.

AUTONOMY AND THE MINIMALLY GOOD HUMAN LIFE

In the real world, this kind of autonomy is characteristic of a minimally good human life (henceforth simply a *minimally good life*).[12] Deep understanding, rewarding struggle, significant achievement, good rela- tionships, virtue, and so forth are some of the things that make a life go minimally well. Autonomy is often necessary for all this. Recall that, to be autonomous, people must be able to reason, make, and carry out simple plans on the basis of their commitments. To create and maintain good relationships, people must usually reason about, make, and carry out plans to spend time with their friends and family from amongst other good options. Planning and carrying out one's plans to learn or develop skills or character traits is often necessary for understanding or significant achievement. And so forth. So, autonomy is characteristic of a minimally good life.

Autonomy is often partly constitutive of a minimally good life as well. *Often*, part of what it means for us humans to live minimally good lives is that:

> [we] have a conception of ourselves and of our past and future. We reflect and assess. We form pictures of what a good life would be, often, it is true, only on a small scale, but occasionally also on a large scale. And we try to realize these pictures. (Griffin 2006: ch. 2)

Those who lack a conception of being a self—persisting through time with a past and a future—may be unable to hope or dream. Those who never pursue their conception of a good life often cannot achieve their goals, carry out projects, or live their lives on their own terms.[13] These things are often part of a minimally good life and they require the reasoning and planning conditions for autonomy (and good options). After all, reasoning is part of reflecting and assessing, and planning is part of trying to realize one's picture of a good life. And, in the real world, people usually need good options to achieve their goals, carry out their plans, and live life on their own terms.[14]

Although people need not control every aspect of their lives or even be very resolute to live minimally good lives, those who lack autonomy are often impaired. Because autonomy is often necessary for securing the things that make a life go minimally well, the non-autonomous are unlikely to live minimally good lives. Because autonomy is often partly constitutive of such a life, even those who secure all of the other things that make a life go minimally well may not live minimally good lives.

On this account, people can have minimally good human lives without autonomy. The severely disabled and very young, for instance, may have such lives. Even if these people cannot reason, form, or carry out plans, they may experience joy and sadness, pleasure and pain, music and light. Disability theorists have convincingly argued that there may be a lot of value in a life without autonomy (Kittay 2005). Although autonomy is characteristic, and often partly constitutive, of a minimally good life, it is *not always* necessary for such a life.

Finally, it is important to reiterate that many other things may be necessary for a minimally good life. Some connection with other people or the natural world may, for instance, be important components of a minimally good life. It is not plausible to say that only autonomy is characteristic, and often constitutive, of such a life.

Nor is it plausible that people only need what enables them to secure autonomy. People may be autonomous – choosing between valuable options like spending time with loved ones or contributing to society – but make poor choices and, so, fail to secure what they need. The fact that people need more than what will enable them to secure autonomy is what distinguishes the minimally good life account of need from autonomy- and personhood-based accounts like those suggested by Gillian Brock and James Griffin.

THE MINIMALLY GOOD HUMAN LIFE ACCOUNT OF NEEDS AND THE DESIDERATA

This chapter has started to explicate the minimally good human life account of needs by arguing that autonomy is characteristic, and often partly constitutive, of a minimally good human life. But does this capture differences in individuals' needs and provide a plausible basis for what decent societies must enable their members to secure? Considering the account's practical implications will help make this case.

This section will explain why, despite individual differences, everyone needs many of the things that appear on traditional lists of needs that decent societies must, plausibly, enable their members to secure—like food and water. It will conclude by considering and responding to a few objections.

Consider, first, how those who lack basic food, water, and health care are likely to suffer from autonomy-undermining disabilities. Malnutrition inhibits one's immune system's ability to fight infection and poor nutrition is linked even more directly to many non-infectious illnesses.[15] Those without basic preventative health care (for example, immunizations) are most at risk for many of these illnesses. Those who cannot secure essential medications (for example, dehydration salts and antibiotics) are most likely to be disabled by these diseases. Often the diseases acquired by those who lack basic food, water, and health care result in severe disabilities. Sometimes they kill people. The very sick and dead are obviously incapable of securing the kind of autonomy this chapter has argued is characteristic of a minimally good life.[16]

Similarly, many of those who lack adequate shelter suffer from autonomy-undermining disabilities. Those without adequate shelter may be exposed to environmental hazards including disasters, pollutants, parasites, and bacteria (for example, in flood water or unsanitary living conditions (Johns Hopkins and the International Federation of Red Cross and Red Crescent Societies 2011)). These "hazards are responsible for about a quarter of the total burden of disease worldwide, and nearly 35% in regions such as sub-Saharan Africa" (World Health Organization 2011). Bed nets alone could prevent a lot of autonomy-undermining illness.[17]

Less obviously, some of those without basic education, emotional, and social goods suffer from autonomy-undermining disabilities (Woolcock 2001; Doyle 2002). Basic education, emotional, and social goods are often necessary for securing decent living conditions, health care, livelihood opportunities, and earning power (Marmot 2004). Those who lack (formal or informal) elementary education *may* not develop or maintain the reasoning and planning skills they need to secure autonomy (Beaton 2003; Doyle 2002; Marmot 2004).[18] Those who lack basic emotional and social goods are at high risk for mental and physical illness, suicide, and early death from other causes (Cullen and Whiteford 2001; Woolcock 2001; Hudson 2005). "Fear, insecurity, dependency, depression, anxiety, intranquility, shame, hopelessness, isolation and powerlessness [. . .] such experiential elements of a bad life [. . .] [often impact] agency" (Brock 1999: 33). Most people must be able to secure basic education, emotional, and social goods to secure autonomy.

This account fulfills the desiderata from which this chapter started. It is plausible that a decent society must enable most of its members to secure food, water, shelter, education, health care, and social and emotional goods. Most people need these things on the minimally good human life account. Some people will be able to secure autonomy without being able to obtain very much food, water, shelter, education, health care, or social or emotional goods (O'Neill 2005). More may be necessary for others to secure autonomy. So, the minimally good human life account of needs also captures individual differences in need.

One might object that an adequate account of the minimally good life should include much more than the sort of autonomy at issue in this chapter. If autonomy only requires the ability to reason about, make, and carry out plans and good options, some young children are autonomous. At least one could argue that the account of the minimally good life is too minimal; a decent society must enable its members to secure much more than food, water, and so forth. Similarly, saying that everyone needs what will allow them to secure the kind of minimally good life cashed out here will not account for each and every person's needs.

It is true that a *full* account of the minimally good life must include much more than this minimal autonomy but this chapter has only argued that this autonomy is characteristic, and often partly constitutive, of a minimally good life. So, while the sketch has not been filled out enough to provide a complete account of what a decent society must enable its members to secure, it is plausible that decent societies must enable their members to secure at least this much. Similarly, this chapter has not shown that a complete account of the minimally good life will capture each and every person's needs, but the account does capture some important differences in individual needs and it does not say that people need things they do not. Finally, as will become clear below, the account avoids the problematic counter-examples to which the alternatives fall prey.

A more troublesome objection is that it would be too much to require a decent society to enable all of its subjects to secure what they need to attain even the minimal autonomy this chapter has argued is characteristic, and often partly constitutive, of a minimally good life. Some have very expensive health needs and others may lack the social and emotional support they need for minimally good lives even in a decent society.

Perhaps it is implausible to believe that decent societies have to enable all of their subjects to live minimally good lives. If so, however, it is also implausible that these societies have to enable everyone to secure a minimal level of welfare, basic capabilities, or what not. That said, I believe that it *is* plausible that any decent society should enable its members to live minimally good lives when it is possible to do so. Even if this is not realistic or desirable in our world because, for instance, it is too expensive to help some live minimally good lives, that is not necessarily a problem for a theory of needs: There may be a cost threshold limiting what a society is required to provide for its members that is external to an account of what people need. Moreover, there are good reasons to keep the threshold external to an account of what people need. A person who must have expensive medical care to live needs that care, even if that is not the kind of need it is reasonable to require a decent society to meet. Everyone needs some social and emotional support whether or not a society does a good job in creating social spaces that foster supportive communities.

COMPETING ACCOUNTS OF NEEDS

This section argues that the minimally good human life account of needs has some advantages over the most plausible alternatives: harm and social role accounts. The main alternative accounts of need were not designed to fulfill the desiderata with which this chapter started. Harry Frankfurt only tried to account for the presumptive force of needs (Frankfurt 1988). Garrett Thompson wanted to give an account of needs that can explain why one cannot say truly that someone should have different needs (Thompson 2005). David Braybrooke tried to explain what people need in a way that could play a role in guiding public policy (Braybrooke 1987). Still, harm and social role theories are amongst the best developed accounts of needs, so it is worth seeing if they can fulfill the other criteria for a good account of needs set out at the start as well as those they are supposed to fulfill. If they cannot and the minimally good human life account of needs fares better, there is at least some reason to take the minimally good human life account seriously.

Harm-Based Accounts

In *The Importance of What We Care About*, Harry Frankfurt defends one of the most famous accounts of need. Frankfurt argues that people need those things that allow them to avoid harm when they cannot avoid harm in any other way. People need those things that are "necessarily necessary for avoiding harm" (Frankfurt 1988: 112). Although he does not give a complete account of *harm*, Frankfurt says a few things. First, he says, one is harmed if one is made worse off than before. He also claims that, if the only way to keep one's situation from becoming worse is to make it better, one's situation must improve for one to avoid harm. Finally, Frankfurt says that if one remains in a bad condition, one is harmed. He justifies this last claim by noting that more of a bad thing is worse than less of it (ibid.: 110).

There are at least three problems with Frankfurt's account. First, Frankfurt's notion of harm is too inclusive. Intuitively, one may not be harmed if one's bad state merely persists. Some are not made worse off than before by remaining in a bad state that does not become worse. Suppose, for instance, that Grace is in the early stages of Parkinson's syndrome, a degenerative disease. She shakes and has bradykinesia but can still walk and feed herself. Suppose, further, that she is given a new medication that stabilizes her condition. Her condition may remain the same (in at least one sense); she may still shake and have bradykinesia but retain her mobility and ability to feed herself. Even so, it seems that Grace has been helped, not harmed.

Perhaps Frankfurt could say that one's going from a degenerative to a stable condition constitutes a change in one's state. If so, one's bad state does not persist, rather one is in a new stable state. So, he could argue that one has not been harmed by the change. He must say more to show that one cannot benefit from something that keeps a bad state from getting worse in light of the fact that one may be lucky one's state does not deteriorate (note: this is all consistent with the fact that sometimes withholding a benefit can constitute harm).

Alternately, Frankfurt could respond to the Grace case a different way. He might say that Grace is harmed because, absent the disease, she would be much better off. Grace is worse off than she was before she became ill. More generally, Frankfurt could maintain (1) that someone may be harmed if and only if they would otherwise be in a much better state and (2) that people whose bad state persists are worse off than they would otherwise be.

Neither contention is plausible. Adopting this conception of harm for the moment, however, it should be clear that one's bad state persisting does not necessarily make one worse off than one would otherwise be. Grace, for instance, would have been in a worse state if her condition had not stabilized (on any reasonable way of thinking about her state; she would have both lost the use of her legs and continued to degenerate). The fact that her bad state persists does not mean she is worse off than she would otherwise be (though it is plausible that Grace's life goes worse if she is ill for longer).

Saying that the relevant comparison is to the time right before Grace got her degenerative disease will not help. Before getting her degenerative disease Grace may have had a much worse disease. She might, for instance, have had cancer (though her cancer was removed just as she was developing Parkinson's). If so, Frankfurt must agree that (on this conception of harm) Grace has not been harmed by becoming ill. But this is unintuitive.

The second problem for Frankfurt's account is that people do not always need those things that allow them to avoid harm. Some harm is insignificant and people do not need to avoid insignificant harm. I do not need to wear protective clothing even if this is the only way to keep me from getting paper cuts. Even if it is a law of nature that I will get paper cuts if I do not wear protective clothing, I do not need to wear such clothing.

Frankfurt might object that the paper cuts are not harms because they are not severe enough to constitute harms. Alternately, he could say that one does not need to wear protective clothing to avoid paper cuts because the clothing would be more harmful than the cuts.

I do not believe either of these responses goes through. First, it is more plausible that the cuts are minor harms than that they are not harms at all. Second, it is hard to see how protective clothing is harmful. Perhaps the idea is that people may be harmed if they are forced to wear such clothing. But that need not be the case. Suppose, for instance, that a woman raised in a liberal family in the US freely decides to wear a hijab that would protect her from paper cuts. Does she then need to wear a hijab? I think not, or at least not to avoid paper cuts. Perhaps the idea is that the clothing is harmful because it is a nuisance but some may not be bothered by the clothing. Finally, suppose this is wrong and the clothing is harmful. On Frankfurt's account that only seems to imply that people need to avoid the clothing as well as the cuts, not that they do not need to wear the clothing (for without it they will also be harmed by the cuts). If the clothing is not as harmful as the cuts, he will presumably suggest wearing the clothing. But the important point here is just that it is really implausible or at least it is not in line with our ordinary discourse to say that one needs protective clothing to avoid paper cuts.

Frankfurt cannot avoid this problem by suggesting that we need what, all things considered, will prevent the greatest harm. For, sometimes we do need what will prevent lesser harms as well, we just cannot have it. Pregnant women may need anti-inflammatory drugs even if all things considered refraining from consuming them will prevent the greatest harm to the women as well as their fetuses.

Even setting aside these objections from intuition, however, there is another problem with saying that people have a basic need for full body coverings to avoid paper cuts. A good account of need should provide a plausible basis for what, at minimum, a decent society is obligated to enable its members to secure. Decent societies do not always need to enable their subjects to secure full body coverings (even if full body coverings are necessary to avoid paper cuts).

Furthermore, decent societies are not always obligated to enable their subjects to secure even what will enable them to avoid serious harms. Sometimes undergoing significant harm can be beneficial. Enduring significant harm may, for instance, be the only way to secure an even greater benefit. Someone with a good prognosis for recovery who must live through chemotherapy may be harmed by the therapy, but still needs it. Even if chemotherapy is successful it can cause kidney malfunction, infections, blood clots, and many other serious problems for patients (National Cancer Institute 2007). Upon recovery patients may end up with new problems. They may even be sicker than they were when their cancer was first discovered (though they may be better off than they would otherwise be). Usually the harms that result from the treatment are less severe than those that will occur without the treatment, but they are still harms. It may even be the case that a decent society must enable its subjects to secure chemotherapy.

Frankfurt might argue that this is not a good case because one who has to undergo chemotherapy is not harmed by the therapy but is instead helped by it. After all, without the chemotherapy those with cancer often die. At least this seems right if Frankfurt's underlying conception of harm is one on which people can only be harmed by something if they are made worse off than they would otherwise be (Kagan 1998).

Although this chapter did not challenge this way of specifying Frankfurt's conception of harm above, it is implausible. Suppose that George is riding upon his dark steed when he comes across Effe standing on a corner. Being a Very Evil Man, George stabs Effe, grabs her purse, and gallops away. Unbeknownst to George, Effe had just decided to walk down a dark street that she could not see was covered with ice. If George had not interrupted her she would have walked down the street, fallen, hit her head, and died from the injury days later. Because she has been stabbed, however, Effe goes to the hospital instead. It seems that George has still harmed Effe. Frankfurt could not argue that the fact that someone has not been made worse off than they would otherwise be means that that person has not been harmed (see Feinberg 1984).

Even if Frankfurt does not share this intuition and insists on a global theory of harm, his account requires much more defense. It is not clear that his theory can capture all and only the needs of each person. Unless he can say more, his account unintuitively suggests that some people need things they do not (for example, full body coverings) and cannot account for the fact that some people need the things they do (for example, stabilizing medication, if not chemotherapy). So, Frankfurt's account does not provide a plausible basis for what, at minimum, a decent society is obligated to enable its members to secure.

Perhaps a different harm-based account of needs will fare better. In his delightful article "Fundamental Needs," Garrett Thompson argues that "X is a fundamental need for person A" if "X is a non-derivative, non-circumstantially specific and an inescapable necessary condition in order for the person A not to undergo serious harm" (Thompson 2005: 175). Thompson specifies that "a person is harmed when he or she is deprived of engaging in non-instrumentally valuable experiences and activities as well as the possibility of appreciating them" (ibid.: 178).

Unfortunately, Thompson's harm-based account of needs must also be rejected. There is an important ambiguity in the above-quoted claim. It is not clear whether Thompson intends to indicate that: (1) a person is harmed when he or she is deprived of engaging in *any* non-instrumentally valuable experiences and activities as well as the possibility of appreciating them; or (2) a person is harmed when he or she is deprived of engaging in *all* non-instrumentally valuable experiences and activities as well as the possibility of appreciating them. Neither interpretation of Thompson's definition is plausible. The first way of construing his definition must be rejected for the following reason: People are not necessarily harmed by being deprived of some non-instrumentally valuable experiences and activities or the possibility of appreciating them. I may have a non-instrumentally valuable experience looking at a Van Gogh. I will not be harmed if I am deprived of doing so because the museum is closed. Some non-instrumentally valuable experiences are not important enough that being deprived of them constitutes harm. The second way of construing Thompson's definition is also implausible. People may be harmed even if they are not deprived of all non-instrumentally valuable experiences and activities and the possibility of appreciating them. I am harmed if I am not allowed to associate with other humans even if I am not deprived of other non-instrumentally valuable activities or experiences.

Now, Thompson might not be intending to offer a definition of harm but still insist that his account of needs is generally defensible. If a person is deprived of engaging in *all* non-instrumentally valuable experiences and activities as well as the possibility of appreciating them, that person is harmed. Usually those who are deprived of non-instrumentally valuable experiences are harmed.

Although this response is promising, it cannot do. With this analysis, Thompson's account at most offers a characterization of needs. It is not clear that a characterization of needs can help us figure out what each and every person needs or *what a decent society must enable its members to secure.* Furthermore, it is not entirely plausible to characterize needs in this way. In many cases, one can be seriously harmed by being deprived of non-instrumentally valuable experiences without being deprived of what one needs. Even a rich person may be seriously harmed by being deprived of his or her (non-instrumentally valuable) job though the rich person does not need the job. This example might be adapted to provide a general objection to harm theories. It is not always plausible to think the person who is harmed has unmet needs.

Finally, Thompson's account may have to contend with another general objection to harm accounts. Intuitively, some of the things people need they need not merely to avoid harm but in order to flourish. It is possible to argue for this conclusion in several ways. Often people need purely instrumentally valuable goods to flourish. Alternately (though Thompson will not accept this account), consider a conception of harm on which someone can only be harmed if she is made worse off than before. In some developing countries there are ten-year-old children who are working and will not receive a secondary school education. On this conception of harm, these children will not be harmed by failing to receive this education: They are not made worse off than they were before if they are not educated. But, intuitively, most of these children do need education. Intuitively, this is something that a decent society should, at a minimum, enable these children to secure *because* they need it.

Social Role Accounts

The minimally good human life account of needs is not the only account that can explain why people need things that they do not need to avoid harm. David Braybrooke's social role account in *Meeting Needs* has this flavor. Policy-makers can determine the needs of a population via a two-step process. First, they must create a list of necessary goods that enable individuals to fully carry out four social roles—citizen, worker, parent, and housekeeper (Braybrooke 1987). Discussion is essential to determining the exact content of the list. Then, policy-makers must determine the minimal standards of provision for necessary goods. These standards should be set at the level sufficient for each member of the population to carry out each social role. Braybrooke thinks that even those who choose not to occupy a particular social role need many of the same things that those who occupy all of the roles need.

Unfortunately, some people do not need the things that would let them occupy Braybrooke's social roles and others need things that they do not need to occupy these roles (especially if they hope to occupy other roles). A monk who never wants to have children may not need to have them or be a worker, but may need religious freedom.

Even if Braybrooke agrees that the monk needs religious freedom, he might suggest that this freedom is just a part of the freedom of conscience necessary for the social roles at issue in his account. He might maintain that people need freedom of conscience to be good citizens, for instance. Perhaps some freedom of religion is necessary for the kind of freedom of conscience people need to be good citizens, workers, parents, and housekeepers.

It is not clear, however, that people need the kind of religious freedom the monk needs to fulfill Braybrooke's social roles. Many of those in the world's most oppressive regimes who lack freedom of conscience as well as freedom of religion are parents, housekeepers, workers, and citizens, for instance.

Perhaps Braybrooke could maintain that the monk only needs the *opportunity* to have jobs and children. Perhaps his idea is just that people need to have the opportunity to fulfill their social roles. Maybe old monks do not need to be able to have children but when they are young, everyone should have this option.

Unfortunately, Braybrooke cannot claim that people just need to have the opportunity to fulfill his (their) social roles. If the monk, for instance, never wants to have children nor wants the opportunity to do so, it would be strange to say he needs this opportunity. At least the monk does not need the opportunity to have children if he stays a monk who does not want children. Though, if the monk did decide that he wanted to have children, he may need the option.

Braybrooke would probably respond to this last worry by saying that he is only concerned to give an account of what people *typically* need in a way that could be presented to the public. For, he explicitly says that not everyone will need to play every social role on his list and emphasizes that he is not concerned about idiosyncratic, or episodic needs. Most people need what will allow them to have children and homes. Few people need the kind of religious freedom monks need. Similarly, most people need what will allow them to work and to have citizenship in some country, though some extraordinary individuals do fine without these things. For Braybrooke, needs are (rebuttably) universal propositions for people in their prime who are not disabled (Braybrooke 1987: S2.33). Braybrooke is only trying to give an account that can form the basis for social policy.

This, however, is just to say that Braybrooke is engaged in a quite different project than the one in which this chapter is engaged. Although Braybrooke's project is also quite valuable, his account cannot be used for this chapter's purposes. Braybrooke's account does not fulfill the desiderata with which this chapter started. It does not capture all the differences in individual needs because, intuitively, some needs are not even rebuttably universal (that is, few would think everyone needs the kind of religious freedom the monk needs). So it does not capture these individuals' needs. Braybrooke's account, like harm accounts of needs, also suggests that some people need things that they do not (some do not need work or children but these are rebuttably universal needs).[19] Perhaps for this reason, decent societies need not enable their members to secure all and only those things Braybrooke's account suggests. Decent societies need not enable their members to fulfill all the social roles if they do not want to do so. They need not, for instance, enable monks who do not want to have children to do so. Decent societies may, however, have to enable monks to secure significant religious freedom. The claim is not that what people need is determined by what they want but that the life plans people pursue are relevant to what they need.

Braybrooke might object that a good account of needs must provide a basis for public policy. He might argue that the minimally good life account of needs cannot play that role. Few people understand, never mind agree on, the value of autonomy that is central to the account (Braybrooke 1998). Policy-makers need a simple, concrete list of what most people need, not a highly philosophical account of needs.

The minimally good life account of needs might provide a basis, however, for public policy. People do understand what it means to reason and plan and so on, so policy-makers could just talk about the abilities constituting what this chapter has called autonomy, rather than using the term "autonomy" when talking about these components of a minimally good life. Furthermore, the minimally good life account can provide the basis for a simple, concrete list of needs. To create such a list, policy-makers just have to focus on what *most* people need to live a minimally good life.

Note that, in providing concrete policy advice, the minimally good life account may fare no better than Thompson's account. Unlike Thompson's account, however, it is plausible that the minimally good life account, when it is not being used for policy purposes, captures all and only the things each person needs. So, even if it is not good to use a highly philosophical account of needs as the basis for public policy, such an account may be useful for other (that is, philosophical) purposes. Once again, this is just to say that harm, social role, and minimally good life accounts of need may be part of different, but valuable, projects.

HARM, SOCIAL ROLES, AND THE MINIMALLY GOOD HUMAN LIFE

Intuitively, not everyone needs everything that will allow them to avoid harm or fulfill traditional social roles and some people need other things. Still, there is a close connection between meeting needs, avoiding harm, and fulfilling traditional social roles. If the minimally good human life account of needs is defensible, it may be able to explain this connection. People are usually harmed if their ability to live a minimally good life is undermined. Those who cannot live a minimally good life are often unable to do so because they have been harmed or are prevented from fulfilling important social roles. People may not be able to live minimally good lives if they are prevented from working and earning enough to feed themselves, for instance. Similarly, people are often incapable of fulfilling social roles and avoiding harm because they cannot live minimally good lives. Those who cannot secure autonomy, for instance, may not be able to fulfill important social roles or avoid serious harms. The minimally good human life account may retain some of the advantages of the traditional accounts. It also avoids some of their implausible consequences. The account does not fall prey to the above counter-examples to harm and social role based accounts. Most rich people do not need jobs to live minimally good lives, but they do need human interaction. Most monks do not need to be workers or parents to live minimally good lives, but most children need education to live such lives.

CONCLUSION

The minimally good human life account of need, unlike its main competitors, can fulfill the desiderata for a good account with which this chapter started. Both harm and social role theories capture some things it seems that people do not need, and/or neglect other things it seems that people do need. Because of this, it is not plausible that a decent society must enable its subjects to secure what they need to avoid harm or fulfill social roles. The minimally good human life account of needs fares better. It is plausible that each person needs whatever will enable them to live a minimally good life and nothing else. It is plausible that a decent society should enable its subjects to secure what they need for a minimally good life. Like its competitors, the minimally good human life account requires further cashing out. There is, however, reason to take it seriously.

Notes

1. The author would like to thank Gillian Brock, David Braybrooke, Allen Buchanan, Thomas Pogge, Thomas Christiano, Michael Gill, Jerry Gaus, Keith Lehrer, Susan Wolf, Allen Buchanan, Alex London, James Griffin, Dale Dorsey, and audiences at the University of Arizona, ATINER 3rd International Conference on Philosophy Northwest Philosophy Conference, and KwaZulu-Natal University for helpful comments. Finally, she is terribly grateful for the support she received from the American Association of University Women, the University of North Carolina Chapel Hill, Duke University, the Earhart Foundation, the Falk

Foundation, Stanford University's Center for Ethics in Society, and the United Nations University's World Institute for Development Economics Research for their support during the course of this project. She apologizes to anyone she has so carelessly forgotten to mention. Some of the arguments advanced here appeared first in Hassoun 2009b. The author would like to thank *Res Philosophica* for permission to reprint some of the arguments that appear in the following publication here: Nicole Hassoun, "Human Rights and the Minimally Good Life," *Res Philosophica*, vol. 90, no. 3 (July 2013), pp. 413–38, DOI: 10.11612/resphil.2013.90.3.6.

2. For discussion of the idea that justice should respond to individual differences in this way, see Nussbaum (2000) and Pogge (2002).
3. I have argued elsewhere that there are significant obligations to help those in need and suggested something like this account. See for instance Hassoun (2012, 2013). I have also advanced some constraints on an adequate theory for how institutions should meet need in Hassoun (2009a).
4. If these things include welfare, capabilities, resources, or opportunities, this account may overlap in part, or whole, with versions of welfare, capability, resource, or opportunity accounts of what decent societies must enable most of their members to secure.
5. Ultimately, Arneson rejects this kind of perfectionism because he does not think it can accommodate cheap thrills. I do not find this particularly compelling but if cheap thrills are essential to human wellbeing, maybe humans and other animals need cheap thrills to live minimally good lives.
6. Hurka uses Kripkean thought experiments to argue for this contention.
7. Neither author uses the exact phrase "minimally good life" but, as I explain below, the exact phrase is not important.
8. On this account, people would need: life, health, nourishment, bodily integrity, shelter, reproductive choice, sensation, imagination, reason, adequate education and freedom of expression, the ability to experience emotions, pleasure and avoid non-beneficial pain, to form attachments, to form a conception of the good life, affiliate with others, and have the social bases of self-respect. They might also need to be able to care for and live in relation to other parts of the natural world, play, participate effectively in politics, and have equal rights to employment and property (Nussbaum 2007: 23–4).
9. As David Brink puts it, "This perfectionist conception of the significance of choice or post-deliberative desire may sound remarkably like an informed desire conception of practical reason or the good. But notice some important differences. First, an informed desire conception defines normatively significant desire by appeal to a *counterfactual* condition. Is the desire one which *would* emerge from some suitable idealization of the agent's current desires? By contrast, the perfectionist conception appeals to an *historical*

condition. Is the desire one which was produced or is sustained by a suitable kind of deliberation?" (2008: 41; original emphasis). Still, "it is choice, rather than desire, as such, that has normative significance" (ibid.: 40).

10. Some have suggested autonomy-based accounts of need. On such accounts, people need whatever will enable them to live autonomous lives. The problem with autonomy-based accounts of needs is that some people cannot secure autonomy, but even these people have some needs.

11. Although it will not do here to go into Hurka's argument for this conclusion, he basically uses a scientifically informed Kripkean conceptual analysis to reject other perfectionist conceptions because they fail two tests. They either fail to retain the appeal of the idea that human nature is morally significant or have implausible consequences by suggesting that human nature includes things that lack moral significance. See Hurka (1993: 9). As Richard Kraut puts it, perfectionist theories are developed via "two-stage processes in which a broad account that applies universally is then made more specific by being tied to the peculiarities of the human situation." See Kraut (1994: 48).

12. This does not mean that autonomy's value is completely derivative from its role in enabling people to live a minimally good life or that the minimally good life's value depends entirely on the value of autonomy.

13. Again, the kind of reasoning and planning one must be able to do need not be particularly complex. For an interesting discussion of non-intellectual pleasures that may contribute to a minimally good life, see Braybrooke (1989).

14. At least this seems right on the conditions for autonomy this chapter has defended.

15. Scurvy results from a lack of vitamin C, beri-beri from a lack of thiamine, pellagra from niacin deficiency, and macrocytic and microcytic anemia from folic acid and iron deficiencies, for instance. There is also a lot of evidence that decent nourishment is important for good cognitive functioning. Children's mental functioning can even be impaired if their mothers do not receive proper nourishment during pregnancy (see Leathers and Foster 2009).

16. The feedback loop between malnutrition and illness also goes in the other direction—illness can promote dietary deficiencies just as dietary deficiencies can promote illness (ibid.).

17. Bed nets can prevent many cases of dengue fever and malaria, for instance. See Center for Disease Control and Prevention (2011).

18. Stress may contribute to a host of autonomy-undermining mental disorders. Stress can, for instance, cause panic attacks and depression. Psychological disorders can reduce the ability of one's immune system to fight infection. See Beaton (2003).

19. In conversation Braybrooke has resisted the idea that people need children but I can see no other way that one might be a parent.

References

Alkire, Sabina (2002), *Valuing Freedoms*, Oxford: Oxford University Press.

Anscombe, Elizabeth (1958), "Modern Moral Philosophy," *Philosophy*, vol. 33, no. 124, pp. 1–19.

Arneson, Richard (1999), "Human Flourishing Versus Desire Satisfaction," *Social Philosophy & Policy*, vol. 16, no. 1, pp. 113–42.

Beaton, David B. (2003), "Effects of Stress and Psychological Disorders on the Immune System," Rochester Institute of Technology Working Paper, New York: Rochester Institute of Technology.

Bratman, Michael (2005), "Planning Agency, Autonomous Agency," in J. S. Taylor (ed.), *New Essays on Personal Autonomy and Its Role in Contemporary Moral Philosophy*, Cambridge: Cambridge University Press, pp. 33–57.

Braybrooke, David (1987), *Meeting Needs*, Princeton, NJ: Princeton University Press.

Braybrooke, David (1989), "Review: Thoughtful Happiness," *Ethics*, vol. 99, no. 3, pp. 625–36.

Braybrooke, David (1998), "The Concept of Needs, with a Heartwarming Offer of Aid to Utilitarianism," in G. Brock (ed.), *Necessary Goods: Our Responsibilities to Meet Others' Needs*, New York: Rowman & Littlefield, pp. 57–72.

Brink, David (2008), "The Significance of Desire," in R. Shafer-Landau (ed.), *Oxford Studies in Metaethics*, vol. 3, Oxford: Oxford University Press, pp. 5–46.

Brock, Gillian (ed.) (1998), *Necessary Goods: Our Responsibilities to Meet Others' Needs*, New York: Rowman & Littlefield.

Brock, Karen (1999), *"It's Not Only Wealth that Matters – It's Peace of Mind Too": A Review of Participatory Work on Poverty and Illbeing*, Brighton: Institute of Development Studies.

Buchanan, Allen (2004), *Justice Legitimacy and Self-Determination: Moral Foundations for International Law*, Oxford: Oxford University Press.

Center for Disease Control and Prevention (2011), *Vector Control*, Atlanta: Center for Disease Control and Prevention, <http://www.cdc.gov/nceh/ehs/etp/vector.htm> (last accessed 26 October 2015).

Christman, John (ed.) (1989), *The Inner Citadel: Essays on Autonomy*, Oxford: Oxford University Press.

Copp, David (1998), "Equality, Justice, and the Basic Needs," in Gillian Brock (ed.), *Necessary Goods: Our Responsibilities to Meet Others' Needs*, New York: Rowman & Littlefield, pp. 113–34.

Cullen, Michelle and Harvey Whiteford (2001), "Inter-relations of Social Capital with Health and Mental Health," Mental Health and Special Programs Branch Commonwealth Department of Health and Aged Care Discussion Paper, Canberra: Commonwealth Department of Health and Aged Care.

Doyle, Rodger (2002), "Calculus of Happiness: Assessing Subjective Well-Being Across Societies," *Scientific American* (November), p. 32.

Feinberg, Joel (1984), *Harm to Others*, Oxford: Oxford University Press.

Frankfurt, Harry (1988), *The Importance of What We Care About: Philosophical Essays*, Cambridge: Cambridge University Press.

Griffin, James (2006), *Human Rights: The Incomplete Idea*, Working Draft, Corpus Christi College, Oxford.

Hassoun, Nicole (2009a), "Meeting Need," *Utilitas*, vol. 21, no. 3, pp. 250–75.

Hassoun, Nicole (2009b), "Human Rights, Needs, and Autonomy," in P. Hanna (ed.), *An Anthology of Philosophical Studies*, vol. 3, Athens: AITNER, pp. 277–88.

Hassoun, Nicole (2012), *Globalization and Global Justice: Shrinking Distance, Expanding Obligations*, Cambridge: Cambridge University Press.

Hassoun, Nicole (2013), "Human Rights and the Minimally Good Life," *Res Philosophica*, vol. 90, no. 3 (July), pp. 413–38, DOI: 10.11612/resphil.2013.90.3.6.

Hill, Thomas (1989), "The Kantian Conception of Autonomy," in J. Christman (ed.), *The Inner Citadel: Essays on Individual Autonomy*, Oxford: Oxford University Press: Oxford, pp. 91–105.

Hudson, Christopher G. (2005), "Socioeconomic Status and Mental Illness: Tests of the Social Causation and Selection Hypotheses," *American Journal of Orthopsychiatry*, vol. 75, no.1, pp. 3–18.

Hurka, Thomas (1993), *Perfectionism*, Oxford: Oxford University Press.

Johns Hopkins and the International Federation of Red Cross and Red Crescent Societies (2011), "Control of Communicable Diseases," <http://www.jhsph.edu/bin/k/c/Pages_from_Chapter_7_.pdf> (last accessed 25 October 2015).

Kagan, Shelley (1998), *Normative Ethics*, Boulder, CO: Westview Press.

Kittay, Eva Feder (2005), "At the Margins of Moral Personhood," *Ethics*, vol. 116, pp. 100–31.

Kraut, Richard (1994), 'Desire and the Human Good', Presidential Address delivered before the Ninety-Second Annual Central Division Meeting of the American Philosophical Association in Kansas City, Missouri, May 6, *Proceedings and Addresses of the American Philosophical Association*, vol. 68, no. 2, pp. 39–54.

Leathers, Howard D. and Phillips Foster (2009), *The World Food Problem: Toward Ending Undernutrition in the Third World*, 4th edn, Boulder, CO: Lynne Rienner.

Marmot, Michael (2004), *Status Syndrome: How Your Social Standing Directly Affects Your Health and Life Expectancy*, London: Bloomsbury.

National Cancer Institute (2007), "Coping with Side Effects," *Chemotherapy and You: A Guide to Self-Help During Cancer*, <http://www.cancer.gov/publications/patient-

Nickel, James (2006), *Making Sense of Human Rights*, Oxford: Oxford University Press.

Nussbaum, Martha (2000), *Women and Human Development: The Capabilities Approach*, Cambridge: Cambridge University Press.

Nussbaum, Martha (2007), "Human Rights and Human Capabilities," *Harvard Human Rights Journal*, vol. 20, pp. 21–4.

O'Neill, Onora (1986), *Faces of Hunger: An Essay on Poverty, Justice and Development*, London: Allen & Unwin.

O'Neill, Onora (2005), 'The Dark Side of Human Rights', *International Affairs*, vol. 81, no. 2, pp. 427–39.

Pogge, Thomas (2002), "Can the Capability Approach be Justified?," *Philosophical Topics*, vol. 30, no. 2, pp. 167–228.

Rawls, John (1971) *A Theory of Justice*, Cambridge, MA: Belknap Press.

Raz, Joseph (1998), *The Morality of Freedom*, Oxford: Clarendon Press.

Reader, Soran (2006), "Does a Basic Needs Approach Need Capabilities?," *Journal of Political Philosophy*, vol. 14, no. 3, pp. 337–50.

Thompson, Garrett (2005), "Fundamental Needs," in Soran Reader (ed.), *The Philosophy of Need*, Cambridge: Cambridge University Press, pp. 175–86.

Vallentyne, Peter (2005), "Debate: Capabilities Versus Opportunities for Well-Being," *Journal of Political Philosophy*, vol. 13, no. 3, pp. 359–71.

Woolcock, Michael (2001), "The Place of Social Capital in Understanding Social and Economic Outcomes," *Canadian Journal of Policy Research*, vol. 2, no. 1, <http://www.oecd.org/innovation/research/1824913.pdf> (last accessed 25 October 2015).

World Health Organization (2011), "10 Facts on Preventing Disease Through Healthy Environments," Geneva: World Health Organization, <http://www.who.int/features/factfiles/environmental_health/environmental_health_facts/en/> (last accessed 25 October 2015).

Part II

The Applicability of Global Principles – Some Contemporary Dilemmas

Chapter 4

TOWARD ANOTHER KIND OF
DEVELOPMENT PRACTICE

Julian Culp

INTRODUCTION

In this chapter I will defend the thesis that there are good reasons to support certain forms of the practice common among states of giving and receiving official development assistance (ODA).[1] These reasons are grounded in a discourse-theoretic, internationalist account of global justice and represent a novel moral rationale for certain forms of this international development practice. By *moral rationales for international development practice* I refer to moral justifications for the promotion of development activities across national borders. This promotion is conducted both by governmental and intergovernmental institutions such as, respectively, the British Department for International Development and the United Nations Development Programme. However, we will see that the forms of international development practice that discourse-theoretic Internationalism supports are recognizably different from the ones generally practiced today.

This discourse-theoretic, internationalist moral rationale agrees with theorists of global distributive justice – like Beitz, Pogge, Caney, and Brock – that participation in certain forms of international development practice can count as a demand of *justice* instead of solely a demand of *humanity*. Yet it also rejects their view that the moral rationale for international development practice is to further realize an ideal of global distributive justice. Rather, I will present a different moral rationale, contending that this practice can contribute to establishing certain domestic socio-political structures that are required by global discursive justice. This is because, by fostering in various ways democratic practices at the domestic level, certain forms of international development practice help to satisfy the intranational conditions of a fundamentally

79

just global basic structure. Thereby the processes of opinion and will formation at the international level can *eventually* be properly structured so as to permit the discursive justification of principles of global distributive justice that one may reasonably presume to be justified. I emphasize 'eventually', since, in addition to the fulfillment of the intranational conditions, certain international conditions regarding the degree of inequality in justificatory power at the international level must also be satisfied.

The argument for the thesis that there is such a 'Discourse-Theoretic Rationale' for certain forms of international development practice begins with a juxtaposition of two different and very influential moral rationales for this practice. These are the 'Humanitarian Rationale' and the 'Distributive Rationale', based respectively on considerations of humanity and global distributive justice. Note that the Humanitarian Rationale is a moral rationale for certain forms of international development practice, *not* for humanitarian aid. It is labeled 'humanitarian' because it is based on the so-called duty of humanity.[2]

This chapter agrees with the Distributive Rationale that the Humanitarian Rationale must be rejected, because the Humanitarian Rationale accepts the existing global distribution of holdings as just. However, this chapter argues against the Distributive Rationale and in favor of the Discourse-Theoretic Rationale by showing that the latter can more convincingly counter frequently voiced criticisms of actual international development practice.

Before I present this argument, I introduce the Discourse-Theoretic Rationale in the third section by suggesting a discourse-theoretic internationalist account of global justice that provides the basis for the novel, discourse-theoretic moral rationale for international development practice. I then also substantiate in detail this particular Discourse-Theoretic Rationale, arguing that certain forms of international development practice can effectively contribute to satisfying the intranational conditions of global justice by contributing to the establishment of more democratic socio-political institutions.

The fourth section confronts the Distributive Rationale and the Discourse-Theoretic Rationale with two very prominent criticisms that post-development theorists put forward against actual international development practice – the charge of ethnocentrism and the hermeneutic critique – and argues that the Discourse-Theoretic Rationale is better equipped to respond to them than the Distributive Rationale. The concluding section observes that the Discourse-Theoretic Rationale not only represents a well-grounded moral foundation for certain forms of the international development practice but also strengthens the case for discourse vis-à-vis distributivist theories of justice more generally.

MORAL RATIONALES FOR INTERNATIONAL DEVELOPMENT PRACTICE: HUMANITY AND JUSTICE

For more than six decades states have been engaging in the *global,* international practice of providing and receiving ODA. Statements by bureaucrats and government officials participating in the international development practice usually stress a moral rationale for the activity. One prominent example is World Bank president McNamara's 1973 Nairobi speech, in which he pointed out:

> In my view the fundamental case for development assistance is the moral one. The whole of human history has recognized the principle – at least in the abstract – that the rich and the powerful have a moral obligation to assist the poor and the weak. (McNamara 1973: section 3)[3]

Many empirical studies (McKinlay and Little 1977), development organizations (World Bank 1990: 127–8, 1998: 40–1) and commentators (Niggli 2008: ch. 7), however, contend that richer states participate in this practice simply to advance their foreign-policy objectives – specifically, that they provide ODA in order to gain political support from the poorer states in international negotiations or to pursue domestic economic interests abroad. It is very likely that such prudential considerations often do constitute the *actual rationales* for the provision of ODA. In fact, several studies (McGillivray 1989, 2004; White and McGillivray 1992, 1995; Alesina and Dollar 2000; Birdsall et al. 2003; Berthélemy and Tichit 2004) that strive to explain the actual rationale for international development practice by investigating the allocation of ODA flows among ODA recipients found support for this interpretation.

This chapter, however, does not pursue the empirical question of why richer or poorer states engage in international development practice. Rather, it asks whether there is a *moral rationale* for at least certain forms of this practice, that is, whether there exist moral considerations that justify states' continued participation in certain forms of international development practice. This inquiry thus also differs from prescriptive studies that ask how ODA flows ought to be allocated once one accepts a certain normative purpose of the ODA flows as given. The Oxford and World Bank economists Collier and Dollar (2001, 2002), for instance, propose 'optimal aid allocation rules' that would maximize the impact of ODA in reducing absolute poverty as defined by the World Bank's $1-per-day poverty line.[4] Others (Llavador and Roemer 2001; Cogneau and Naudet 2007) have suggested 'fair aid allocation rules' on the assumption that the purpose of ODA is to ensure that individuals have an equal opportunity to escape from poverty. By contrast, this chapter pursues the question of what, if anything, one ought to accept as the normative purpose of at least some forms of international development practice.

Many advocates of international development practice argue for the view that considerations of *humanity* provide the overriding moral rationale for this activity. This Humanitarian Rationale begins with the general principle that human beings have a moral duty to relieve human suffering whenever they can do so at a small personal cost. This moral principle, together with the further empirical claim that some forms of international development practice indeed allow members of richer states to reduce human suffering abroad at a small personal cost to them, ground a moral obligation to engage in the practice. Therefore, institutions' engagement in international development practice mediates duties of humanity that members of richer states have vis-à-vis members of poorer states.[5]

In a similar vein, other theorists emphasize that the reduction of human need constitutes a moral rationale for international development practice. There are at least two major differences, however, between such a 'Needs-Based Rationale' and the Humanitarian Rationale. First, the Needs-Based Rationale does not focus on human suffering generally but only on needs. Second, it generally assumes that the presence of needs provides a basis for claims to fulfill those needs, irrespective of the costs that others have to bear in order to satisfy them.[6] Utilitarians also have argued that *individuals* from richer countries have obligations to donate a substantial portion of their holdings to non-governmental organizations or to international institutions even if doing so entails incurring more than just a small personal cost. After all, if individuals from richer countries would give large amounts of their resources to charitable organizations, this would eventually increase the total amount of human welfare. A 'Utilitarian Rationale' for international development practice, based on a similar reasoning, would emphasize that financial support of certain forms of international development practice has the capacity to further overall human welfare (cf. Singer 1972; Unger 1996).[7]

Many other theorists, however, reject the Humanitarian Rationale as the sole moral foundation for certain forms of international development practice. These theorists argue instead that considerations of *global distributive justice* morally justify the practice. They claim that the validity of some egalitarian (Beitz [1979] 1999: 172–3; Pogge 1989, 1994; Moellendorf 2002: 61) or sufficientarian (Miller 2007: ch. 9; Brock 2009: ch. 5) distributive principle of justice is global in scope and therefore morally grounds a practice that can bring the actual distribution of holdings into closer conformity with the distribution of holdings that justice requires.

Among the specific possible actions, Pogge (1989: 256 n. 18, 264–5, 1994: 202) proposes an international tax on the extraction of nonrenewable resources and Brock (2009: 136, 122) suggests a more complex international taxation scheme to raise revenues for a 'global justice fund' that would provide the 'revenue that is badly needed in developing countries'. David Miller (2007: 254–7) also acknowledges some sufficientarian duties of global distributive justice that can be said to ground a Distributive Rationale, even if these duties, according to Miller, hold only on the condition that nobody in the country in which people live below the sufficiency threshold bears (outcome) responsibility for this state of affairs.

The defenders of the Distributive Rationale (Beitz [1979] 1999: 127, 172–3; Miller 2007: 260–1) stress that it is crucial to acknowledge that the moral foundation for participating in international development practice is based on considerations of justice and not only on considerations of humanity. This matters, they argue, because if these forms of international development practice were grounded on considerations of humanity alone, then their moral justification could vindicate only those forms of this practice that would not place more than a certain threshold of demand upon the givers.[8] As just mentioned, considerations of humanity establish a duty to relieve human suffering only on the condition that this can be done at small personal cost. Thus, if one were to propose establishing a form of international development practice that required of any given individual more than what he or she could provide at a small personal cost, such a practice would not be justifiable by a purely humanitarian rationale.

On the other hand, if a particular form of international development practice is justified on the basis of considerations of global distributive justice, then this justification cannot be rejected on the ground that it might require some individuals to incur more than a small personal cost. After all, if justice calls for a particular practice, no one can under-mine the claim of justice simply by objecting that it is very burdensome to carry it out. One would not think, for instance, that a slaveowner could ask not to participate in the institutional reform of a slaveholding society, simply because freeing the slaves would impose on him or her a substantial economic cost.

In addition, such global distributivist theorists also object that the Humanitarian Rationale – by suggesting that richer states ought to transfer some of *their* holdings to poorer states – accepts the existing global distribution of holdings. This is because moral considerations of humanity concern what one ought to do with one's *own* holdings in order to relieve human suffering. This fact, in turn, means that any claim owed as a matter of humanity presupposes an assumption about the just distribution of holdings. Kant, for one, doubts that people who have accrued their holdings unjustly can in any way use such holdings beneficently to further the well-being of someone else:

> Having the resources to practice such benevolence as depends on the goods of fortune is, for the most part, a result of certain human beings favored through the injustice of the government, which introduces an inequality of wealth that makes others need their beneficence. Under such circumstances, does a rich man's help to the needy, on which he so readily prides himself as something meritorious, really deserve to be called beneficence at all? (Kant [1797] 1996: 203)

Barry powerfully expresses a similar thought:

> We cannot sensibly talk about humanity unless we have a baseline set by justice. To talk about what I ought, as a matter of humanity, to do with what is mine makes no sense until we have established what is mine in the first place. (Barry [1982] 2008: 206–7)

Hence, the criticism runs, humanitarian advocates of international development practice who formulate a moral rationale for the practice *only* in terms of humanity accept the given global distribution of holdings as just. This, however, constitutes a grave moral flaw in the eyes of the distributivist theorists. After all, their argument for morally grounding the international development practice on an account of global distributive justice involves precisely the claim that the current global system decreeing what persons are entitled to is unjust.

The critique of the Humanitarian Rationale from the distributive point of view is very appealing. For why should one assume that the global distributional status quo is morally acceptable? If one does not want to follow Nagel (2005) and restrict the scope of justice arbitrarily to the boundaries of the state,[9] then it would be necessary to argue up front for a certain conception of global justice that vindicates the actual distribution of global holdings as just. However, there is no compelling conception of global distributive justice so far that would defend the view that the current global distribution of holdings is just.

Even the conservative statist (Blake 2001; Miller 2007: ch. 9; Brock 2009: ch. 3) conceptions of global distributive justice would consider it an injustice if a certain level of sufficiency remained globally unmet. Hence the Humanitarian Rationale rests on philosophical premises that still wait to be convincingly theorized and defended. This is not to say, of course, that constructing a defense of this position would be impossible. However, the Humanitarian Rationale would have to occupy an outlying position in the debate about global distributive justice, a position opposed to the view (held by the vast majority of theorists) that assuring some level of sufficiency to all is a minimal demand of global distributive justice.

Before presenting, in the fourth section, the arguments that demonstrate the deficiencies of the Distributive Rationale, I will next introduce the Discourse-Theoretic Rationale in greater detail. I begin by articulating briefly the central features of discourse-theoretic Internationalism. Then I make the case that this version of a discourse theory of global justice provides a sound moral rationale for at least certain forms of international development practice – a moral rationale, that is, for *another kind* of international development practice.

A DISCOURSE-THEORETIC RATIONALE FOR ANOTHER INTERNATIONAL DEVELOPMENT PRACTICE

The Humanitarian Rationale is not only problematic, because it pre-sumes the justice of the global distribution of holdings but also, one should add, the justice of the actual practices of justification and thus the global political system that authorizes who makes the decisions (and how they are made) about the socio-economic order that influ-ences the production and distribution of justice-relevant goods. This raises the question of whether a discourse theory of global justice could serve as a convincing basis for a moral rationale of certain forms of international development practice. In the remainder of this section I will answer this question in the affirmative, first by sketching an internationalist account of global discursive justice and, second, by explicating how such an account can ground a novel moral rationale for another kind of international development practice.

Global Discursive Justice – An Internationalist Account

A fundamental requirement of a discourse theory of justice is the establishment of basic structures of justification that enable persons 'to demand and provide justifications and to challenge false legitimations' (Forst 2011: 9). While on the domestic level this substantive, fundamen-tal requirement can be institutionally instantiated by a certain form of deliberative democracy,[10] it is far less clear how, in the absence of a world state, this fundamental requirement can be met on the global level.[11]

In a very schematic and admittedly cursory way, I outline in this sub-section an *internationalist* interpretation of this fundamental demand of discursive justice on the global level.[12] This internationalist account of global discursive justice demands on the *inter*national level that representatives of internally sufficiently just states ought to have suf-ficient justificatory power[13] in international processes of opinion and will formation that affect the lives of their members. Representatives of internally sufficiently just states would participate in discursively constructing the internationally valid, substantive principles of justice upon which the specific shape and contours of a just international order would then be erected. This demand holds for existing international institutions as well as for future international institutions that might be created with this specific purpose.[14]

With respect to the globally just distribution of justice-relevant goods, this means that the internationalist account does not argue for the implementation of a certain ideal of global distributive justice. Instead it urges that those affected by such distributive principles are entitled to provide the justifications that establish the normative validity of these principles, even if this means initially only that international processes of justification have to mediate the justifications of members of states via their government officials. I say 'initially' because there may exist further channels through which members of states may have influence upon international decision-making processes. The focus here, however, is on some minimal conditions that fundamental international justice requires, even if it is very likely that there will be further demands that go beyond these minimal conditions.

Second, since the justifications for any kind of international order must be ultimately justifiable to the states' members, the internationalist account also calls for appropriate structures of justification on the *intra*national level. Domestically, structures of justification must enable members of states 'to demand and provide justifications and to challenge false legitimations' (Forst 2011: 9) of the particular shape of their domestic social and political orders.

As long as this domestic requirement remains unmet, international practices of justification lack the normative quality necessary to ground a reasonable presumption of the moral acceptability of the agreements reached in international processes of opinion and will formation. For without the effective political opportunity to question the opinions expressed and decisions made by the representatives of states, members of states are not sufficiently taken into account when states' international priorities are determined.

In a nutshell, then, the internationalist account of global discursive justice consists of a two-pronged approach that requires the establishment of properly shaped structures of justification on both the inter- and intranational levels, which enable justificatory discourses to construct the principles that determine the fundamental shape of socio-political orders. It spells out the conditions whose fulfillment would make the global basic structure fundamentally just. The next sub-section will explain how one can employ such a discourse-theoretic and internationalist account of global justice as the foundation of a moral rationale for another kind of international development practice.

Global Discursive Justice and Another Kind of International
Development Practice

The internationalist account of global discursive justice can ground a moral rationale for another kind of international development practice, because certain forms of this practice can effectively contribute to the establishment of fundamentally just basic structures of justification on the *intra*national level. Hence this chapter assumes that international development practice can evolve in such a way as to become effective in fulfilling the conditions of global justice that discourse-theoretic Internationalism sets out.[15]

By focusing on this particular task, international development practice can help to achieve the fundamental requirement of an *inter*national basic structure of justification, which, as just mentioned, presupposes that the states that form this international structure are internally ordered in a fundamentally just way.

More specifically, certain forms of international development practice can facilitate the moral objective of discourse-theoretic Internationalism by empowering people to possess the capabilities that they require in order to gain the justificatory power necessary to participate in constructing and challenging of the institutional setup of their socio-political community. For instance, in states where *some* members are prevented from participating in political life because they are constantly preoccupied with their survival and sustenance, improving the socio-economic conditions *of the least powerful* would be an effective means to realize global discursive justice. Development policies directed at ameliorating conditions of health and education can likewise be morally grounded by the internationalist account of global discursive justice, but only on the condition that these policies function as effective means to create the political capabilities that confer more justificatory power on the least powerful members of a given state.[16]

The internationalist account of global discursive justice, thus, can substantiate a novel Discourse-Theoretic Rationale for certain forms of international development practice. Distinct from the Distributive Rationale, the Discourse-Theoretic Rationale does not suggest that the proposed kind of international development practice needs to be instrumental in bringing the actual distribution of goods into closer conformity with some (egalitarian or sufficientarian) ideal of global distributive justice. Rather, the Discourse-Theoretic Rationale starts from the observation that the very conditions under which representatives of states could engage internationally in a discursive construction of the normative principles determining a just global distribution of goods are currently absent, and that therefore the primary purpose of international development practice should be to fulfill those conditions.

As long as, in many states around the world, large segments of the population lack sufficient justificatory power and are thereby excluded from playing a relevant role in their domestic political procedures, international processes of opinion and will formation fail to ascertain valid principles of justice for the international order. Yet another kind of international development practice could help to overcome this fundamental injustice of the international order by fostering establishment of the domestic social and political conditions necessary to grant *all* members of states sufficient justificatory power to co-determine the concrete shape of their socio-political orders.

Even though this promotion of another kind of international development practice is meant to respond to considerations of *inter*national justice, by facilitating social and political changes on the *intra*national level of those states that lack properly organized structures of justification, it actually also contributes toward identifying the changes that international justice requires in those states that already possess a potentially fundamentally just structure of justification. As long as the global institutional order is based on international processes of opinion and will formation that do not possess the reasonable presumption of identifying valid principles of justice, no state can reasonably assume that its internal order is compatible with an international order that would have emerged from morally valid international processes of opinion and will formation. Hence, if effective, this novel form of international development practice would not only further international justice, but would also advance domestic justice in *all* states, whether or not they already have established a structure of justification internally that is *pro tanto* fundamentally just.

The next section argues that the Discourse-Theoretic Rationale can respond more convincingly than the Distributive Rationale to eminent critiques from post-development theorists who radically challenge the moral legitimacy of current international development practice. It is important to consider these critiques carefully, even if both the Distributive Rationale and the Discourse-Theoretic Rationale provide moral rationales for a new kind of international development practice different from the currently existing one that often appears to have as its main objective the furthering of donor countries' foreign policy goals. This is because the post-development theorists' objections are of such a general character that they seem to be addressing *any form* of international development practice.

Finally, the concluding section of this chapter will point out that the Discourse-Theoretic Rationale's ability to answer these critiques more convincingly than the Distributive Rationale also supports the soundness of discourse-theoretic formulations of justice vis-à-vis distributivist theories of justice more generally. This is because it shows that the considered moral judgments regarding the practical conclusions that result from the application of a discourse theory of justice are more robust than those that emerge from distributivist theories of justice.

THE POST-DEVELOPMENT CRITIQUES

In this section I present two post-developmental criticisms of international development practice and argue that the Discourse-Theoretic Rationale is better equipped to respond to these criticisms than the Distributive Rationale.[17] Thereby I make the comparative argument that we have more reason to endorse the Discourse-Theoretic than the Distributive Rationale as a moral foundation for certain forms of international development practice.

The Charge of Ethnocentrism

First, we will consider the charge of ethnocentrism, which alleges that current international development practice is based on the misapplication of the normative code of one (Western) socio-political context to a different context.[18] The objection to this transfer of a certain normative code from one context to another is that it fails to take into account the distinct characteristics of the two contexts that would call for applying different normative codes to their different socio-political circumstances. Escobar, for instance, whose important book *Encountering Development* acutely depicts existing international development practice as the product and medium of an asymmetric, dominating international discourse about development, argues:

Ethnocentrism influenced the form development took. Indigenous populations had to be 'modernized', where modernization meant the adoption of the 'right' values – namely, those held by the white minority or a mestizo majority and, in general, those embodied in the ideal of the cultivated European. (Escobar 2012: 43)[19]

The charge of ethnocentrism can be directed forcefully at a Distributive Rationale that is based on a theory of egalitarian global distributive justice. In this case, the ethnocentrism charge would consist of the claim that international development practice functions as a vehicle to model societies in light of a conception of distributive justice that is foreign to them and that is therefore not sufficiently context-sensitive. This critique is less plausible when it addresses forms of the Distributive Rationale that are based on sufficientarian conceptions of global distributive justice, because these can grant that states ought to be structured internally according to principles of justice formulated specifically for their own domestic contexts.

But the charge carries considerable force when targeting versions of the Distributive Rationale that are based on egalitarian conceptions of global distributive justice, because these exemplify the extrapolation of one particular domestic conception of justice to the world at large. After all, these globalist theorists (Beitz [1979] 1999; Pogge 1989; Moellendorf 2002; Tan 2004; Caney 2005), whether they endorse practice-dependent or practice-independent justifications, offer *arguments by analogy* that hold that the domestic and the global case are relevantly similar in moral respects. As Beitz ([1979] 1999: 128) explicitly states: "It is wrong to limit the application of [egalitarian] contractarian principles of social justice to the nation-state; instead, these principles ought to apply globally." But how, if at all, is this idea of a single morally valid conception of global egalitarian distributive justice defensible against the charge of ethnocentrism?

Some defenders of the Distributive Rationale, such as Pogge (1989: 271), argue that if an intercultural, global dialogue about principles of global distributive justice were to take place, the resulting consensus would consist precisely of the egalitarian ideal that the theorists have already envisioned. Others, like Moellendorf (2002: 24), respond that the moral conception of the person that grounds the globally valid egalitarian distributive principles is universal in kind and hence cannot be reasonably rejected.

The problem that these responses to the charge of ethnocentrism share, however, is that they attempt to ground the validity of global egalitarian principles of distributive justice without addressing the core of the objection, namely that the distributive principles are not sufficiently context-sensitive. This is because they do not actually present any argument as to why the distributive norms of one socio-political system are suitable to serve as a global, regulative, distributive ideal, despite the existence of considerable global social, economic, political, and cultural heterogeneity. Rather, they beg the question either by postulating that a global, intercultural dialogue would lead to a consensus in favor of their distributive norms or by suggesting that basic moral concepts alone, such as a conception of a moral person, would lead directly to substantive distributive ideals of global justice.[20]

By contrast, those espousing the Discourse-Theoretic Rationale can respond to the objection of ethnocentrism by clarifying that their moral defense of another kind of international development practice does not rely on any substantive, full-fledged ideal of global distributive justice. As outlined above, the Discourse-Theoretic Rationale calls for the establishment of domestic and international basic structures of justification that allow the members of these structures to determine themselves the substantive distributive norms that are to regulate these contexts.

In this way the Discourse-Theoretic Rationale can accommodate the core concern behind the charge of ethnocentrism, which is that the norms underlying the moral rationale for certain forms of international development practice are not sufficiently context-sensitive. For the Discourse-Theoretic Rationale asks those affected by principles of justice to discursively construct these principles themselves. It thereby concurs that principles of distributive justice should be sufficiently context-sensitive and calls for the establishment of institutions that take this idea seriously.

Nevertheless, proponents of the Discourse-Theoretic Rationale must concede that the internationalist account of global discursive justice also involves a substantive, universal account of the demands of justice (although not *distributive* justice). It contains the requirement to establish properly arranged domestic and international structures of justification and is based on the fundamental moral idea of the equal dignity of all humans as reason-exchanging beings. So how can proponents of this moral rationale defend themselves against the charge that this requirement expresses the misapplication of a normative code from one socio-political context to another?

It is an attractive feature of the Discourse-Theoretic Rationale that it can respond to this version of the ethnocentrism charge by demonstrating that the charge itself presupposes the moral validity of the foundational principle on which the Discourse-Theoretic Rationale is grounded. For those who raise the ethnocentrism charge implicitly base their claim on the idea that persons should be subject only to those principles of justice that they could have endorsed themselves in light of their particular socio-political context. The basic idea of the ethnocentrism charge precisely consists in the idea that any set of principles of justice has to be appropriate for its context of application, and that whether this is the case, can ultimately be decided only by the addressees of the principles of justice. Once we formulate it in this way, it becomes clear that the ethnocentrism charge invokes the same foundational principle as the Discourse-Theoretic Rationale. For it is a central tenet of the discursive theory of global justice that principles of justice can be morally valid only if they emerge from properly structured political discourses among those who are subject to these principles. This is implicit in the basic idea that the 'first question of justice' concerns relations of justification and thus involves the discursive or justificatory power 'to demand and provide justifications and to challenge false legitimations' (Forst 2011: 9).

Hence the Discourse-Theoretic Rationale can respond effectively to the charge of ethnocentrism, demonstrating that it does not put forth context-insensitive distributive principles by clarifying that it refrains from spelling out any substantive, full-fledged ideal of distributive justice. Rather, it calls for the institutionalization of adequately regulated structures of justification that enable political discourses that can, in turn, construct distinct distributive principles of justice for distinct social and political contexts.

The Discourse-Theoretic Rationale can further respond that the foundational principle underlying the charge of ethnocentrism also underlies the Discourse-Theoretic Rationale. The idea that normative principles, like principles of justice, must be context-sensitive, because they must be based on the views of those who are part of this context, is of central importance for *both* the ethnocentrism charge and the Discourse-Theoretic Rationale.

The next sub-section argues similarly that the Discourse-Theoretic Rationale can counter the hermeneutic critique of international development practice more convincingly than the Distributive Rationale (regardless of whether the Distributive Rationale is based on an egalitarian or a sufficientarian conception of global distributive justice).

The Hermeneutic Critique

Many theorists (Gupta 2009; Rahnema 2010) criticize current international development practice as pervaded, if not constituted, by the donors' misunderstanding and misrepresentation of the recipients' situation. They point out that the donors interpret the recipients' socio-political context against the background of experiences and value judgments drawn from their own socio-political upbringing and environment. The donors thereby fail to properly grasp the recipients' understanding of the actual situation and consequently can represent it only inadequately.

As a result of this misunderstanding and misrepresentation, donors tend to formulate policies that do not address the types of socio-political changes that the recipients themselves would like to see. The central objection of the hermeneutic critique, then, is that actual international development practice fails to take seriously the recipients' understanding of their socio-political constellations.

The thrust of this hermeneutic critique can be observed by considering the international development community's pivotal concern with poverty. Many scholars (Noël 2006; Hulme and Fukuda-Parr 2009) argue that ever since the adoption of the United Nations Millennium Declaration in 2000, the eradication of poverty has moved to center stage of international development practice and represents a 'global anti-poverty consensus' (McDonnell et al. 2003: 7). While this heightened focus on poverty may itself express the overcoming of the previous misunderstanding that all states should strive for industrial modernization or growth in the market value of produced goods and services,[21] even this apparently innocuous concern manifests problems of misunderstanding and misrepresentation. These problems arise because despite a generally shared understanding of the concept of poverty, various conceptions of poverty can substantiate its concrete meaning very differently.[22] Rahnema articulates clearly:

The word 'poverty' is, no doubt, a key word of our times, extensively used and abused by everyone. [. . .] Strangely enough, however, no one, including the proposed 'beneficiaries' of these [development] activities, seems to have a clear and a commonly shared, view of poverty. For one reason, almost all the definitions given to the word are woven around the concept of 'lack' or 'deficiency'. Yet, on that basis, perhaps not a single human being could be found who would not feel 'lacking' in some thing. What makes the difference between the poor and the 'non-poor' would only be, then, the nature and the perception of the 'lack'. (Rahnema 1991: 4)

Hence, a heuristically adequate conception of poverty would have to be established by reference to a *thick* characterization of the socio-political context of those potentially affected by international development practice. Such thick characterizations, proponents of the hermeneutic critique argue, will not only vary substantially across different social and political contexts, but also will have to rely upon the narratives or self-descriptions of those constituting these contexts.

International development practice, in contrast, ignores these facts by putting forward an allegedly universally valid conception of poverty[23] that merely reflects a supposedly valid generalization of a local or domestic understanding of poverty. This practice effectively fails, therefore, to pursue articulating the actual problem of poverty in a sufficiently context-sensitive manner.[24] Shiva, for example, criticizes international development practice for defining poverty in a too narrowly and market-oriented way:

Culturally perceived poverty need not be real material poverty: subsistence economies which serve basic needs through self-provisioning are not poor in the sense of being deprived. Yet the ideology of development declares them so because they don't participate overwhelmingly in the market economy, and do not consume commodities provided for and distributed through the market. (Shiva 1988: 10)

The hermeneutic critique presents a serious problem for the Distributive Rationale. For the theory of global distributive justice that underlies the Distributive Rationale employs *one single metric* – for example, of resources or of primary goods – relative to which it assesses whether a certain egalitarian or sufficientarian distributional requirement is met at the global level. Thus, it has to argue for the global validity of one particular understanding of justice-relevant goods, one specific 'currency' of justice, despite the fact that, as the hermeneutic critique urges, adequate interpretations of the situations of those subject to development policies are context-bound and not reducible to a single global understanding of what constitutes the currency of justice. Hence, those defenders of a Distributive Rationale that endorse some *sufficientarian* ideal of global distributive justice are likely to encounter problems similar to those that confront formulations of an allegedly universal conception of poverty. And those who base their claims on an *egalitarian* ideal will find it arguably even more difficult to determine a context-sensitive way to define how people are equal on a global scale. This weakness is evidenced by the many reformulations that global egalitarians (Moellendorf 2002, 2009; Caney 2001, 2007) have undertaken in light of criticism (Boxill 1987; Miller 2005) that points to the inadequacy of their metrics of equality.[25]

Moreover, the Distributive Rationale is predominantly 'forward-looking', in the sense that it calls for the future achievement of one global distributional pattern of some kind, rather than the rectification of unjust behavior in the past.[26] This forward-looking character of the Distributive Rationale *reinforces* the hermeneutic critique that international development practice does not pay sufficient attention to the way in which people themselves characterize their socio-political context. This is because 'backward-looking' accounts ground normative claims by investigating whether and how past relations among individuals within a particular socio-political context give rise to certain demands. Forward-looking accounts, by contrast, dispense – at least by and large – with justificatory narratives that consider past events.

The way in which this forward-looking character of the Distributive Rationale aggravates the hermeneutic critique of current international development practice can be illustrated by considering another hermeneutic criticism of the international development community's concern with poverty. Gupta points out that the attempt to reduce 'global poverty' concentrates exclusively on achieving 'a world free of poverty'[27] in the future without taking into consideration how people have been brought into poverty in the first place:

The numbers that capture the phenomenon of global poverty [. . .] do not tell anything about why a certain group of people at a certain place has fallen into poverty. So the notion of global poverty is in that respect to a large extent based on a decontextualized and static understanding of social relations. (Gupta 2009: 133; my translation)

If the moral rationale of international development practice is the necessity of achieving a global distribution of holdings where all individuals live above a specified threshold of sufficiency, then it is vulnerable to this version of the hermeneutic critique. For by determining a certain level of sufficiency that everyone ought to reach, the Distributive Rationale, and the forms of international development practice oriented to it, abstracts from the concrete socio-political contexts that allow people to fall below the threshold of sufficiency in the first place.

This approach neglects, however, the complexities of phenomena like poverty that can only be adequately conceptualized by an account that is historically, socially, and politically situated. As Gupta (2009: 135; my translation) goes on to assert: "Context-sensitive conceptions of poverty [must] acknowledge the historically grown inequalities that have brought several social groups in certain regions into situations of material emergency." The forward-looking character of the Distributive Rationale further intensifies, then, its difficulty in responding to the hermeneutic criticism of international development practice, which the Distributive Rationale's reliance on a single, globally valid currency of distributive justice has already brought to the fore.

Defenders of the Discourse-Theoretic Rationale can argue, in contrast, that their moral case for international development practice already incorporates the insights contained in the hermeneutic critique. This is because a discourse theory of global justice refrains from defending a substantive metric by reference to which the extent of global distributive justice or injustice could be determinately identified. In fact, a discourse theory argues precisely that the formulation of metrics of justice requires that members of socio-political contexts themselves provide the necessary thick characterizations of their situation. There is no other way to ground claims as to who ought to receive and produce which goods within the Discourse-Theoretic Rationale, which takes the relations of justificatory power, rather than the distribution of goods, as fundamental. Thereby an international development practice based on a Discourse-Theoretic Rationale would be less likely to generate the kinds of misunderstandings and misrepresentations that the hermeneutic critique says it is doomed to reproduce.

Furthermore, the discourse-theoretic account of justice that grounds the Discourse-Theoretic Rationale of the international development practice is in many important ways backward-looking. This is because this account of justice asks those who will be affected by certain principles of intra- and international justice to employ their justificatory power in order to construct these principles. This discursive construction of principles of justice has to be based, therefore, on the characterizations of those who constitute a particular socio-political context. Thereby it will unavoidably involve considerations that look back at the past social and political relations of those among whom principles of justice are being generated.

Otherwise they would fail to capture the specificity of the socio-political context in question, the accurate description and interpretation of which is one central point of a discourse theory of justice. Because of this backward-looking character, the Discourse-Theoretic Rationale can accommodate the hermeneutic critique's objection that existing international development practice employs an ahistorical, static, and context-insensitive account of poverty. Thus the international development practice need not be based on a moral rationale that tends to engender misunderstanding and misrepresentation of the situation of those whom it addresses.

CONCLUSION

In this chapter I have presented the Discourse-Theoretic Rationale as a novel moral rationale for certain forms of international development practice. For this purpose I sketched a discourse-theoretic internationalist account of global justice that laid a political and philosophical foundation for a discourse-theoretic moral rationale for international development practice. I supported moreover this Discourse-Theoretic Rationale by showing that it is better placed than the Distributive Rationale to counter the eminent objections alleging that present-day international development practice is guilty of and vulnerable to a hermeneutic critique.

Thereby I made the case for replacing the Distributive Rationale, which is one of the strongest candidates for a moral rationale for certain forms of international development practice. Despite its own problems, the Distributive Rationale is more equipped than the Humanitarian Rationale to serve as a foundation for international development activity, because it does not share the Humanitarian Rationale's implicit acceptance of the actual global distribution of holdings. Such acceptance would require an argument for a conception of global distributive justice that affirms the status quo; the Humanitarian Rationale fails to provide any such account. Accepting the status quo would also mean taking a stance in opposition to the consensus of a broad range of theories of global distributive justice and therefore would be very difficult to defend.

The comparative superiority of the Discourse-Theoretic Rationale also further strengthens the case for discourse-theoretic accounts of justice, given that the considered moral judgments regarding the practical conclusions about international development practice that can be drawn from one of them. Therefore beyond my central objective in this chapter to articulate and defend the Discourse-Theoretic Rationale for the international development practice, I also provided an additional argument that supports discourse-theories of justice more generally.

Notes

1. I presented earlier versions of this chapter at the University of Bayreuth *Philosophy & Economics* Summer Meeting of Young Philosophers and Economists in August 2010, the Governance of Relief – Post-Colonial and Cold War Humanitarian Aid conference in Mannheim in December 2010, the Colonial Legacies, Postcolonial Contestations conference in Frankfurt in June 2011, the Global Justice – Assessing International Aid conference in Lisbon in July 2011 and the *Justitia Amplificata – Rethinking Justice: Applied and Global* World Poverty, Global Justice and Humanity workshop at the Forschungskolleg Humanwissenschaften in Bad Homburg in May 2012. I would like to thank the audiences at these events as well as Amy Allen, Paulo Barcelos, Gabriele de Angelis, Allen Buchanan, Franziska Dübgen, Stefan Gosepath, Nicole Hassoun, Uchenna Okeja and Philippe Van Parijs for their extremely helpful comments. My work on this chapter benefited from a scholarship of the Cluster of Excellence *Normative Orders* at the University of Frankfurt. This chapter appeared as 'Toward another Kind of Development Practice' in Julian Culp, *Global Justice and Development* (New York: Palgrave Macmillan, 2014), ch. 7, and is reproduced with permission of Palgrave Macmillan.

2. See my *Global Justice and Development* (Culp 2014: ch. 1), for a characterization of the duty of humanity, which is often also referred to as the
   'principle of mutual aid'.
3. In his Four Point Speech US President Truman (1949) also insisted: 'Only by
   helping the least fortunate of its members to help themselves can the human
   family achieve the decent, satisfying life that is the right of all people.'
4. The World Bank now defines extreme poverty by a $1.25-per-day poverty
   line.
5. For the idea of the mediation of duties via institutions, cf. Shue (1988).
6. See Streeten and Burki (1978); Streeten (1981, 1984); Stewart (1985).
   See Culp (2014: ch. 6), for a formulation of the basic needs approach to
   development.
7. The Utilitarian Rationale is not further pursued here, because utilitarian
   moral and political philosophy rests on a number of very problematic
   assumptions (for example, the commensurability of different values) and
   involves certain counter-intuitive assumptions (for example, that there are
   no supererogatory acts).
8. As Beitz argues, different from the 'duty of mutual aid to help those who,
   without help, would surely perish [. . .], [o]bligations of justice might be
   thought to be more demanding than this, to require greater sacrifices on
   the part of the relatively well-off' (Beitz [1979] 1999: 127).
9. I offer a critique of Nagel's position in Culp (2014: ch. 3).
10. Cf. Habermas (1996: ch. 8); Forst (2012: ch. 7).
11. To the extent that it is a fundamental concern that *individuals* are enabled
    to occupy spaces that allow them to effectively shape their socio-political
    environments, the internationalist account is in a certain sense strongly
    cosmopolitan.
12. See Culp (2014: ch. 5) for a fuller articulation of discourse-theoretic
    Internationalism.
13. 'Sufficient' rather than 'equal' justificatory power, because to demand
    equal justificatory power is incompatible with the current condition of the
    natural world.
14. Habermas (2008: 333–4), for instance, calls for the creation of a transna-
    tional negotiation system of which states would form a constitutive part.
15. Note, however, that current international development practice over
    the last six decades has failed to deliver on its promise to spur economic
    growth in the poorer countries. Economists who contend on the basis of
    econometric analyses that the actual international development practice
    has in general not been effective in that respect include Mosley et al.
    (1987), Boone (1996), Burnside and Dollar (2000), Easterly (2002, 2006,
    2008), and Rajan and Subramanian (2005). However, Minoiu and Reddy
    (2009) show that investing resources with the purpose of promoting

growth in poorer countries can effectively achieve this goal in the long run. Other social scientists, including Kabou (1993), Ellerman (2005), and Moyo (2010) seek to explain by reference to the structure of the donor–recipient relationship, albeit in very different ways, why actual international development practice has been ineffective in promoting economic growth in poorer countries. For philosophical discussions of the relevance of the fact of international development work's practical effectiveness to the question of whether to support the international development practice from a moral point of view, see Wenar (2003, 2007), Jamieson (2005), and Hassoun (2012: ch. 4). These philosophical discussions tend to conclude that while one ought to support international development practice, careful, cautious deliberation is needed as to which particular activities of the international development practice should continue.

16. Arguably, it is a serious challenge for the Discourse-Theoretic Rationale that the strongly inter-governmental character of bilateral aid makes it very difficult for the system to bring about changes in the lives of the politically least powerful individuals and groups within states. Non-governmental organisations may promise to be more successful in such contexts – and thus they often receive additional ODA funds to carry out precisely these tasks.

17. For similar criticisms that address theories of global distributive justice more directly, see Benhabib (2004: 106–8), who differentiates between epistemic, hermeneutic, and democratic objections against ideals of global distributive justice.

18. This 'normative' version of the charge of ethnocentrism can be separated from another 'positive' version of the charge of ethnocentrism that criticizes international development practice for implementing of economic strategies in poor countries that are based on extrapolations from factors of economic success in rich countries. Many earlier development economists (Bauer and Yamey 1957: 66; Higgins 1959: 256) argued, for instance, that the reduction of family size would be a necessary condition for economic growth; during the 1970s the World Bank rewarded states that implemented birth-control policies (Sinding 2007: 5). Hirschman (1965) discusses illuminatingly the positive version of ethnocentrism.

19. In a similar vein, Illich (1970: 140) argued: 'There is a normal course for those that make development policies [. . .]. It is to define development and to set its goals in ways with which they are familiar.'

20. Moellendorf (2009: ch. 3) has recently taken up a noticeably more context-sensitive position. He now argues that in light of the type of association for which principles of justice are sought, subject-specific contents of justice have to be justified in conjunction with a context-insensitive, egalitarian distributive presumption.

21. The earlier shift towards focusing development policies on basic needs, initiated by former World Bank president Robert McNamara (1973), found support from many like-minded public initiatives (cf. Dag Hammarskjold Foundation 1974, 1975; International Labour Organization 1976).
22. Sen (1981: 17) formulates the concept of poverty as follows: 'Indeed, there is an irreducible core of *absolute* deprivation in our idea of poverty, which translates reports of starvation, malnutrition and visible hardship into a diagnosis of poverty without having to ascertain first the relative picture.'
23. Consider the World Bank's $1.25- and $2-per-day poverty lines, or the multidimensional understanding of poverty that the UN Millennium Development Goals 1 to 6 incorporate.
24. Some also stress that, in some contexts, international development practice has induced in many people the self-image of a poor person. Norberg-Hodge (1992) describes how externally initiated development interventions aimed at the people of India's Ladakh region introduced among these people the previously absent belief that they are poor.
25. Cf. Brock (2009: ch. 1) for an overview and critique of global egalitarianism's reformulations. Culp (2014: ch. 3) discusses the global validity of the principle of fair equality of opportunity and concludes that the validity of a particular principle of fair equality of opportunity presupposes a properly structured political practice that allows people to co-determine the notion of 'success' relative to which chances are to be equalized.
26. Indeed, theorists of the Distributive Rationale are backward-looking when it comes to questions of non-ideal theory, that is, questions as to how to go about the transition from an unjust status quo to the realization of an ideal of justice. However, the formulation of the ideal of justice itself seems to be solely forward-looking. By contrast, in a discourse-theoretic account of justice the very formulation of the ideal of justice has to be both backward- and forward-looking.
27. The World Bank's motto declares that the bank is 'Working for a World Free of Poverty'.

References

Alesina, Alberto and David Dollar (2000), 'Who Gives Foreign Aid to Whom and Why?', *Journal of Economic Growth*, vol. 5, no. 1, pp. 33–63.

Barry, Brian [1982] (2008), 'Humanity and Justice in Global Perspective', in T. Pogge and D. Moellendorf (eds), *Global Justice – Seminal Essays*, St. Paul: Paragon House, pp. 179–209.

Bauer, Peter and Basil Yamey (1957), *The Economics of Under-Developed Countries*, Chicago: University of Chicago Press.

Beitz, Charles [1979] (1999), *Political Theory and International Relations*, 2nd edn, Princeton, NJ: Princeton University Press.

Benhabib, Seyla (2004), *The Rights of Others: Aliens, Residents, and Citizens*, Cambridge: Cambridge University Press.

Berthélemy, Jean-Claude and Ariane Tichit (2004), 'Bilateral Donors' Aid Allocation Decisions – A Three-Dimensional Panel Analysis', *International Review of Economics & Finance*, vol. 13, no. 3, pp. 253–74.

Birdsall, Nancy, Stijn Claessens and Ishac Diwan (2003), 'Policy Selectivity Forgone: Debt and Donor Behavior in Africa', *The World Bank Economic Review*, vol. 17, no. 3, pp. 409–35.

Blake, Michael (2001), 'Distributive Justice, State Coercion, and Autonomy', *Philosophy & Public Affairs*, vol. 30, no. 3, pp. 257–96.

Boone, Peter (1996), 'Politics and the Effectiveness of Foreign Aid', *European Economic Review*, vol. 40, no. 2, pp. 289–329.

Boxill, Bernard (1987), 'Global Equality of Opportunity and National Integrity', *Social Philosophy and Policy*, vol. 5, no. 1, pp. 143–68.

Brock, Gillian (2009), *Global Justice: A Cosmopolitan Account*, Oxford: Oxford University Press.

Burnside, Craig and David Dollar (2000), 'Aid, Policies, and Growth', *The American Economic Review*, vol. 90, no. 4, pp. 847–68.

Caney, Simon (2001), 'Cosmopolitan Justice and Equalizing Opportunities', *Metaphilosophy*, vol. 32, no. 1–2, pp. 113–34.

Caney, Simon (2005), *Justice Beyond Borders: A Global Political Theory*, Oxford: Oxford University Press.

Caney, Simon (2007), 'Global Poverty and Human Rights: The Case for Positive Duties', in T. Pogge (ed.), *Freedom from Poverty as a Human Right: Who Owes What to the Very Poor?*, Oxford: Oxford University Press, pp. 275–302.

Cogneau, Denis and Jean Naudet (2007), 'Who Deserves Aid? Equality of Opportunity, International Aid, and Poverty Reduction', *World Development*, vol. 35, no. 1, pp. 104–20.

Collier, Paul and David Dollar (2001), 'Can the World Cut Poverty in Half? How Policy Reform and Effective Aid Can Meet International Development Goals', *World Development*, vol. 29, no. 11, pp. 1787–802.

Collier, Paul and David Dollar (2002), 'Aid Allocation and Poverty Reduction', *European Economic Review*, vol. 46, no. 8, pp. 1475–500.

Culp, Julian (2014), *Global Justice and Development*, New York: Palgrave Macmillan.

Dag Hammarskjold Foundation (1974), 'Cocoyoc Declaration', *Development Dialogue*, no. 2, pp. 88–96.

Dag Hammarskjold Foundation (1975), 'What Now? Another Development', *Development Dialogue*, no. 1–2, pp. 1–129.

Easterly, William (2002), *The Elusive Quest for Growth*, Cambridge, MA: MIT Press.

Easterly, William (2006), *The White Man's Burden*, New York: Oxford University Press.

Easterly, William (2008), 'Can the West Save Africa?', <http://www.nber.org/papers/w14363.pdf> (last accessed 26 October 2015).

Ellerman, David (2005), *Helping People Help Themselves*, Ann Arbor: University of Michigan Press.

Escobar, Arturo (2012), *Encountering Development: The Making and Unmaking of the Third World*, 2nd edn, Princeton, NJ: Princeton University Press.

Forst, Rainer (2011), 'Transnational Justice and Democracy', *The Formation of Normative Orders Working Papers*, no. 4, pp. 1–18.

Forst, Rainer (2012), *The Right to Justification – Elements of a Constructivist Theory of Justice*, New York: Columbia University Press.

Gupta, Akhil (2009), 'Nationale Armut, Globale Armut und Neoliberalismus: Eine anthropologische Kritik', in H. Büschel and D. Speich (eds), *Entwicklungswelten – Globalgeschichte der Entwicklungszusammenarbeit*, Frankfurt and New York: Campus, pp. 113–42.

Habermas, Jürgen (1996), *Between Facts and Norms – Contributions to a Discourse Theory of Law and Democracy*, Cambridge, MA: MIT Press.

Habermas, Jürgen (2008), 'A Political Constitution for the Pluralist World Society?', in *Between Naturalism and Religion*, Cambridge: Polity Press, pp. 312–53.

Hassoun, Nicole (2012), *Globalization and Global Justice*, Cambridge: Cambridge University Press.

Higgins, Benjamin (1959), *Economic Development – Principles, Problems and Policies*, London: Constable.

Hirschman, Albert (1965), 'Obstacles to Development: A Classification and a Quasi-Vanishing Act', *Economic Development and Cultural Change*, vol. 13, no. 4, pp. 385–93.

Hulme, David and Sakiko Fukuda-Parr (2009), 'International Norm Dynamics and "the End of Poverty": Understanding the Millennium Development Goals', Brooks World Poverty Institute Working Paper, no. 96, pp. 1–38.

Illich, Ivan (1970), *Celebration of Awareness: A Call for Institutional Revolution*, New York: Penguin Books.

International Labour Organization (1976), *Employment, Growth and Basic Needs: A One World Problem*, Geneva: International Labour Organization.

Jamieson, Dale (2005), 'Duties to the Distant: Aid, Assistance, and Intervention in the Developing World', *Journal of Ethics*, vol. 9, no. 1–2, pp. 151–70.

Kabou, Axelle (1993), *Weder arm noch ohnmächtig*, Basel: Lenos.

Kant, Immanuel [1797] 1996, *The Metaphysics of Morals*, ed. Mary Gregor, Cambridge: Cambridge University Press.

Llavador, Humberto and John Roemer (2001), 'An Equal-Opportunity Approach to the Allocation of International Aid', *Journal of Development Economics*, vol. 64, no. 1, pp. 147–71.

McDonnell, Ida, Henri-Bernard S. Lecomte and Liam Wegimont (2003), 'Public Opinion Research, Global Education and Development Co-operation Reform: In Search of a Virtuous Circle', OECD Development Centre – Working Paper, no. 222, pp. 1–38.

McGillivray, Mark (1989), 'The Allocation of Aid Among Developing Countries: A Multi-Donor Analysis Using a Per Capita Aid Index', *World Development*, vol. 17, no. 4, pp. 561–8.

McGillivray, Mark (2004), 'Descriptive and Prescriptive Analyses of Aid Allocation: Approaches, Issues, and Consequences', *International Review of Economics & Finance*, vol. 13, no. 3, pp. 275–92.

McKinlay, Robert and Richard Little (1977), 'A Foreign Policy Model of US Bilateral Aid Allocation', *World Politics*, vol. 30, no. 1, pp. 58–86.

McNamara, Robert (1973), 'Address to the Board of Governors, Nairobi, Kenya, September 1973', Washington, DC: The World Bank.

Miller, David (2005), 'Against Global Egalitarianism', *The Journal of Ethics*, vol. 9, no. 1–2, pp. 55–79.

Miller, David (2007), *National Responsibility and Global Justice*, Oxford: Oxford University Press.

Minoiu, Camelia and Sanjay Reddy (2009), 'Development Aid and Economic Growth: A Positive Long-Run Relation', IMF Working Paper WP/09/118, Washington, DC: International Monetary Fund.

Moellendorf, Darrel (2002), *Cosmopolitan Justice*, Boulder, CO: Westview Press.

Moellendorf, Darrel (2009), *Global Inequality Matters*, New York: Palgrave Macmillan.

Mosley, Paul, John Hudson and Sara Horrell (1987), 'Aid, the Public Sector and the Market in Less Developed Countries', *Economic Journal*, vol. 97, no. 387, pp. 616–41.

Moyo, Dambisa (2010), *Dead Aid*, London: Penguin Press.

Nagel, Thomas (2005), 'The Problem of Global Justice', *Philosophy & Public Affairs*, vol. 33, no. 2, pp. 113–47.

Niggli, Peter (2008), *Der Streit um die Entwicklungshilfe: Mehr tun – aber das Richtige!*, Zurich: Rotpunktverlag.

Noël, Alain (2006), 'The New Global Politics of Poverty', *Global Social Policy*, vol. 6, no. 3, pp. 304–33.

Norberg-Hodge, Helena (1992), *Ancient Futures: Learning from Ladakh*, Delhi: Oxford University Press.

Pogge, Thomas (1989), *Realizing Rawls*, Ithaca, NY: Cornell University Press.

Pogge, Thomas (1994), 'An Egalitarian Law of Peoples', *Philosophy & Public Affairs*, vol. 23, no. 3, pp. 195–224.

Rahnema, Majid (1991), 'Global Poverty: A Pauperizing Myth', *Interculture*, vol. 24, no. 2, pp. 4–51.

Rahnema, Majid (2010), 'Poverty', in W. Sachs (ed.), *The Development Dictionary*, 2nd edn, London: Zed Books, pp. 158–76.

Rajan, Raghuram and Arvind Subramanian (2005), 'Aid and Growth: What Does the Cross-Country Evidence Really Show?', International Monetary Fund Working Paper, 05/127, Washington, DC: International Monetary Fund.

Sen, Amartya (1981), *Poverty and Famines*, Oxford: Oxford University Press.

Shiva, Vandana (1988), *Staying Alive: Women, Ecology, and Development*, London: Zed Books.

Shue, Henry (1988), 'Mediating Duties', *Ethics*, vol. 98, no. 4, pp. 687–704.

Sinding, Steven (2007), 'Overview and Perspective', in W. Robinson and J. Ross (eds), *The Global Family Planning Revolution: Three Decades of Population Policies and Programs*, Washington, DC: The World Bank, pp. 1–13.

Singer, Peter (1972), 'Famine, Affluence, and Morality', *Philosophy & Public Affairs*, vol. 1, no. 3, pp. 229–43.

Stewart, Frances (1985), *Planning to Meet Basic Needs*, Basingstoke and London: Macmillan.

Streeten, Paul (1981), *First Things First: Meeting Basic Human Needs in the Developing Countries*, Washington, DC: The World Bank.

Streeten, Paul (1984), 'Basic Needs: Some Unsettled Questions', *World Development*, vol. 12, no. 9, pp. 973–8.

Streeten, Paul and Shahid Burki (1978), 'Basic Needs: Some Issues', *World Development*, vol. 6, no. 3, pp. 411–21.

Tan, Kok-Chor (2004), *Justice Without Borders*, Cambridge: Cambridge University Press.

Truman, Harry (1949), *Inaugural Addresses of the Presidents of the United States*, Washington, DC: US GPO, <http://www.bartleby.com/124/pres53> (last accessed 26 October 2015).

Unger, Peter (1996), *Living High and Letting Die: Our Illusion of Innocence*, New York: Oxford University Press.

Wenar, Leif (2003), 'What We Owe to Distant Others', *Politics, Philosophy and Economics*, vol. 2, no. 3, pp. 283–304.

Wenar, Leif (2007), 'The Basic Structure as Object: Institutions and Humanitarian Concern', in D. Weinstock (ed.), *Global Justice, Global Institutions*, Calgary: University of Calgary Press, pp. 253–78.

White, Howard and Mark McGillivray (1992), 'Descriptive Measures of the Allocation of Development Aid', International Institute of Social Studies of Erasmus University Working Paper Series, no. 125, pp. 1–22, <http://repub. eur.nl/pub/18825/wp125.pdf> (last accessed 26 October 2015).

White, Howard and Mark McGillivray (1995), 'How Well is Aid Allocated? Descriptive Measures of Aid Allocation: A Survey of Methodology and Results', *Development and Change*, vol. 26, no. 1, pp. 163–83.

World Bank (1990), *World Development Report 1990*, Washington, DC: Oxford University Press.

World Bank (1998), *Assessing Aid – What Works, What Doesn't, and Why*, Washington, DC: Oxford University Press.

Chapter 5

THREE APPROACHES TO GLOBAL HEALTH CARE JUSTICE: REJECTING THE POSITIVE/ NEGATIVE RIGHTS DISTINCTION

Peter G. N. West-Oram

INTRODUCTION

There are two questions that we need to answer when embarking on a discussion of global duties to aid.[1] First, 'What do we need to do to discharge our obligations to people in other countries?', which is a question about what needs to be done as much as it is about what duties we actually have.

The second, and more philosophically interesting, question is 'Why do we have these obligations?' This relates to the reasons we have such duties and the justifications that exist for our global duties to aid. This is a prior question because the way in which we answer it will affect the way that we can answer the first question posed. Without an adequate definition of the reasons for our duties, we will struggle to provide a comprehensive description of what those duties are.

In this chapter I focus on three cosmopolitan approaches to answering this second question in the context of global health care justice: Pogge's negative duties based approach (Pogge 2008: 15), Brock's minimal needs view (Brock 2009: 54–5) and Henry Shue's model of basic rights (Shue 1980: 18). While these approaches share a common focus on attempting to justify the existence of global duties to aid, held by the wealthy and owed to the global poor, each offers a distinct interpretation of why such duties exist and suggests a range of options for fulfilling them. Importantly, while I argue that Shue's approach to our global duties is the most effective of the three, I consider they all offer important insight into the problem of global poverty and provide a variety of possible practical solutions to this problem.

I will argue that Shue's model offers the most comprehensive justification of global duties and in fact can be seen as accommodating or incorporating the other two approaches. The efficacy of Shue's approach can be seen to have its foundation in his rejection of the positive/negative rights dichotomy. Shue's rejection of this widely, and mistakenly, held view of rights and duties is central to his argument for global duties to aid, as I discuss below. However, it is first important to explain my use of health care as an example for this chapter. In the following two sections I first consider why health care should be considered an important good and go on to examine why we should consider it a question of justice.

WHY HEALTH AND HEALTH CARE

Each of the approaches I consider in this chapter is primarily concerned with deprivation and poverty generally, with the inequity of access to health care being considered as one issue amongst many. In this chapter I concentrate on access to health care for two reasons.[2] First, health care can be easily recognised as a fundamental requirement of living even a minimally decent human life. Lacking health, or being unable to 'access' it, through lack of access to essential health care services for example, is profoundly unpleasant at best and completely debilitating to the point of preventing enjoyment of even a basic standard of living at worst. Health care is also of importance because of its role in enabling many aspects of human life; for example, Nussbaum includes 'bodily health' in her capabilities list (Nussbaum 2003: 41–2), David Held recognises the importance of physical and mental health for democratic participation (Held 1995: 192, 194–5) and Gillian Brock includes health in her list of requirements for human agency (Brock 2009: 66). Similarly, Henry Shue argues that health and health care are necessary for the enjoyment of all other rights (Shue 1980: 23–5).

There are those, such as Thomas Nagel, who regard the provision of basic welfare services, such as health care, as a charitable, humanitarian issue, rather than a question of justice (Nagel 2005: 118). This position is based on a restricted understanding of what we should consider our obligations to those living in poverty to be, and suggests that while we should help the global poor, such action would be supererogatory, rather than simply a moral obligation. I shall to a certain extent assume that this position is incorrect. What I am concerned with is answering the question of why we have duties to distant others, rather than establishing exactly what they are. Of course, since I am concerned with three specific cosmopolitan justifications for our duties to aid I will implicitly argue against Nagel's more restrictive view of moral obligation, though this is not the main focus of this chapter.

AN EXAMPLE: THE GLOBAL BURDEN OF TUBERCULOSIS

To clarify why access to health care should be considered a question of justice it is helpful to look at the example of the global distribution of cases of tuberculosis (TB). Tuberculosis is a useful example for four key reasons. First, it is a disease which is debilitating and which can kill, so we can consider the disease to have a severe adverse effect on personal welfare. Second, it is a disease that is both preventable and curable. Third, it is a disease which is far more dangerous to people with a weakened immune system, so we can reduce vulnerability by addressing those conditions, such as malnutrition, which adversely affect general health.

This focus on general health promotion as a means of addressing the spread of tuberculosis is a key part of the World Health Organization strategy for addressing TB (World Health Organization 2010a: 9). The argument behind these first three points is that since the disease has a major adverse effect on personal welfare, and we are able to help those at risk of tuberculosis and those currently infected, we cannot argue that the alleviation of suffering caused by the disease is beyond existing medical and social capabilities.

A final point about tuberculosis and justice is demonstrated by the distribution of cases globally. Tuberculosis predominantly affects those living in poorer parts of the world, with roughly two thirds of the incidences of the disease occurring in Africa and South-East Asia (World Health Organization 2010b). Wealthier countries, such as the United States and the UK, are relatively unaffected by comparison (ibid.). This disparity is important because it suggests that there is something that rich countries are doing that poor countries are not, which means that they are less affected than they would be otherwise. In itself this may not be a compelling reason to regard access to health care as an issue of justice. However, when we consider Pogge's (2008: 118–20) arguments on the impact of large-scale economic activity in exacerbating global poverty, the disparity in incidences of tuberculosis seems more likely to be a possible case of injustice. In line with Pogge's thinking generally about wealth disparities, and the causal role wealthy countries have in exacerbating them, the disparity of tuberculosis incidence rates between rich and poor countries may indicate that poor countries are unable to replicate certain conditions that keep these rates low in wealthier countries. Therefore, by exacerbating poverty, wealthy countries may be encouraging, or at least allowing, the circumstances in which diseases like tuberculosis can thrive. In the following section I examine the first of the three approaches to global justice that this chapter is concerned with: Thomas Pogge's negative duties based approach.

APPROACH ONE: POGGE'S NEGATIVE DUTIES APPROACH

Pogge's argument is based on the claim that there is a negative duty not to cause harm. He accepts, at least for the purposes of his argument, the negative view of rights and attempts to provide a justification for global duties of aid based on the empirical claim that the actions of agents in wealthy nations are in fact causing harm to the poor through economic, social and diplomatic practices, so that these agents are failing in their duties not to cause harm (ibid.: 148–50).[3] For the purposes of this chapter I shall assume that all of Pogge's claims about the harmful effects of the actions of wealthy nations are correct and that we are actually causing harm to the global poor through our actions. Pogge offers a variety of examples of the ways in which the actions of the wealthy affect the global poor. However, it is not the empirical data which concerns me, but rather the basis of his philosophical position which seems to leave him vulnerable to a problematic objection.

Pogge's argument is almost deceptively simple: there is a duty not to harm, currently we (in wealthy countries) do harm people, and therefore we fail in our duty. Therefore, to fulfil our duty not to harm we must change our behaviours. In the case of tuberculosis, we could say that since our actions encourage poverty, we restrict the extent to which poor countries can provide their citizens with adequate social services and so encourage the conditions in which tuberculosis and diseases like it thrive. Therefore, we are failing in our duty not to cause harm by encouraging poverty and hence disease so we must refrain from certain behaviours and increase our proactive involvement in activities which address global poverty and deprivation.

There are three main options open to those who would criticise Pogge's argument.

First, there are two types of possible empirical objections, which

Pogge acknowledges, and I believe, successfully rejects. Specifically, there are those criticisms that deny the causal responsibility of wealthy nations for conditions in poor countries (ibid.: 12–15), and there are those that accept causal responsibility but deny that there is a better alternative available (ibid.: 6–11).[4]

An example of the case of the first objection can be found in John Rawls's *The Law of Peoples*, where he states that conditions in poor countries are likely to be the result of 'oppressive governments and corrupt elites' (Rawls 1999a: 77; Pogge 2008: 295, fn. 238). This claim may be partially correct; corruption and oppression can hardly be thought to be to the benefit of the global poor. However, as Pogge notes, this explanation ignores the role that wealthy countries have in supporting those governments and elites, and the responsibility that obtains as a result of such support. As such, the claim is hard to substantiate given the range of examples offered by Pogge of the impact that the actions of wealthy nations can have on the global poor (Pogge 2008: 118–22, 148). Similarly, Leif Wenar has drawn attention to the impact that our engagement through trade with authoritarian regimes in resource-rich countries actively harms the citizens of such countries by depriving their citizenry of resources which should be used for their benefit (Wenar 2008: 3–4).

The more subtle claim, that there is no better alternative to the existing world order, may be based on a variety of empirical arguments. For the purposes of this chapter I shall briefly consider two of these possible approaches. First, as Pogge notes (2008: 9–10), it may be objected that the cost of helping the poor achieve a higher standard of living would impose such hardship on the wealthy that the outcome would be worse than the current global situation in terms of overall welfare (Rorty 1996: 14–16). Second, as Pogge also recognises (Pogge 2008: 7–9), it may be argued that by helping the poor we inadvertently contribute to the worsening of everyone's long-term welfare. See, for example, Garrett Hardin's article 'Living on a Lifeboat' (1974) in which he argues that rapid population growth will lead to the inevitable exhaustion of the world's natural resources and hence a far greater loss of general welfare (and life) than would be the case if we maintained our current position of not helping.

The first of these claims – that by attempting to improve the lives of the global poor we may be forced to drastically and unjustifiably reduce our own standard of living – Pogge argues is simply mistaken; the cost of massively improving the lives of the global poor is not so vast as to damage the welfare of the wealthy. For example, Pogge states that the cost to wealthy countries of lifting the 950 million people around the world out of extreme poverty and into the 'higher' economic category of 'severe poverty' would cost roughly $38 billion annually. A large sum certainly, but the impact on wealthy countries would, according to Pogge, reduce 'our share from 78.98 percent of the global product down to 78.90 percent' (Pogge 2008: 105), hardly an immense loss.

Pogge also provides a convincing response to the 'population explosion' claim suggested by Hardin. Hardin's position may initially seem convincing; drawing attention to the great difference between population growth rates in wealthy and poor countries,[5] he raises concerns about the sustainability of such rapid population growth in a world of scarce resources. However, as Amartya Sen has noted (1994), there is an inverse correlation between improved economic status and population growth; that is, when income and welfare go up, the birth rate decreases. To suggest that rapid population growth is a threat to everybody, and that the preventable deaths of millions are in some way necessary, is to ignore significant empirical data which demonstrate the exact opposite of what is argued: that alleviating poverty is an effective way of controlling population growth.

Pogge counters the empirical objections to his thesis, but it is a philosophical question that presents a more troubling problem for his position. Pogge explicitly claims that 'human rights entail only negative duties' (Pogge 2008: 72). By rejecting any positive interpretations of duties, Pogge ignores a significant aspect of human rights as there will inevitably be cases where merely refraining from harmful action will be insufficient to guarantee the entitlements provided by a human right. Even if we accept, as I think we should, the suggestion that Pogge's position demands that we not be passive bystanders to injustice, this can readily be interpreted as a positive demand for action, rather than a negative demand for passivity in the face of opportunities to harm.

Further, and perhaps more problematically for Pogge, the ease with which it is possible to rephrase certain 'negative' duties as 'positive' requirements highlights the inadequacy of a purely negative model of duty. Even if one acknowledges that Pogge's argument demands that we must actively engage with making global institutions just, this seems to be an obviously positive duty and one which his approach is ill suited to account for. It seems to be the case that Pogge's account of duty does actually imply positive duties, but in explicitly stating his support for a 'negative duties alone' model (ibid.: 26) he leaves himself without the right tools to include the positive steps needed to facilitate those duties.

Further, focusing purely on negative duties ignores the importance of assistance after harms have occurred, and cases where a person has suffered significant damage to his or her welfare through brute bad luck, rather than the actions of any identifiable agent. I shall call this the 'sorry but . . .' argument. This claim would allow opponents of duties to the global poor to acknowledge that harm has been done, but then to deny that they have any responsibility to actually do anything to help as they were not responsible for the harms caused. For example, such an argument could accept that we should refrain from harming, but deny that there is a corresponding duty to help, as such an obligation would be a positive duty and as such would be an unwarranted restriction on liberty.[6]

This is difficult to address within Pogge's framework precisely because he explicitly accepts the negative rights view, and thus gives too much space for his opponent to reject all non-negative duties. Therefore, even though for Pogge the duties are negative, they clearly contain significant positive elements which cannot be accounted for under his model and which weaken the claim that human rights and justice require only negative duties. If one does not accept the existence of duties to the global poor, or if one is committed to a purely negative view of those duties, it is far too easy, on acceptance of Pogge's view, to reject essential demands of human rights as being beyond the scope of negative duty. Thus, his argument is vulnerable to an objection grounded on the same foundations as his own – the negative view of duties.

As I have stated above, Pogge successfully rejects the empirical objections to his position. However, by embracing a 'negative duties only' model, he does not seem to be able to account for the full range of duties demanded by human rights. Before I discuss this problem in more detail I will first examine the second of the three approaches to global justice that I am concerned with in this chapter, Brock's minimal needs approach.

APPROACH TWO: BROCK'S MINIMAL NEEDS APPROACH

Where Pogge approaches a justification of our global duties using a negative duty not to harm, Gillian Brock is primarily concerned with meeting basic needs. She proposes a minimum threshold-based approach which is reminiscent of the argument presented by Peter Singer in 'Famine, Affluence, and Morality' (1972) in that she argues that since we are able to lift those living in severe poverty above a minimum acceptable welfare threshold at little cost to ourselves, we have an obligation to do so.

Brock's focus is on shared fundamental human needs, including things such as certain basic liberties and protection from common causes of harm (Brock 2009: 52). These basic needs, Brock argues, should concern us as a matter of justice because they are so fundamental to living an autonomous human life that those without them do not enjoy even a minimally acceptable welfare standard.

While Brock's conclusion is similar to that offered by Singer, her justification for that conclusion is profoundly Rawlsian, based as it is on a variation on the original position which Brock calls the 'ideal choosing situation' (ibid.: 52). Brock argues that in the ideal choosing situation, which includes a modified veil of ignorance, participants would select a minimum threshold model as the fairest way to guarantee an acceptable welfare standard for all persons. Such a solution would be just, she argues, because it represents a rational choice for persons to make as it offers a broader set of guarantees, compatible with all views of the good, than those suggested by Rawls as arising from the original position.

Brock reinforces her argument with reference to empirical studies conducted by Frohlich and Oppenheimer (1992) which confirm the results of the thought experiment. In these studies, which were conducted internationally, participants from a variety of cultural backgrounds were asked to select a just system of guaranteeing individual welfare from four options. Importantly, the studies were conducted under similar conditions to those endorsed by Brock in her ideal choosing situation, with particular emphasis on 'conditions of impartiality' (Brock 2009: 54). The four options available included: first, a Rawlsian difference principle (Rawls [1971] 1999b: 65) for maximising the income of the worst off; second, a principle to maximise the average income, following Harsanyi (1953); third, a principle 'maximising the average with a floor constraint of $____'; and, fourth, a principle which maximised 'the average with a range constraint of $____' (Brock 2009: 54–5). Overwhelmingly, a safety net or minimum threshold model (the third option) was selected as the most just or fairest way of guaranteeing individual welfare (ibid.: 55).

As with Pogge, I think Brock's argument has considerable force and covers much ground that Pogge does not. However, I do have a concern with one consequence of Brock's focus on individual needs and a minimum acceptable welfare standard: it is difficult following Brock to assign responsibility to specific persons, an advantage that Pogge, and Shue, has over Brock. This is perhaps not terribly problematic as we can readily assign responsibility through reference to our shared needs or a reciprocity agreement. 'Why me?' can be answered: 'because you would get the same help if you were in their place'. And, of course, institutions play a key role in actual distributions, so their role in facilitating existing deprivations as well as potential solutions should not be overlooked as a basis for justifying their obligations to help. However, reciprocity and empathy are not the best justifications for duties to aid available to us. For reciprocity we must answer concerns about duties to those who cannot reciprocate, and empathic arguments depend on acknowledging that we would have a duty to help in the first place, something that many governments and individuals are of course notoriously unwilling to consider.

DEFINING THE PROBLEM

As mentioned above, Pogge's acceptance of the negative view of duties presents significant difficulty when attempting to justify certain kinds of positive action, such as providing aid to the deprived. In contrast, as I discuss below, Shue rejects the classification of rights and duties as being either positive or negative and can therefore justify a wider range of moral obligations than is available to Pogge. Brock's focus on individual needs, derived from a variation of the original position, avoids the problem of justifying positive action by emphasising the importance of certain social goods. However, Brock's position presupposes that others will share her recognition of the need to guarantee these goods, and it is by no means clear that such recognition is widespread. Therefore, it is difficult for Brock to make demands of specific agents as she does not provide a comprehensive justification of who should do what. By comparison, Shue can justify a much closer link between specific agents and positive behaviours, because he adopts a rights-based approach, thereby implying the assignation of duties, but he rejects the negative/positive distinction which creates such problems for Pogge. In the rest of this chapter, I argue that Shue's approach provides the kind of comprehensive argument necessary for a full justification of global duties to aid.

APPROACH THREE: SHUE AND BASIC RIGHTS, REJECTING THE POSITIVE/NEGATIVE RIGHTS DISTINCTION

As mentioned in the previous section, there are a variety of problems associated with the justifications of our global duties offered by Pogge and by Brock. Each has its own difficulties, but they share a common issue in that both models assume the validity of the distinction between positive and negative rights and duties. This distinction is based on the claim that there is a significant difference between positive rights, which entitle rights holders to demand that others perform certain actions, and negative rights, which entitle the holder to demand that duty bearers refrain from certain behaviours.

Contrary to this, Henry Shue claims that there is no basic right which can be classified as either positive or negative. As such, arguments which rest on the assumption that the positive/negative distinction is correct will present an incomplete picture of the kinds of duties that are required for global justice.

Shue describes three categories of basic rights: to security, to subsistence and to liberty. Each of these basic rights is made up of various constitutive elements. Thus, the right to security includes rights to protection from harm and against theft of one's property; the right to subsistence contains rights to things like adequate nutrition, sanitation and basic health care; and the right to liberty contains rights to personal freedoms, such as self-determination and political participation. Shue considers these rights to be fundamental prerequisites for the enjoyment of any other rights; they are basic because without them, according to Shue, we cannot have any rights at all. In this way he shares similarities with both Pogge and Brock. Like Pogge he derives his argument about duty from a logical extension of what it means to have a right, but like Brock his concern is for establishing a minimum threshold of entitlement. These rights are basic, according to Shue, not only because they enable the enjoyment of other rights, but also because they guarantee the ability to have a 'decent life' (Shue 1980: ix).

It is important to note that as well as being necessary for non-basic rights, each of the three basic rights is dependent on each of the others: the enjoyment of security depends on our enjoyment of liberty and subsistence rights, and so on. For example, we cannot enjoy a right to liberty if we are starving to death, no more than we can if we must risk being assaulted in order to vote. Similarly, a right to security or to subsistence is worth little if we are at the mercy of some temporarily 'benevolent dictator', as Shue puts it (ibid.: 74–5). Each of the basic rights cannot therefore be classified as either positive or negative, their interdependence demands both that we are guaranteed protection from and assistance in the case of certain harms, just as they also entitle us to demand that others not perpetrate certain acts against us; positive and negative demands respectively. 'It is impossible', Shue argues, 'for any basic right – however "negative" it has come to seem – to be fully guaranteed unless all three types of duties are fulfilled' (ibid.: 53).

For example, the right to political participation, itself one aspect of the right to liberty, entails both negative and positive requirements. The entitlement to vote, or to engage in political protest, obviously requires that rights holders not be subject to violence or intimidation when attempting to cast their ballot, so there is a negative duty not to attempt to limit a person's entitlement to participation through such means. But the right also requires that laws and the means to enforce them exist so that rights holders are protected from 'those who do not choose not to violate [the right to political participation]' (ibid.: 39). The right to political participation therefore requires both negative and positive duties. It is simply not enough that we not perform certain actions; we also have to ensure that those who would choose to restrict the rights of others are unable to do so (ibid.: 61). Fulfilment of the 'positive' condition of the right to liberty can be constructed as a duty to contribute fairly to taxation so that the means of law enforcement are funded in such a way as to be able to enforce the duties relating to a specific right. Of course, the creation and maintenance of a system of laws also demands the existence of a duty to contribute fairly through taxation.

This rejection of the positive/negative rights distinction is central to Shue's argument, and is the theoretical foundation which allows him to offer a more comprehensive position than either Pogge or Brock. By arguing that rights require both positive and negative duties, Shue can avoid Pogge's difficulty with justifying positive action and assign responsibility to specific agents more effectively than Brock.

To account for the broad requirements of the interrelated basic rights Shue offers the following 'tripartite' (ibid.: 53) model of duty, which includes both positive and negative requirements:

   I.   To avoid depriving.
  II. To protect from deprivation
       1. By enforcing duty (I) and
       2. By designing institutions that avoid the creation of strong
           incentives to violate duty (I).
 III. To aid the deprived
       1. Who are one's special responsibility,
       2. Who are the victims of social failures in the performance of
           duties (I), (II-1), (II-2) and
       3. Who are the victims of natural disasters. (Shue 1980: 60)

Like Pogge, Shue includes a proscription against harming (or depriving) under duty one, and like Brock, he recognises the importance of basic needs by demanding a duty to aid under duty three. Importantly, duty two offers an intermediate step between the other two and serves to support the duty not to cause harm. This duty recognises the existence of harms that we can prevent or at least whose risk of occurring we can minimise – it requires duty bearers to enforce the duty to avoid depriving, and to establish institutions which do not incentivise violations of that duty. Importantly, according to Shue, each of the duties can be held by both individuals and institutions, though the requirements may vary according to the agents (ibid.: 60–1).

THE IMPLICATIONS OF SHUE'S MODEL FOR HEALTH CARE

If we relate this model to health care we can see that duty one would require us to avoid behaviours likely to cause harm, for example drunk driving. Looking beyond individuals, the way that the TRIPS regime within the pharmaceutical industry excludes the poor from essential medicines is an example of corporate or governmental failure to meet the duty to avoid depriving.[7]

The TRIPS regime is problematic for the latter two of Shue's three duties, but it also violates the duty to avoid depriving. Prior to the advent of the TRIPS regime, manufacturers of generic medicines in countries such as India could work under domestic patent laws which allowed the production of generic drugs by providing patents only on processes rather than products. This allowed manufacturers to develop generic versions of drugs for sale to those who would be unable to afford the monopoly prices demanded for branded medicines (Barton

2004: 147). In contrast, TRIPS provides patents for products rather than processes, meaning that generic manufacturers are now unable to offer generic versions of drugs which are still under patent.[8] The effect of this change is that the TRIPS regime has deprived the global poor of their main source of essential medicines by rendering the process by which affordable medicines are created illegal (ibid.: 149–52).

The second duty requires that both individuals and institutions contribute fairly to the maintenance of health-promoting or protecting institutions, for example a duty to pay our fair share of the tax burden to ensure that adequate sanitation is provided to all people. Similarly, the duty to protect also implies the existence of meaningful laws which enforce the duty to avoid depriving and reduce the likelihood of risks to health occurring in the first place.

Shue acknowledges that in a world of perfect beneficence, where everyone fulfilled their duty to avoid depriving, there may be less need for a duty to protect (Shue 1980: 61). However, he rejects this possibility as unrealistically utopian and argues that while people and corporations may restrain themselves under threat of the law, they are far less likely to do so when not so restricted. Accordingly, Shue argues that a duty to protect is necessary to ensure good behaviour by those who may cause harm (ibid.: 61). In the case of the right to health care, as with other rights, while perfect beneficence and adherence to duty might be theoretically possible, it is extremely unlikely, so the relevant laws and regulations are necessary as a matter of practicality.

The duty to aid most closely corresponds to Brock's argument. It is a duty to ensure that in cases where we were unable to prevent harm those affected are not ignored or left to die. In the case of health care this duty would require the provision of treatment for disease or injury. Similarly, the duty would require the provision of support in terms of sanitation, sewerage and nutrition to those affected by natural disasters.

Like the three basic rights, Shue's three duties are interconnected, so a right which did not entail the fulfilment of all three types of duty would lack significant force. In the absence of the duty not to harm, the duty to protect could soon be overwhelmed by the needs of those harmed by the actions of the malevolent or negligent. Similarly, in the absence of the duty to protect, the right not to be harmed would become dependent on luck, while the duty to aid would face far greater demands, prevention being better, and usually cheaper, than cure. Finally, refusing a duty to aid overlooks the fact that duties are often ignored and that poor luck can have consequences as bad as, if not worse than, malicious action. As such, ignoring an obligation to provide aid would turn the duties to avoid depriving and to protect into the worst kind of threshold, one which merely described a line beneath which the unfortunate were condemned to struggle.

RESOLVING THE PROBLEM

I mentioned above that the main concern I have with Pogge's justification of global duties to aid arises because of his acceptance of the negative view of rights and duties. This view holds that moral duties can only demand that we refrain from engaging in certain types of behaviours,[9] and, as such, Pogge's acceptance of the view makes it difficult for him to move from responsibility for harms to any demands for positive action. In contrast, Brock's focus on individual needs provides a sound justification of why certain goods, such as health care, are important, because they enable human agency (Brock 2009: 66). However, her model does not provide as convincing an argument as to why specific agents have a responsibility to guarantee access to those goods as that provided by Shue. Shue's approach offers a stronger argument for assigning duties as well as a way to avoid the problems of positive duties associated with Pogge's position.

Shue recognises the importance of a duty to avoid harming, but he makes no claim that this is based on a negative model of rights; it is simply a requirement of having a right that others not violate it. So he can account for Pogge's approach here. Similarly, Brock's approach can be accounted for by Shue's acknowledgement of the significance of positive action. We have to have some duty to protect and to aid, else the duty not to harm really does become, as Shue puts it, 'the only poison they [the vulnerable] need' (Shue 1980: 19). The interrelatedness of Shue's three basic rights is fundamental to his argument and provides the basis for his rejection of the positive/negative rights distinction, itself an integral part of Shue's argument. By emphasising the relationship between the three basic rights, and arguing for the necessity of both 'positive' and 'negative' duties in his tripartite account of duty, Shue can place a wider range of obligations on duty bearers by drawing attention to the need for active, 'positive' engagement in the fulfilment of rights, such as the right to liberty, which are frequently, and mistakenly, thought of as purely negative rights.

Furthermore, he can also make claims about responsibility in a stronger manner than Brock, because he grounds his argument in an analysis of rights and argues that we have to have rights to certain things if we are to have any rights at all. By doing so he can point at a right to life (or the kind of goods that he and Brock are both concerned with) and demand, 'do you think that we have this?'[10] If the answer is yes, then we are committed at least to his framework of basic rights. If the answer is no, then it seems that the respondent is suggesting some kind of Hobbesian state of nature where no rights were guaranteed, which seems, at least intuitively, inherently unsatisfying.

CONCLUSION

My aim in this chapter has been modest. I do not wish to assert that either Pogge's or Brock's argument is untenable or should be ignored. Much can be learned from both positions and both offer a significant contribution to a comprehensive approach to global justice. Pogge's 'Global Resource Dividend' (Pogge 2008: 202), and his involvement in the development of the 'Health Impact Fund' (Hollis and Pogge 2008; Bannerjee et al. 2010), as well as Brock's 'Global Justice Fund' (Brock 2009: 136), offer excellent practical suggestions for addressing global poverty. However, neither Pogge nor Brock can offer a fully satisfying argument for the existence of our global duties to aid. Pogge's account gives too much to the neo-liberal position by tacitly accepting that we should only view negative duties as having any weight, and by doing so he allows room for a critic to argue that because we only have negative duties we are only under obligation to stop harming, something which can be interpreted minimally, and not to actually help. In contrast, Brock's position can offer an argument as to why someone should help, but a much weaker explanation of *why* any specific agent should help than can be provided under Shue's model.

Shue meanwhile does give us a reason to care about a minimum threshold, and provides explanation of why specific agents should consider themselves responsible. For Shue, the varied responsibilities under his tripartite account of duty can be assigned to everyone, because that responsibility is simply a requirement of the existence of rights. Exactly what those responsibilities are will vary according to the agent-specific context, which may include factors such as ability, culpability and relationship to the specific right holder. However, while the specifics of how rights are to be fulfilled may vary, we can readily assign general duties to specific agents in a far simpler manner than is available to Brock. Where Brock must move from a need-based model to duty, Shue works within the model of rights and duties and challenges mistaken preconceptions about them. Thus, Shue has a much simpler path to the assignation of specific duties.

Neither Pogge nor Brock offers a full justification of our duties to aid. They offer partial solutions, and each of them is vulnerable to the questions I have set out. In contrast, if we follow Shue's approach, we are provided with a comprehensive argument which avoids the objections simply by rejecting the classification of rights and duties as positive or negative. And this is the key strength of Shue's argument: by rejecting the false dichotomy of positive/negative rights he removes a significant argument against duties to aid, that we have only negative duties. By classifying rights as having a broader set of requirements than what would be allowed under a purely negative model, Shue demands that if we acknowledge a right to anything, we must fulfil certain positive and negative obligations. We cannot deny a duty simply because it is positive and hence too demanding, because to do so turns rights and duties into meaningless decoration used to disguise the fact that such 'quasi-rights' offer no more protection than being lucky enough to avoid disease or violence.

Rejecting the positive/negative distinction enables us to justify a better system of rights and duties relating to health care or to other issues of justice than is available if we follow either Pogge's or Brock's approach. If the foundation of Shue's argument is that if we have a right to something we must also have a right to the things necessary for it, the framework of the argument is that to classify a right as either positive or negative is simply to misunderstand what a right is. In the case of health care, declaring that we have a right only to non-interference means only that we are free to die of the first disease that is severe enough. If we only have a right to protection, then we only have a right to health care until that protection fails; if we catch some unpreventable disease or are in a car accident, we are on our own. Finally, if we have only a right to assistance, then we are entitled to help, but that help can at best restore us to health and not compensate us for being harmed in the first place. And, in any case, even if we are returned to full health, we have still been harmed, and a reason to think health is important is because lacking it can be catastrophic. Any actual basic right must entail a comprehensive set of corresponding duties beyond mere non-interference if it is going to be worth anything, and Shue's approach offers the best way of justifying such duties.

Notes

1. I am deeply grateful to Professor Heather Widdows (the University of Birmingham), the participants and organisers of the Global Economic Justice: Assessing International Aid conference, held at the Universidade Nova, Lisbon, Portugal, and to Patrick Andelic for their very helpful comments on an early draft of this chapter. In addition, I am grateful to the UK Arts and Humanities Research Council (AHRC) for their generous financial support whilst writing this chapter during my time as a PhD student at the University of Birmingham.
2. It may be objected that since health is the objective of health care, we should talk in terms of access to health rather than health care. This is a profoundly complicated question and I do not wish to go into it here; instead, I shall use the term 'health care' in a very loose sense, and leave discussion of whether we have a right to health or health care for another time.
3. I take 'agents' to include individual persons, corporations, as well as governments.
4. Pogge refers to these arguments as 'easy reasons to ignore world poverty' (Pogge 2008: 6).
5. At the time Hardin's article was published population growth in wealthy countries was at a rate that would double the population every eighty-seven years, while the same effect in poor countries took only thirty-five years (Hardin 1974: 564).
6. I discuss this issue in greater detail in 'Approach Three: Shue and Basic Rights, Rejecting the Positive/Negative Rights Distinction' and 'The Implications of Shue's Model for Health Care' below.
7. The Trade Related Aspects of Intellectual Property Rights (TRIPS) regime is an agreement between member states of the World Trade Organization which provides guaranteed monopolies to the creators of certain kinds of intellectual property, including trademarks, industrial designs and patents (World Trade Organization 1994: 319). Importantly, the TRIPS agreement also provides protection for pharmaceutical products, thus granting patent holders a monopoly on the production and sale of potentially life-saving drugs. TRIPS has been widely criticised, both for its alleged ineffectiveness (Hubbard and Love 2004) and for the way that it allows pharmaceutical companies to charge extremely high prices for medicines which may make them inaccessible to those with insufficient funds (Barton 2004: 149–50; Hollis and Pogge 2008: 1).

8. Of course, it may be objected that what is relevant in this case is that the original producer of drugs loses out on a potential market for their products if other companies can manufacture generic versions of their products and undercut them on price. However, we should remember that the people who are most in need of cheap drugs and who have been most harmed by the limitations placed on their production are the same people who would simply not have been able to purchase brand-name drugs in the first place. Given the inability of the global poor to pay monopoly prices for brand-name drugs, a market which caters to their unmet needs, such as the Indian generic pharmaceuticals industry, does not remove a potential or former market for pharmaceutical companies; rather, it provides the benefits of medical technology to those who would otherwise not have been able to benefit from it. Hollis and Pogge discuss this in more detail in *The Health Impact Fund: Making New Medicines Accessible for All* (Hollis and Pogge 2008: 64–6).
9. As opposed to legal duties which may involve positive obligations.
10. Shue and Brock share a sufficientarian concern with establishing a minimum threshold of entitlement to certain basic goods. However, where Brock writes in terms of goods, Shue is focused on rights and duties, another reason it is easier, using his approach, to assign responsibility to specific persons.

References

Bannerjee, Amitava, Aidan Hollis and Thomas Pogge (2010), 'The Health Impact Fund: Incentives for Improving Access to Medicines', *The Lancet*, no. 375, pp. 166–9.
Barton, John H. (2004), 'TRIPS and the Global Pharmaceutical Market', *Health Affairs*, vol. 23, no. 3, pp. 146–54.
Brock, Gillian (2009), *Global Justice: A Cosmopolitan Account*, Oxford: Oxford University Press.
Frohlich, Norman and Joe Oppenheimer (1992), *Choosing Justice: An Experimental Approach to Ethical Theory*, Berkeley and Los Angeles: University of California Press.
Hardin, Garrett (1974), 'Living on a Lifeboat', *Bioscience*, vol. 24, no. 10, pp. 561–8.
Harsanyi, John C. (1953), 'Cardinal Utility in Welfare Economics and in the Theory of Risk-taking', *Journal of Political Economy*, vol. 61, no. 5, pp. 434–5.
Held, David (1995), *Democracy and the Global Order: From the Modern State to Cosmopolitan Governance*, Oxford: Polity Press.
Hollis, Aidan and Thomas Pogge (2008), *The Health Impact Fund: Making New Medicines Accessible for All. A Report of Incentives for Global Health,*

<http://healthimpactfund.org/wp-content/uploads/2012/11/hif_book.pdf>
(last accessed 26 October 2015).

Hubbard, Tim and James Love (2004), 'A New Trade Framework for Global Healthcare R&D', *PLoS Biology*, vol. 2, no. 2, pp.147–50.

Nagel, Thomas (2005), 'The Problem of Global Justice', *Philosophy and Public Affairs*, vol. 33, no. 2, pp. 113–47.

Nussbaum, Martha (2003), 'Capabilities as Fundamental Entitlements: Sen and Social Justice', *Feminist Economics*, vol. 9, no. 2–3, pp. 35–59.

Pogge, Thomas (2008), *World Poverty and Human Rights*, 2nd edn, Cambridge: Polity Press.

Rawls, John (1999a), *The Law of Peoples; with, The Idea of Public Reason Revisited*, Cambridge, MA: Harvard University Press.

Rawls, John [1971] (1999b), *A Theory of Justice: Revised Edition*, Cambridge, MA: Harvard University Press.

Rorty, Richard (1996), 'Who Are We?: Moral Universalism and Economic Triage', *Diogenes*, vol. 44, no. 173, pp. 5–15.

Sen, Amartya (1994), 'Population: Delusion and Reality', *New York Review of Books*, vol. 41, no. 15, pp. 62–71.

Shue, Henry (1980), *Basic Rights: Subsistence, Affluence and U.S. Foreign Policy*, Princeton, NJ: Princeton University Press.

Singer, Peter (1972), 'Famine, Affluence, and Morality', *Philosophy and Public Affairs*, vol. 1, no. 3, pp. 229–43.

Wenar, Leif (2008), 'Property Rights and the Resource Curse', *Philosophy and Public Affairs*, vol. 36, no. 1, pp. 2–32.

World Trade Organization (1994), *Annex 1C: Agreement on Trade Related Aspects of International Property Rights*, <http://www.wto.org/english/docs_e/legal_e/27-trips.pdf> (last accessed 26 October 2015).

World Health Organization (2010a), *Global Tuberculosis Control: WHO Report 2010*, WHO Press, <http://reliefweb.int/sites/reliefweb.int/files/resources/F530290AD0279399C12577D8003E9D65-Full_Report.pdf > (last accessed 26 October 2015).

World Health Organization (2010b), 'Tuberculosis', Fact Sheet no. 104, <http://www.who.int/mediacentre/factsheets/fs104/en/index.html> (last accessed 26 October 2015).

Chapter 6

RESTITUTION AND DISTRIBUTIVE JUSTICE

George F. DeMartino and Jonathan D. Moyer

INTRODUCTION

There is no question but that historical injustices perpetrated by some people and nations against others continue to cast a shadow over contemporary economic, social, and political circumstances.[1] Current disparities between racial and ethnic groups within countries and between nations—in wealth and income, human capital, privilege, freedom, and technology—in part reflect egregious historical violations of fundamental rights. Examples of this include, though are certainly not limited to, the colonial expansion by Europeans and others from the late sixteenth to the mid-twentieth century as well as the enslavement of Africans in Europe and North America from the late fifteenth through the nineteenth century (Brennan 2011). In the United States, racial injustice in the form of explicit (legal) discrimination in employment, housing, voting, and access to education and other government services carried on for well over a century after emancipation. Indeed, even today many racial minorities in the US face substantial barriers to the achievement of genuine equality. *Prima facie* evidence of the effects of past injustice is found today in racially differentiated rates of educational attainment, employment, health, incarceration, income, political representation, and wealth.

The continuing, compounding effects in the present of past historical injustice raise the question whether governments today ought to enact restitution[2] that would bring about some sort of monetary transfer or other compensation from its beneficiaries to its victims. Restitution for past injustices has been advocated in all manner of contexts—both within countries and between sovereign states, with varying impacts. Table 6.1 provides a selection of restitution cases and their current

Table 6.1 Cases Involving Restitution

Injustice	Suggested Restitution Amount	Outcome
Trans-Atlantic slave trade	The African World Reparations and Repatriation Truth Commission in 1999 demanded 777 trillion USD from Western Europe and the Americas; also called for Africa's debts to be unconditionally cancelled.	No payment made.[a]
Austrian treatment of Jews during WWII	Payment of 25 million USD in 1990 to survivors of Holocaust.	Payment made.[b]
German treatment of Jews during WWII	More than 50 billion USD from Germany to victims.	Payment made over decades since the war.[b]
Japanese Americans jailed during WWII	20,000 USD in 1990 to survivors.	Restitution paid to survivors in 1988 Civil Liberties Act. Total of 1.2 billion USD paid.[b,c]
Japanese treatment of South Koreans during WWII	800 million in 1965 USD from Japan as (a) 300 million USD grant, (b) 200 million USD in low-interest loans, (c) 300 million USD in private credits.	Payment made over 10 years starting 1965.[d]
Argentina military junta's treatment of dissidents	Range of restitution based on degree of violation determined by Argentine law.	In 2004, victims of unlawful detention were given 3 billion USD.[e,f]
Colombian treatment of dissidents	Fourteen extradited warlords paid 4.6 million USD in 2008; Chiquita Brands fined 25 million USD in 2007 for making payments to paramilitary groups that engaged in human rights violations and murders; establishment of a reparation fund. Also, Chiquita now faces lawsuits from family members of people killed or disappeared in the fighting, which could represent 4,000 claims.	Fine paid.[f,g]

Table 6.1 (continued)

Injustice	Suggested Restitution Amount	Outcome
Chilean treatment of dissidents	The Chileans offered a few restitution options to the family members: a lump sum payment, monthly payments based on the average wage of the disappeared or killed family member, scholarships for secondary and university education of the children of killed or disappeared people until age 35, and free medical and psychological care.	Restitution paid.[f]
Chemical weapons used on Kurdish minorities in Northern Iraq during Iran–Iraq war sold by Dutch national to Iraq	Dutch criminal court ruled that victims could receive no more than 680 EUR in 2005; 15 Kurds sought this payment as civil parties to the case but the Dutch Supreme Court ruled their claims were too complicated and they must seek compensation through civil courts.	Dutch national convicted of war crimes, original plaintiffs still not compensated.[h]
Iraqi treatment of property owners during Saddam Hussein's rule	Court treatment of restitution involving repayment for those forcibly removed from land and reconciliation with current land-owners.	Over 40,000 decisions made out of more than 140,000 cases.[f]
Iraqi treatment of Kuwait in 1991	UN Security Council mandated restitution of all cultural property seized and Iraq must pay 5 percent of its oil revenues into a special UN reparations account until all claims deemed worthy by the UN have been satisfied.	Iraq has paid 25 billion USD to Kuwait for the 1990 invasion.[i,j]
Bosnian treatment of Serbs	Court ordered payment of 2.4 million USD in 2003 of government funds to the creation of a cemetery and memorial fund, along with property restitution for nearly 2.2 million internally displaced persons and over 400 houses damaged or destroyed.	By 2003 more than 92 percent of claims settled.[f]

Table 6.1 (continued)

Injustice	Suggested Restitution Amount	Outcome
Rwandan genocide	Returning of all looted items, establishment of memorial sites with sales tax revenue, no full monetary restitution for victims.	Many goods returned, many people participate in community service.[f]
South African apartheid	Payment to surviving victims benchmarked to family income with ceiling and floor.	Payment made.[f]
Canadian Indian Residential Schools	In 1999, 350 million CAD was given to the Aboriginal Healing Foundation for healing services and revitalization of Aboriginal culture. In 2007 the Indian Residential Schools Settlement Agreement provided 10,000 CAD to all survivors of the IRSs with an extra 3,000 CAD for every year attended. Compensation up to 275,000 CAD for abuse. 60 million CAD for a Truth and Reconciliation Commission to work for 5 years. Another 125 million CAD to the Aboriginal Healing Foundation and 20 million CAD for memorials.	By 2008 the government had issued payment to 68,000 survivors.[k,l]
Morocco "Years of Lead," the brutal oppression from 1956 to 1990	The Advisory Council on Human Rights (CCDH) was established in 1990 and in 1998 recommended the formation of an official body to compensate victims of past human rights abuses. The Independent Arbitration Commission awarded about 100 million USD in reparations but many were unhappy with the IAC's methods. So the Equity and Reconciliation Commission (IER) was formed in 2004.	The IER has distributed 85 million USD to around 9,000 people. However, the communal reparations programs are still in their initial phase.[m]

Table 6.1 (continued)

Injustice	Suggested Restitution Amount	Outcome
Killed and disappeared people during the Brazilian military dictatorship	The Special Commission on Political Deaths and Disappearances disbursed nearly 40 million BRL in 1995 to over 300 families. In 2001, the Amnesty Commission decided that the victims of political persecution were entitled to reparations.	As of January 2011, 35,000 victims of political persecution have been paid reparations, totaling 2.4 billion BRL in 2010.[n]
DRC crimes against humanity and war crimes	In 2006 four cases in the DRC were awarded reparations by military courts and tribunals. These cases recommended the payment of 987,317 USD to victims of the abuses.	As of 2012, the reparations had not been paid.[o]
Use of child soldiers in the DRC	The ICC found Lubanga guilty of conscripting child soldiers and decreed that reparations are due. Since Lubanga does not have the funds, the Trust Fund for Victims (TFV—funded by ICC members) will be paying the reparations.	As of March 2015 the exact amount of reparations due was still being decided by the TFV.[p]

Sources: [a] BBC News 1999; [b] du Plessis 2003; [c] O'Brien and Fugita 1991; [d] Manyin 2001; [e] United States Institute of Peace 2011; [f] Ferstman et al. 2009; [g] CNN World 2011; [h] van Hasselt 2010; [i] United Nations News Centre 2011; [j] *The Daily Star* 2012; [k] ICTJ 2008; [l] Aboriginal Healing Foundation 2014; [m] ICTJ 2009; [n] Mezarobba 2010; [o] Parmar 2012; [p] ICC 2015.

status. Table 6.2 provides estimates of US restitution for historical injustices.

The intuition behind campaigns promoting restitution is clear: where some have been systematically or significantly wronged, and where the effects of those wrongs extend into the present, they or their descendants ought to be compensated by those who perpetrated the wrongs, or by their descendants who are the innocent beneficiaries of the wrongs. Where the injustice involved the actions of members of some groups against members of another, the case can be and is made that restitution should involve inter-group transfer. This may occur alongside cases of restitution involving particular individuals when particular rights violators and their victims can be identified.

Table 6.2 Estimated Restitution for US Slavery

Estimation of Restitution to African Slaves in US	Source
Restitution was 3.4 billion USD, calculated from the value of slave production not returned as food or shelter and summed over the years 1805–60 in current dollars	Ransom and Sutch (1990)
Taking wage for a free person as a proxy, calculated restitution is 1.4 trillion USD in 1983	Neal (1990)
Income diverted from enslaved Africans during slavery calculated restitution to be a range of 2.1 trillion to 4.7 trillion USD in 1983, depending on the rate of return	Marketti (1990)
Taking the "40 acres and a mule" as a basis, author calculates restitution to be 1.3 trillion USD in 2008	Darity (2008)

Programs of restitution intend to achieve three things: "acknowledgement of a grievous injustice, redress for the injustice, and closure of the grievances held by the group subjected to the injustice" (Darity 2008: 656). The three objectives build incrementally: acknowledgment precedes redress, redress precedes closure. Restitution claims can be organized into three types: (1) those of individuals who suffered injustice who are still alive at the time of restitution (for example, Japanese Americans and World War II); (2) those made by communities on behalf of previous promise breaking (for example, Native American petitioning of US government); and (3) claims made by individuals who are descendants of victims of injustice (for example, the African American attempt to achieve restitution for the harms associated with slavery and legal segregation) (Thompson 2001: 114–15).

As the foregoing suggests, the end goal of restitution can differ widely from retribution to rehabilitation. Restitution can be tied to the claim that wrong-doers be punished, with restitution to victims forming a part of the punishment—the treatment of Germany after World War I provides one notable example. But this approach is available only when the wrong-doers are both identifiable and surviving. A second claim casts a much broader net: Restitution is intended to restore those whose rights were violated, or those who suffer today from the past rights violations of others (such as their ancestors), to the position they had enjoyed prior to the rights transgression; or, more ambitiously, to the situation they would enjoy today had the past violation not occurred. This second claim founds restitution proper (independent of retribution); it applies both in cases where the unjust act or practice is very recent and where it is long since passed; and where the perpetrators and victims of injustice are individually identifiable, and where they are not. Here the drive is not to punish, but to overcome some of the damage from past transgressions. Punishment and restitution proper are not inconsistent, of course: but they are nevertheless distinct. In what follows, we will focus exclusively on restitution proper and leave aside the matter of retribution.

If the intuition founding the case for restitution proper is clear, restitution is nonetheless fraught with complexities. As Vernon states: "although there is, in principle, a clear case of restitutive justice, its elements rarely, if ever, exist in the real world in an unmixed state" (Vernon 2003: 542). Restitution claims require all sorts of empirical and normative judgments about which reasonable people may and certainly do disagree. Not least, even if we agree on the contours of a past injustice that continues to generate inequality in the present, we may very well disagree about whether restitution is *the* or even *an* appropriate means for addressing it. Might not it be better, the welfare consequentialist might argue, to let bygones be bygones and instead search for non-restitutive policies that will best promote social welfare in the future? Moreover, especially in post-conflict environments (such as civil wars involving genocide and other atrocities), it can well be argued that the promotion of peace and prosperity are better advanced by truth and reconciliation processes that acknowledge but do not attempt to provide payment for past injustices. People might rightly fear in this context that restitution processes could re-inflame passionate antipathies. Restitution following World War I is a widely recognized determinant of the rise of fascism in post-war Europe, for example.

Here we do not take a position on if and when restitution is an appropriate response to past injustice. This reflects in part our awareness of the salience of the particular circumstances surrounding each case and associated complexities. What is both warranted and efficacious in one context might be unwarranted and self-defeating in another. This implies that determinations about if and when restitution should be made ought not to be rule-based, but instead tied to the very specific contexts in which one group continues to suffer the effects of past injustices.

Our goal is more limited. We seek to demonstrate that careful consideration of restitution, where it is taken to be an appropriate means for responding to past injustices, involves substantial normative work.

One cannot hope to offer well-reasoned and compelling answers to questions like which historical practices and institutions warrant restitution, and what magnitude of restitution is sufficient to redress historical wrongs, if one has not first worked out the normative criteria that will guide these judgments. Indeed, whether restitution is warranted at all will depend on a normatively inscribed reading of history. Like so many other areas of social investigation, analyses of past injustice are founded upon a thorough integration of the normative and the positive. In this context, and as we hope to show, the mathematical calculations required to quantify the effects of past injustice are shot through with prior choices that are far from value-neutral.

Of the many normative matters that arise in the context of restitution, we will focus here on just one: on the question of justice. The tie between conceptions of justice and the project of restitution is signaled by the "theory of restitution" itself. This theory is founded on a strong empirical premise that is in turn predicated on a claim of justice, described by Richard America as follows: "Whenever nations, races or other large social groups have chronic grievances, a fundamental issue is invariably the sense that one party has perpetuated unremedied historical economic injustices" (America 2005: 327). Substantiating this claim is by no means straightforward. It requires an account of justice against which one can assess the historical record. And while it might be the case that some social practices achieve notoriety under virtually all accounts of justice, it is very likely that others will be normatively contested—indicted under one or more accounts, but validated under others.

The restitution project may also require the quantification of the impact of historical wrongs, which presumes of course that such an accounting can in fact be done. In America's words,

> The theory of restitution is based on the intuition that it is possible to reconstruct historic economic relations; to specify "fair" standards [. . .] that were violated, usually by force; to audit the historical pattern of transactions between the groups and compare the actual with the "fair" standard; to then estimate the deviation from "fairness." (America 2005: 327)

This exercise, too, certainly requires that normative judgments be made—as the term "'fair' standards" makes clear. What forms of economic enrichment are just, and which are unjust? If my grandfather got the better of your grandfather in a voluntary economic transaction, is that indictable against a standard of fairness—and ought it to appear today in the restitution board's ledger of past injustices? And just what do we mean by "voluntary" in this context—what if your grandfather was coerced into accepting unfavorable terms from my grandfather, owing to the specific conditions under which they confronted each other? Should Milton Friedman or Karl Marx be our guide in assessing the presence of "coercion"? Clearly, these decisions, too, will depend on the normative framework that guides the assessment.

The notion of justice has been the site of intense controversy in moral and political philosophy, political economy, and beyond over the past several centuries. Indeed, it is likely to remain contested in perpetuity. The question that naturally arises, then, is whether the striking lack of consensus on what makes for just social arrangements is problematic for the project of restitution. It does not necessarily follow that it is: It may very well be that alternative, respected accounts of justice reach substantial agreement in their interpretations of the historical record (as concerns, for example, the practice of slavery), in which case the lingering philosophical controversy need not overly concern those who press for restitution. On the other hand, if it is the case that different accounts of justice produce disparate assessments of the historical record, then we must take account of these differences as we undertake the work of identifying historical wrongs and estimating magnitudes of restitution. Our claim is that we must pay explicit attention to the various plausible justice frameworks before engaging in politically charged discussions like those surrounding issues of restitutions.

In what follows we explore the extent of consensus and disagreement among alternative contemporary accounts of justice on the matter of the kinds of events that might warrant restitution and, consequently, the computation of the magnitude of restitution. The goal is not to adjudicate the relevant normative controversies, but rather to illustrate the significance of normative theory for the restitution project. For purposes of demonstration, we focus on three important traditions in the recent scholarship on economic justice; and we focus in particular on one theorist from each tradition. The first is the libertarian tradition of political philosophy; our exemplar is the work of Robert Nozick. The second is the liberal contractarian approach, and we focus on the work of John Rawls. The third is the capabilities approach, a chief advocate of which is Amartya Sen.

This narrow focus allows us to achieve the objective of demonstrating that normative controversy surrounding the concept of justice bears heavily on considerations pertaining to restitution. Even limiting our attention to these three perspectives we find striking disagreement regarding the practices and outcomes that warrant redress and, consequently, the appropriate magnitudes that would suffice as restitution. This is particularly notable because of the parallels between Rawls and Sen.[3] This implies that a wider review of accounts of justice would likely yield even more disagreement about restitution than we find among the three scholars we examine here. We will see that these three approaches yield overlapping but distinct conclusions about which kinds of historical practices might warrant restitution today and, were restitution to be pursued, what would be the magnitude of the required payments. The chapter concludes with some thoughts about how to take account of this normative controversy in the restitution project.

A STYLIZED HISTORICAL ACCOUNT

For simplicity of exposition, let us presume a stylized account of certain features of international affairs during the sixteenth through twentieth centuries. During this long historical epoch European and other powers exerted extensive colonial control over regions in Asia, Africa, the Americas, and beyond. Salient features of colonialism included the proliferation of enforced labor and exploitation through taxation and other enforced transfers from indigenous populations to the colonizers. Colonialism was also associated with what at best might be thought of as "uneven exchange" in markets involving colonizers and colonized but often entailed little more than piracy, plunder, and simple expropriation of resources. Colonial relationships could also involve the destruction of the indigenous economy, especially those industries in the periphery that might otherwise have presented competition to the colonizers' industries back home. Moreover, colonialism could be and sometimes was associated with genocide and indigenous cultural collapse—sometimes as a consequence of explicit policy and other times as a consequence of the material, political, and social transformations that colonizers imposed on those under their domain.

Though not a necessary feature of colonialism, slavery also proliferated during this historical period and was likewise associated with international conquest. For instance, the African–North American slave trade endured for several centuries. The seized African slaves were traded for profit and exploited in agriculture, mining, manufacturing, and other sectors. The harms of the trade were not only borne by the enslaved themselves, but also by the communities from which they were abducted.

We presume that these transgressions continue to reverberate today in terms of intra-national and international inequalities. Following America (2005), we presume that part of the existing inequality in economic development across countries today stems from the colonial history and enslavement of previous centuries. Moreover, we will presume that within national contexts, such as the US, part of the inequality that persists today between racial minorities (most importantly, African Americans and Native Americans) and the Anglo majority is rooted in its history of enslavement and colonialism.

For present purposes we will consider just three types of interaction that may arise between members of any two distinct groups. While by no means exhaustive, these three interaction types cover many of the practices that proliferated during the colonial era, and that might and do form the basis for restitution claims:

1. *Extra-market appropriations, takings or transfers*: Interactions from which one community secures appropriations from another community through force, coercion, or other illicit activity. These might entail enslavement and other forms of forced labor, theft, fraud, destruction of property or community, systematic terror and murder that yield economic advantage and disadvantage, and related practices.
2. *Market-based appropriations*: Interactions from which one community secures market-based appropriations from another community.[4] These interactions might entail "unequal exchange" that results from discrimination (such as in the labor market), the exercise of monopoly power, and so on. For our purposes unequal exchange refers to transactions where the terms of the exchange (such as the content, quality, or price of the goods or services being exchanged) reflect an asymmetry in bargaining power of the respective agents, perhaps owing to differences in their opportunity sets or fall-back positions.

3. *Differential gains*: Interactions that benefit both communities, but
   from which the gains enjoyed by one systematically exceed those
   enjoyed by the other. The causal drivers in this case may be the same
   as, similar to, or different from those described under case 2, above.[5]

The inequalities in evidence today, across nations and across distinct
groups within nations, reflect *inter alia* some combination or other of
these three kinds of processes. The nature and extent of inequality
results from the interplay of all three processes, of course, which complicates greatly the task of computing the contribution of each for the
purpose of restitution. Different economic perspectives (for example,
Marxian versus neoclassical theory) would also undoubtedly reach different conclusions about the contribution of each kind of social process
to inequality. Any account of restitution should address in one way or
another each of these types of misappropriation. For present purposes,
we will assume that reasonable estimates (of upper and lower bounds)
could be made of the contribution of each kind of process to existing
inequality.

Formalizing, we have the following equation:

$$D = \sum_{i=1}^{n} (X_i + M_i + G_i)(1 + r)^{(n-1)} + f\left[\sum_{i=2}^{n} D_i\right]$$

where D is the cumulative difference in capacities (as represented, for
instance, by income) between two groups of people (such as two racial
or ethnic groups, or two nations) in any year n; X_i is net extra-market
appropriations between the two groups in year i (1, above), M_i is net
market-based appropriations (2, above), and G_i the net difference in
gains from interaction between the two groups (3, above). The term r is
the compound rate, and allows for the calculation of the present value
of past and present differential impacts.

The final term in the equation, $f\left[\sum D_i\right]$, captures the present effect
of past differential impacts that exceed the normal compound rate.
Continuing our previous example, if in some period i the Anglo
American community secured a positive D, then it is likely that
in period i + 1 it will enjoy the potential to convert that past gain
into greater capacity (for entrepreneurship, technological innovation,
human capital formation, and so forth) than is given by any standard

compound rate (such as the rate of interest). The f [D_i] term therefore reflects cumulative causation where, over time, advantage yields further advantage. For the African American community, which suffers a loss in period i, the result will be the opposite: It will experience a diminution in its capacities in period i + 1 that is independent of its interaction with Anglo Americans in period i + 1, and which exceeds the standard compound rate. The inclusion of this term, then, reflects the fact that the differential impact is not fully reducible to resource flows in any given year, or even to the present value of the sum of such flows over an extended period. These flows—and the means deployed for securing them—may be expected to induce additional effects that are likely to amplify inequality over time. Hence, the differential in any given year is theorized to be the result from the contributions in that year of X, M, and G, as well as the contribution in that year of the differences in capacity that resulted from earlier differentials.

COMPETING CONCEPTIONS OF DISTRIBUTIVE JUSTICE

The three accounts of justice surveyed here are among the most influential in contemporary debates over social arrangements and policy.

Libertarian Justice

The contemporary libertarian account of justice that appears in the work of Robert Nozick (1974) descends from the work of John Locke and other theorists in the liberal tradition. Locke asserts that an individual has property rights in those elements of nature with which he or she has mixed his or her labor. This right to appropriation is a natural right, one that precedes the intervention of civil society. Moreover, and more importantly for present purposes, this natural right extends to those things produced by the resources one owns and hires, such as the labor of others (MacPherson 1962: 219–20; Locke [1690] 1999).

The right of property, including the right to alienate what one owns, provides the basis for establishing the legitimacy of market transactions, regardless of the patterns of inequality that may emerge therefrom. Locke's liberalism defends formal liberty rather than substantive equality—it privileges the right of the individual to contract freely in most cases over fairness of outcomes. The Lockean defense of market exchanges and outcomes as fair regardless of the substantive inequality that emerges therefrom, provided the transactors are formally free to contract as they see fit, certainly carries forward to contemporary libertarian thinking.[6]

For Nozick, the defense of market-based distributions builds upon his view of rights as "side-constraints" that may not be violated regardless of the social benefit that rights violations might promote. In the side-constraint view of rights, the interests of the group (in economic efficiency, "justice," and so on) cannot trump the right of the individual to live his or her life free from coercion. If we recognize the inviolability of this right, then we are led to see that market exchanges between free transactors must not be constrained by the state so as to promote greater income equality, wealth, or other measures of human welfare.

Nozick's "historical" account of justice follows from these insights. The account is historical in the sense that the justice or injustice of a distribution depends strictly on how it came about. In his words, "A distribution is just if it arises from another just distribution by legitimate means. [. . .] Whatever arises from a just situation by just steps is itself just" (Nozick 1974: 151).

Nozickean justice requires justice in the *"original acquisition of holdings"* and justice in the *"transfer of holdings* from one person to another" (ibid.: 150; original emphasis). Justice in acquisition speaks to "the appropriation of unheld things": the manner in which unowned assets or goods are initially claimed. Following Locke, Nozick appends a proviso to his account of justice in acquisition: An agent may not properly appropriate unheld assets to such a degree that the position of others is jeopardized. In Locke's words, the appropriator must leave "enough and as good [. . .] in common for others" (cited in ibid.: 175). For instance, justice in acquisition does not permit the right to monopolize a scarce source of potable water in the desert.[7] Justice in transfer refers to processes by which assets justly acquired can come under the ownership of another. Such processes include exchange, gifting, bequeathing, and other mechanisms by which those with an ownership right over a good may sacrifice that right.

Were there no violations of the principles of justice in acquisition and transfer, there would be nothing further to say about the justice of existing distributions. Virtually no extent of inequality would be indictable so long as it results fully from agents acting in accordance with their rights of acquisition and transfer. But Nozick's historical account of justice recognizes that rights violations do take place, and that current distributions of goods and income are shaped in part by these historical injustices. In Nozick's words,

> Some people steal from others, or defraud them, or enslave them, seizing their product and preventing them from competing in exchanges. None of these are permissible modes of transition from one situation to another. And some persons acquire holding by means not sanctioned by the principle of justice in acquisition. (Nozick 1974: 152)

Hence, the need in the Nozickean framework for a third justice principle: the "rectification of injustice in holdings" (ibid.: 152). The effects of past injustice must be rectified by transfers from beneficiaries to victims of past injustice before we can validate current distributions. Establishing the magnitude of the warranted rectification requires the use of "historical information about previous situations and injustices done in them (as defined by the first two principles of justice and rights against interference), and information about the actual course of events that flowed from these injustices, until the present . . ." (ibid.: 152).

One final point warrants attention in this regard. Nozick counterposes his historical account of justice (which he claims is implicitly shared by socialist thought) to what he calls "time-slice" accounts of justice. Time-slice (or "patterned") accounts judge who gets, has, or enjoys what in the present against "some *structural* principle(s) of just distribution" without attention to whether that distribution came about through voluntary exchange or through violence and plunder. Utilitarianism represents one such approach, insofar as it judges any particular distribution by the criterion of maximum aggregate utility. And so does standard welfare economics, since "the subject is conceived as operating on matrices representing only current information about distribution" (ibid.: 154). Nozick ridicules this kind of reasoning for focusing on the wrong set of facts. Is there no difference, Nozick asks us, between two distributions that are identical in every respect except for the fact that one came about through extortion while the other came about through a voluntary transaction that both parties took to be beneficial? It bears reiteration that what ought to matter in ascertaining the legitimacy of a distribution, for Nozick, is how it came about—not who currently has what.

Rawlsian Contractarian Justice

Rawls's theoretical work is perhaps the best-known approach to distributive justice outside of the field of political philosophy. Rawls (1971) argues that distributive outcomes are just only if they would result from the rational deliberations of a hypothetical committee of representatives of all the groups that constitute society, with these deliberations occurring behind a "veil of ignorance." The deliberators operate in the "original position." That is, this hypothetical body is to do its work prior to any of the participants knowing to which group they will be assigned, and in the absence of specific knowledge of their own respective comprehensive accounts of society. The deliberators are taken to be disinterestedly rational, and are driven in their deliberations exclusively by "general considerations" (ibid.: 118).

For Rawls, the committee of disinterested, rational representatives would generate two principles of justice. The first is taken to be paramount: It concerns the equal distribution across individuals of what he calls "primary goods" which are theorized as general-purpose means that people need to achieve that which they have reason to value. In his words, "a) Each person has an equal right to the most extensive scheme of equal basic liberties compatible with a similar scheme of liberties for all" (Rawls 1993: 271).

Primary goods include, *inter alia,*

political liberty [. . .] freedom of speech and assembly; liberty of conscience and freedom of thought; freedom of the person along with the right to hold (personal) property; and the freedom from arbitrary arrest and seizure as defined by concept of the rule of law. (Rawls 1971: 61)

The second principle is the "difference principle." This principle provides for deviations from the equal distribution of primary goods under two conditions: "Social and economic inequalities are permissible provided that they are i) to the greatest expected benefit of the least advantaged; and ii) attached to positions and offices open to all under conditions of fair equality of opportunity" (Rawls 1993: 271). The intuition underlying the difference principle is appealing, though in fact it is obviously correct only in very simple cases. For instance, those cast adrift in a lifeboat might rightly distribute more food and water to those who will perform the onerous task of rowing the boat, since this unequal distribution would better serve all in the boat (including those who are too weak to row) than would an equal distribution. Importantly, the two principles working in concert seem to allow for even rather substantial inequality in economic circumstances, provided they improve the condition of those who are worst off. But the principles do not countenance the sacrifice of any and all rights in pursuit of economic improvement. For Rawls, the principles are lexically ordered, with priority given to equality of political rights over economic gain. In his words, "being arranged in a serial order they do not permit exchanges between basic liberties and economic social gains" (Rawls 1971: 63). These features bear directly on restitution, as we will see momentarily.

We will argue below that Rawlsian justice can found a case for restitution of certain past injustices. But we note here that Douglas Ficek (2002) has argued that the Rawlsian account of justice does not permit an adequate conception of restitution to victims of racial oppression. For Ficek, the deficiencies in the Rawlsian account stem from "the racist baggage of being a theoretical extension of Kantian deontology; and second, the inability of color-blind theorizing to appreciate the distinct historicities of racialized Others (or 'non-Others', as Lewis R. Gordon has argued) and their specific claims of justice" (ibid.: 2). To make this case, Ficek demonstrates the under-specification (by Rawls) of and consequent confusion surrounding the information and knowledge that the deliberators in the original position would have. They are to have "the general facts about human society" but no specific knowledge of particulars—of "contingencies that set them in opposition" (ibid.: 3). But, then, what are we to presume they would know about race, if they are to have no knowledge of the "concrete historicity and intentionality" that define racism and racial oppression? And if they are to have access to an account of history that recognizes racial oppression, "who is writing it? Is it Adam Smith or Karl Marx? D.W. Griffith or W.E.B. Du Bois?" (ibid.: 6). Whose account is consistent with "the general facts about human society," access to which is presumed by the Rawlsian original position?

We cannot respond adequately here to the important claims Ficek makes. Instead, we take his essay as further evidence of the claim that founds our own—that is, the demand for restitution depends fully on normative judgments and philosophical inquiry. Whether Rawlsian justice is *the* or even *an* appropriate foundation for the restitution project (in regards to racial or other historical oppressions) depends on a careful specification of just what the framework presumes about what are and what are not violations of rights, duties, and interests that warrant restitution, and the means that it provides for theorizing these violations and the strategies that are appropriate to address them.

Capabilities Equality

Amartya Sen has emerged recently as an important contributor to the debate over distributive justice. Sen's early work in this field (1992) was deeply influenced by the work of Rawls, but he presents an alternative approach to distributive justice that reaches beyond that of Rawls in important respects. For Sen, those advocating equality ought to focus on people's "capabilities to achieve functionings." The term "functionings" refers to states or conditions that people have reason to value, such as being well nourished, well housed, or being politically efficacious. "Capabilities" refer to the complete set of functionings that a person can actually achieve given her allocation of primary goods, the institutional structure of her community, her personal intellectual and physical attributes, and so on. The demand for capabilities equality may be interpreted, then, as a claim that people ought to enjoy equal substantive freedom to live valued lives.

When taken as an approach to distributive justice the capabilities framework differs from the Rawlsian account in one vital respect. Sen's egalitarianism focuses on *actual achievements* that are possible for the individual (given her means and other circumstances), rather than on the *means* to achieve (Rawls's primary goods) (Sen 2009: 66). Because of inter-personal differences, and the differential impact of institutional structures, social practices, and norms on distinct individuals and groups, people will vary in their ability to transform means into achievement. Valuing substantive freedom to achieve, Sen's capability approach to equality therefore demands that we equalize achievements (capabilities) rather than means. Indeed, this approach calls for the unequal distribution of primary goods to offset differences among individuals and groups in the ability to convert means into achievements.

Sen and other theorists operating in the capabilities framework (such as Nussbaum 2000) have paid particular attention to the ways in which group identity can and does affect capabilities. Members of racial, ethnic, or gender groups that are oppressed over time may suffer both in terms of the means they secure to promote their goals, and especially in their ability to convert available means into achievements. Two actors with identical income but from different social groups may face very different opportunities and obstacles as they convert this income into the aspirations for good health and longevity, professional expertise, political efficaciousness, self-respect and other vital functionings. Making matters worse, those who are long denied important freedoms may come to suffer "adaptive preferences" (Elster 1982)—they may come to discount the desirability of the goods or states that they believe to be beyond their reach. Adaptive preference formation may allow the oppressed to achieve a greater degree of happiness, to be sure, since it is easier to live a life believing that you do not want or need what you cannot have. But the psychological adjustment that leads the oppressed to deny the value of what they cannot have represents a significant loss of human freedom—the freedom to imagine and seek a better life (ibid.). Adaptive preferences may then be transmitted inter-generationally, as children are raised within subcultures that deny the value of important goods. All of this implies that historical oppression of social groups may haunt the members of those groups long into the future—even after the formal practices of oppression are terminated.

There is implicit in the capabilities approach an argument (not intended by Sen) against Rawls's difference principle (see DeMartino 2000), which bears directly on the restitution project. We can see this if we disaggregate capabilities into distinct categories such as political capabilities (the ability to be politically efficacious); economic capabilities (the ability to purchase or otherwise acquire primary goods, or to secure valuable work); and cultural and psychological capabilities (the ability to appear in public without shame or feel self-worth in one's community). Disaggregating in this way leads us to appreciate the interdependence of different capabilities, as Sen often emphasizes. A capabilities failure in one realm (for example, the economic) may be expected to generate capabilities failure in others (for example, the political or cultural). A relatively poor person may not only be deprived of important welfare goods, like housing, but may also find it difficult to participate meaningfully in the political life of her community. This then leads to a second critical insight, also emphasized by Sen, that relative poverty might therefore be expected to undermine capabilities across the spectrum. It may be worse in important respects to have a low income in a high-income community than in a community where everyone else is similarly poor. In the former, the poor person may suffer other capabilities failures associated with being relatively poor, while in the latter context, she would not be so disadvantaged.

Taking these two insights together, we discover that Rawls's difference principle is difficult to integrate into the capabilities perspective. A defense of the difference principle would require a demonstration that the capabilities set facing the poor expands as inequality increases. But through the lens of the capabilities perspective, we discern the many pathways by which relative inequality may harm those worst off. Inequality in one domain (such as income) may both undermine equality in others, and may contribute to a general capabilities failure for the relatively impoverished. In short, those advocating the difference principle in a Senian egalitarian framework must bear a very heavy burden of proving that inequality does not impair the capabilities of those with least, taking full account of capabilities interdependence.

It bears emphasis that unlike Nozick's libertarian account of justice, neither Rawls's nor Sen's account appears to be explicitly historical. Both focus attention on what is a just distribution at a given moment in time, and both prescribe a distribution that is, in Nozick's words, "patterned." Upon first approach they seem to be "time-slice" accounts. Indeed, this insight founds part of Ficek's critique of Rawls, as we have seen. But we suggest that this is not the whole story, and for several reasons. First, both frameworks explicitly indict outcomes that arise from unfair processes. On this point, Rawls argues that,

> the distribution resulting from voluntary market transactions (even if all the ideal conditions for competitive efficiency obtain) is not, in general, fair unless the antecedent distribution of income and wealth, as well as the structure of the system of markets, is fair. (Rawls 1993: 266)

Hence, we are required to investigate the historical conditions that yielded the present distribution. Sen surely concurs in this judgment. Indeed, for Sen, unequal capabilities are indictable in part because of the inequality in outcomes (substantive freedoms) to which they give rise.

Second, in both accounts the question arises as to what we are to make of inequalities that develop over time *on account of the decisions actors make as they exercise the freedoms that their primary goods or capabilities afford them.* Two actors who in period *t* make different decisions about, say, investing in their human capital will achieve different levels of capabilities in some future period *t* + *i*. Moreover, an agent may choose to undertake an action, like riding a motorcycle without protective equipment, that interferes with his ability to achieve valued functionings in the future. But then, are these later inequalities indictable, and do they sustain demands for restitution, if they arose from the enjoyment of the freedoms that these approaches provide? Surely, accounts that emphasize positive freedoms must, to some degree or other, hold agents accountable for their actions; otherwise, they would require re-equalization in every period to make up for the "mistakes" that agents made in previous periods.

We find no warrant for thinking that perpetual redistribution to override the outcomes that resulted from the exercise of freedom is entailed in the Rawlsian or Senian frameworks. Far better to presume that in each account the inequality that results from the expression of genuine freedom is not in itself indictable. In Sen's words, "Freedom to choose gives us the opportunity to decide what we should do, but with that opportunity comes the responsibility for what we do – to the extent that they are chosen actions" (Sen 2009: 19). Hence, not all inequalities in the present are to be rectified under these accounts. As with Nozick, then, we need to know under both the Rawlsian and Senian accounts *how existing inequalities came about* before we can say much about whether and how they should be addressed. The Rawlsian and Senian accounts would indict inequalities that result from past interference with the enjoyment of primary goods or capabilities, respectively. And it is this "historical" feature of these accounts, we suggest, that allows us to infer restitution claims.

A further insight complicates the matter, however. If we take seriously the demands of equality in primary goods or capabilities, then we might recognize grounds for periodic redistribution to those who have not fared well over time as a consequence of the unpredictable and uncontrollable contingencies of events (rather than obviously foolhardy decisions or character flaws on their part). For Rawls, the evolution of the background conditions under which actors make their decisions is paramount. "Fair" background conditions (those that entail equality of primary goods) may give way over time to unfair background conditions, even if no actor commits indictable offenses against others. In Rawls's view, "background justice" tends to be eroded

> even when individuals act fairly [. . .]. We might say: in this case the invisible hand guides things in the wrong direction and favors an oligopolistic configuration of accumulations that succeeds in maintaining unjustified inequalities and restrictions on fair opportunity. Therefore, we require special institutions to preserve background justice . . . (Rawls 1993: 267)

For Rawls, examples might include "such operations as income and inheritance taxation designed to even out the ownership of property" (ibid.: 268).

Where does all of this leave us with respect to the question whether the Rawlsian and Senian accounts are compatible with the restitution project? We conclude most importantly that they are—that they do not just permit but even require historical accountings of the sort that the restitution project entails. That they also emphasize that the responsibility of the actor does not contradict the restitutive impulse of these accounts, though it may be that individual responsibility must figure into judgments in any particular case about the appropriateness and magnitude of restitution. Finally, there are also other grounds in these accounts for redistribution from the relatively privileged to the relatively impoverished—grounds that derive not from particular offenses in the past, but from an injustice that inevitably builds up over time as a consequence of agents acting fully within their rights. But we emphasize that redistribution for this reason falls outside the jurisdiction of restitution proper, since the latter involves only those claims that stem from the perpetuation of injustice by one individual or group against another.

RESTITUTION AND JUSTICE

Having briefly sketched some of the chief contours of these three perspectives on justice, we can address the central question of this chapter: What does each account of justice imply about restitution in general, and in the stylized historical case before us?

Nozick's Libertarian Justice

Under Nozick's libertarian account of justice, inhabitants of those countries that were colonized and/or enslaved are due restitution from those of the colonizing nations and enslaving groups since they have suffered the effects of extra-market appropriation (case 1, above). For Nozick, extra-market forms of appropriation of others' property rights are clearly unjust since they certainly violate justice in exchange and may also violate justice in acquisition (Nozick 1974: 152–3, 230–1). In the case before us, this would include enslavement and other forms of forced labor, coercion, theft, fraud, plunder, and all forms of violence against persons, property, and community institutions. Indeed, in cases of colonial exploitation and slavery, there are most certainly egregious violations of the Lockean proviso against appropriating unheld assets to such a degree that the appropriator fails to leave "enough and as good [. . .] in common for others." This provides further grounds for a definitive finding of violations of the justice in acquisition principle.

In contrast, the Nozickean framework does not validate claims for restitution that cite market-based appropriation, such as unequal exchange (case 2), since there is no injustice if in a "voluntary" transaction one party gains at another's expense.[8] This raises the question of just what is meant by "voluntary," of course. For instance, what are we to make of a case in which racial prejudice manifests as a long history of market discrimination that yields depressed wages for African Americans, relative to other groups, both then and now? This outcome is not indictable (or, if morally indictable, not correctable through restitution) so long as the parties who engaged in the transactions were formally free to choose as they saw fit and they acted in accordance with their rights. In this case, the majority enjoys the freedom to associate with each other, even if this results in job segregation and the offer of lower wages to African Americans. That the majority's so choosing diminishes the opportunity set of the minority does not represent a violation of the minority's rights; nor does it diminish the voluntary nature of the minority's behaviors.

Nozick puts the matter this way. Imagine some agent Z whose opportunity set is highly constrained, owing to the decisions taken by all other actors A through Y. Then we must conclude that Z, "does choose voluntarily if the other individuals A through Y each acted voluntarily and within their rights" (ibid.: 263), even if Z's only effective choice is to accept an exploitative wage bargain. He concludes this thought experimenting with the view that "[a] person's choice among differing degrees of unpalatable alternatives is not rendered nonvoluntary by the fact that others voluntarily chose and acted within their rights in a way that did not provide him with a more palatable alternative" (ibid.: 263–4).

This claim bears on the question of restitution for unequal exchange stemming from historical patterns of racial discrimination, of course. So long as post-emancipation African Americans enjoyed the formal right to refuse any market offer that they deemed to be inadequate, they (and their descendants) have no redress for the unpalatable nature of the bargains they were forced to accept. Since both parties acted within their rights, there is no basis now to legislate forced restitution for the consequent patterns of inequality between the two communities. Indeed, in this case, forced restitution by the state would represent a grave injustice – one different in kind from and far more dangerous than the discrimination that it seeks to redress (Nozick 1974; Friedman 1962).[9] Nor, finally, does Nozick's libertarianism permit restitution claims that are based on unequally distributed gains from exchanges that do not violate rights (case 3).

A libertarian account of distributive justice would therefore justify restitution from the beneficiaries to the victims of colonialism and slavery only in case 1 (see Table 6.3). The magnitude of illegitimate harm would be equal to the present value of the sum of net extra-market appropriations (X) over the past several centuries, plus a magnitude that reflects the present value of the cumulative effects of past injustice (D). The expression for restitution (R) is then given by a function (h) of D,[10] defined as follows:

$$R = h(D) = \sum_{i=1}^{n} (X_i) (1 + r)^{(n-1)} + f [\sum_{i=2}^{n} D_i]$$

Rawlsian Justice

Under the Rawlsian approach to justice, restitution is warranted not only in the case of extra-market appropriations, but also in the case of market-based appropriations (cases 1 and 2). Unlike the libertarian approach, the contractarian approach indicts the inequality that exists today that originated in discriminatory market practices since these reflect inequality across social groups (the privileged and the oppressed) in primary goods. Regarding the magnitude of illegitimate harm, Rawls's contractarian approach adds to the libertarian equation the present value of the market-based appropriation (M). It would also include the present value of the cumulative effect of past injustice (D) to take account of the fact that rewards that are founded on prior, illicitly won advantages (the inequality in primary goods) are themselves illicit. It bears repeating in this context that for Rawls, political rights and economic benefits are not fungible. Violations of the political rights that appear among the primary goods are to be avoided at all economic costs.

What might the Rawlsian perspective make of case 3, where both parties gain from the interaction between them, but at differential rates? For the sake of precision in this context it is important to set aside the economic disparities resulting from cases 1 and 2, though in practice they occurred together.[11] Let us imagine that there are at least some differential gains that are not grounded in or do not stem from the practices reflected in the other two cases. Here we confront some ambiguity. On the one hand, the greater benefits that have flowed to the beneficiaries of colonialism and slavery over the past centuries violate the requirement of equal distribution of primary goods for present generations. Some today enjoy greater general-purpose means to achieve their objectives than do others. On these grounds, there appears to be a strong Rawlsian case for restitution for the unequal flows that are captured by the present value of G, the differential gains. But it must be emphasized that this broader claim for restitution is offset by complications stemming from the difference principle to the degree that it can be plausibly argued that the victims of inequality (in income or wealth) today have benefited in an absolute sense from the growing inequality between them and the immediate beneficiaries of unequal gains.

For instance, it might be argued that the extraordinary advances in science and achievements in information and medical technology over the past several decades were funded with the concentration of wealth that is a byproduct of the current inequality that originated in differential gains that were not themselves the consequence of past extra-market and market-based appropriations. Today, the argument goes, the poor benefit tremendously from new technologies—in the form of cell phones, anti-retroviral drugs, micro-nutrient supplements, and so forth. The more equal distribution of income and wealth over the recent and distant past that would have resulted had there been no differential gains might have delayed these developments, to the detriment of all of the world's present population. Those opposing this claim would be forced to produce a plausible counter-factual in which a more equal distribution of the mutual gains would have yielded no fewer advances—or more precisely, no fewer benefits to the poor from these advances. In this case, the Rawlsian indictment of inequality in access to income or wealth (or health care, housing, and other goods) is attenuated. Indeed, those arguing for restitution under a Rawlsian conception of justice must clear an important hurdle: To show counter-factually that the descendants of the victims of colonialism and slavery have not ultimately benefited from the ill-gotten accumulation of wealth by others at least as much as they would have from a more equal distribution of primary goods over the past several centuries. The difficulties of establishing a counterfactual case of this sort that would be convincing to opponents of restitution hardly needs elaboration here.

The expression for restitution under the Rawlsian framework is given, then, as a function of D defined in terms of X and M. It is given by the following:

$$R = h(D) = \sum_{i=1}^{n} (X_i + M_i)\,(1 + r)^{(n-1)} + f\left[\sum_{i=2}^{n} D_i\right]$$

Justice as Equality of Capabilities

The victims of colonialism and slavery are due restitution not only in the case of extra- and market-based appropriation, but even in the case where the effects on the victimized community from its interaction with the beneficiary community, while positive, were less than those flowing to the beneficiaries (cases 1, 2, and 3, above). From a capabilities perspective, the inequality that now exists (for example) between the Anglo and African American communities in the US that resulted from the interaction between them (as a consequence of extra-market and market-based appropriation, and differential gains) is unjust. Hence, in calculating illicit harms, one would add to the Rawlsian equation an estimate of the degree to which the fortunes of the Anglo and African American communities have diverged as a consequence of their interaction over the past several centuries (G). The Senian approach is much less apt to find that any inequality in capabilities over the past centuries (or today) is defensible on grounds of the difference principle, since (as discussed above) any substantive inequality in capabilities is apt to induce absolute capabilities failures for those who are worst off. As a consequence, the capabilities approach is likely to yield a greater magnitude for warranted restitution. The expression for restitution under the Senian approach is given by a function of X, M and, G, as follows:

$$R = h(D) = \sum_{i=1}^{n} (X_i + M_i + G_i)(1 + r)^{(n-1)} + f\left[\sum_{i=2}^{n} D_i\right]$$

The most significant difference between the Rawlsian and Senian approaches to justice may not be quantitative but methodological. In the Rawlsian approach we are directed by the difference principle to explore a confounding counterfactual: How much better or worse off is the victimized group (for example, African Americans) today than it would have been under a more equal distribution of primary goods over the past several centuries? The Senian approach does not appear to demand this counterfactual computation. What is at issue in the capabilities equality approach is extant inequality between the two communities in the extent of their substantive freedoms, not the inequality between the present condition of the victimized community and what it would have been had there been greater equality between the two communities over the past several centuries.

CONCLUSION

Table 6.3 summarizes the results of the preceding investigation of the implications of the three perspectives under review here for the matter of restitution for historical injustice. We emphasize that the analysis that generates these results is exploratory, and based on the highly stylized historical account we provided at the outset. A more comprehensive approach would entail both careful empirical work and more fine-grained theoretical exegesis than we have been able to provide here. We claim to have shown only that distinct approaches to justice yield distinct conceptions of restitution.

Which of these approaches, then, if any, is the right one to adopt

Table 6.3 Accounts of Distributive Justice and Restitution

		Accounts of Justice		
		Libertarian Justice	Rawlsian Justice	Senian Justice
Interaction	Extra-market appropriation (X)	Yes	Yes	Yes
Effects	Market-based appropriation (M)	No	Yes	Yes
	Disparate gains (G)	No	Uncertain	Yes

in approaching the matter of restitution? DeMartino (2000) argues at length that Sen's capabilities approach to equality is extraordinarily fruitful as we encounter the massive inequalities that characterize many societies today, and global affairs. We believe that it is also an appropriate normative standard to apply to the field of restitution, since we share Sen's commitment to the equalization of substantive freedom across members of diverse groups that constitute society. But the goal of this chapter is not to advocate this approach over the others. Instead, it is simply to show that any restitution project must be founded on normative claims, and that the choice of normative grounding matters—perhaps quite significantly in the recognition of indictable harms, and in the computation of the magnitudes of transfers that restitution claims demand.

A pragmatic approach in the face of philosophical disagreement might be to adopt an agnostic normative view, preliminarily at least. This attitude would recommend a consideration of what each of several accounts of distributive justice implies about the validity of restitution claims and the magnitude of the warranted transfers. This would require far more philosophical work than is provided in this chapter, to be sure. A key goal of such an exercise would be to yield a range of magnitudes, from which could be taken upper and lower bounds.

Orthodox economists tend to avoid studiously the value judgments that sorting out competing conceptualizations of distributive justice entails. The agnostic approach of developing multiple estimates based on alternative accounts might therefore encounter least resistance among those economists who are involved in the restitution debate. Moreover, if it is to occur at all, restitution to the victims of past injustice will result from complex negotiations where accounts of justice will be but one factor among many determining the outcome. Hence, providing multiple estimates based on alternative normative accounts may not only be the best that economists can do, it may also be all that we should do if our goal is to facilitate the process of negotiation and reconciliation that restitution will require.

Notes

1. The authors thank Noelle Schaef and Ann Rogers for research assistance on this project; and Paulo Barcelos for comments on a previous draft of this chapter. Any remaining errors are of course the responsibility of the authors alone.

2. Literature in this subject tends to emphasize restitution or reparations. We refer to the less encompassing term of restitution—returning property or economic opportunities to the original owner—instead of reparations—defined as re-establishing just relationships broadly and pertaining to property restitution, but also emotional rehabilitation, and so on. However, the arguments in this chapter apply to both restitution and reparations.

3. Indeed, Sen initially offered the capabilities approach as a friendly amendment to Rawls's framework. Since then Sen has arguably moved further away from Rawls, but there remain important affinities between their respective accounts of justice.

4. Despite the fact that in slave societies markets for slaves exist, the injustice to the slave results not from the terms of the market transaction between buyers and sellers, but from the preceding act of enslavement that permits this trading. Hence, even in this case we theorize the injustice of slavery as an extra-market appropriation.

5. Later on we will distinguish between those differential gains that arise from previous extra-market or market-based appropriations, and those that do not. The distinction will be important in assessing the degree to which differential gains ought to appear as an argument in the Rawlsian function that determines restitution payments.

6. And, it should be said, to neoclassical economic thought. We note that the most ardent defenders of market processes and outcomes tend to draw on both the libertarian emphasis on negative rights, and on the consequentialist welfarism of neoclassical thought. Milton Friedman comes to mind in this regard. In his major philosophical work, *Capitalism and Freedom* (1962), he routinely drifts back and forth between libertarian and welfarist defenses of the free market. This is important for the restitution project: The consequentialist welfarism of neoclassical thought does not provide much basis for theorizing restitution, other than by claiming that failure to provide restitution for past transgressions might induce perverse incentives in the present (by undermining confidence in property rights). There

is a much stronger basis for restitution in the work of those economists, like Friedman, who also draw on libertarian insights.

7. As Nozick (1974) demonstrates, the proviso is complex, and yields competing accounts of which acquisitions are and are not legitimate. See his treatment of the issue on pp. 174–82. While we do not pursue the matter further here, we would note that a violation of the Lockean proviso implies a violation of the justice in acquisition principle, and so warrants rectification (as discussed immediately in the text).

8. The only exception arguably arises in cases that involve the Lockean proviso.

9. Milton Friedman's distinction between "positive" and "negative" harm is relevant in this regard. For Friedman, positive harm results from the use of coercion—what we have called here extra-market appropriation. In his view, and consistent with Nozick, this form of harm should be rectified by the state. In contrast, negative harm results when two nominally free parties fail to reach a bargain that yields a market transaction. In Friedman's view, negative harm does not justify state rectification. Friedman theorizes racial discrimination that prevents a black worker from securing employment from a white employer, or a wage that is equal to that of a white worker, as an instance of negative harm. Such outcomes are regrettable, but they do not justify state intervention. In his words, "I believe strongly that the color of a man's skin or the religion of his parents is, by itself, no reason to treat him differently; that a man should be judged by what he is and what he does and not by these external characteristics. I deplore what seems to me the prejudice and narrowness of outlook of those whose tastes differ from mine in this respect and I think the less of them for it. But in a society based on free discussion, the appropriate recourse is for me to seek to persuade them that their tastes are bad and that they should change their views and their behavior, not to use coercive power to enforce my tastes and my attitudes on others" (Friedman 1962: 111).

10. We say restitution (R) is given by a "function (h) of D" (rather than simply by D) since we recognize that other factors besides justice come into play in determining the amount of warranted restitution.

11. To the degree that we fail to treat case 3 (or either of the other two cases) as distinct, we risk applying to it a normative judgment that ought instead to be applied to one of the other cases. We are mindful, however, that it is far easier to treat case 3 in isolation for analytical purposes than it is to do so in the context of the investigation of any particular historical case. In actual cases of past injustice, it would be necessary to attempt to identify the degree to which differential gains in any one period were the produced result of previous or concurrent extra-market and market-based

appropriations. To the degree that differential gains have tainted origins, the difference principle defense of the gains evaporates. We also note that those differential gains that arise as a consequence of prior extra-market or market-based appropriations are already incorporated in the restitution function in the term f [$\sum$ Di].

References

Aboriginal Healing Foundation (2014), *Summary Points of the SHF Final Report*, <http://www.fadg.ca/downloads/rapport-final-eng.pdf> (last accessed 26 October 2015).

America, Richard (2005), "The Theory of Restitution," in Cecilia Conrad, John Whitehead, Patrick Mason, and James Stewart (eds), *African Americans in the U.S. Economy*, Lanham, MD: Rowman & Littlefield, pp. 327–33.

BBC News (1999), "Trillions Demanded in Slavery Reparations," 20 August, <http://news.bbc.co.uk/2/hi/africa/424984.stm> (last accessed 26 October 2015).

Brennan, Fernne (2011), "Slave Trade Legacies, Reparations and Risk Allocation," *International Journal of the Humanities*, vol. 8, no. 10, pp. 117–25.

CNN World (2011), "Florida Judge Allows Suits Against Chiquita to Move Forward," 3 June, <http://edition.cnn.com/2011/WORLD/americas/06/03/florida.colombia.chiquita.lawsuits/> (last accessed 26 October 2015).

Daily Star (2012), "Iraq and Kuwait Mull Reparations 'Fund': UN," 22 January, <http://www.dailystar.com.lb/News/Middle-East/2012/Jan-22/160728-iraq-and-kuwait-mull-reparations-fund-un.ashx#axzz1p6UF6E1t> (last accessed 26 October 2015).

Darity, William (2008), "Forty Acres and a Mule in the 21st Century," *Social Science Quarterly*, vol. 89, no. 3 (September), pp. 656–64.

DeMartino, George (2000), *Global Economy, Global Justice: Theoretical Objections and Policy Alternatives to Neoliberalism*, London: Routledge.

du Plessis, Max (2003), "Historical Injustice and International Law: An Exploratory Discussion of Reparation for Slavery," *Human Rights Quarterly*, vol. 25, no. 3, pp. 624–59.

Elster, Jon (1982), "Sour Grapes – Utilitarianism and the Genesis of Wants," in A. Sen and B. Williams (eds), *Utilitarianism and Beyond*, Cambridge: Cambridge University Press, pp. 219–38.

Ferstman, Carla, Mariana Goetz, and Alan Stephens (eds.) (2009), *Reparations for Victims of Genocide, War Crimes, and Crimes Against Humanity*, Leiden: Martinus Nijhoff.

Ficek, Douglas (2002), "Rawls, Race and Reparations," *Radical Philosophy Review*, vol. 5, no. 1/2, pp. 1–9.

Friedman, Milton (1962), *Capitalism and Freedom*, Chicago: University of Chicago Press.

International Center for Transitional Justice (ICTJ) (2008), "Canada, Submission to the Universal Periodic Review of the UN Human Rights Council Fourth Session: February 2–13, 2009," <https://www.ictj.org/sites/default/files/ICTJ-Canada-Periodic-Review-2008-English.pdf> (last accessed 26 October 2015).

International Center for Transitional Justice (ICTJ) (2009), "Truth and Reconciliation in Morocco," <https://www.ictj.org/sites/default/files/ICTJ-Morocco-TRC-2009-English.pdf> (last accessed 26 October 2015).

International Criminal Court (ICC) (2015), "Lubanga Case: ICC Appeals Chamber Amends the Trial Chamber's Order for Reparations to Victims," <http://www.icc-cpi.int/en_menus/icc/press%20and%20media/press%20releases/pages/pr1092.aspx> (last accessed 26 October 2015).

Locke, John [1690] (1999), *Two Treatises on Government*, ed. Peter Laslett, Cambridge: Cambridge University Press.

MacPherson, C. B. (1962), *The Theory of Possessive Individualism: Hobbes to Locke*, Oxford: Oxford University Press.

Manyin, Mark (2001), *North Korea–Japan Relations: The Normalization Talks and the Compensation/Reparations Issue*, Congressional Research Service Report for Congress, <http://www.globalsecurity.org/military/library/report/crs/RS20526.pdf> (last accessed 26 October 2015).

Marketti, James (1990), "Estimated Present Value of Income Diverted During Slavery," in Richard America (ed.), *The Wealth of Races: The Present Value of Benefits from Past Injustices*, New York: Greenwood Press, pp. 107–23.

Mezarobba, Glenda (2010), "Between Reparations, Half Truths and Impunity: The Difficult Break with the Legacy of the Dictatorship in Brazil," *SUR – International Journal on Human Rights*, vol. 7, no. 13, pp. 7–25.

Neal, Larry (1990), "A Calculation and Comparison of the Current Benefits of Slavery and an Analysis of Who Benefits," in Richard America (ed.), *The Wealth of Races: The Present Value of Benefits from Past Injustices*, New York: Greenwood Press, pp. 91–105.

Nozick, Robert (1974), *Anarchy, State and Utopia*, New York: Basic Books.

Nussbaum, Martha (2000), *Women and Human Development: The Capabilities Approach*, Cambridge: Cambridge University Press

O'Brien, David J. and Stephen S. Fugita (1991), *The Japanese American Experience*, Washington, DC: Library of Congress.

Parmar, Sharanjeet (2012), "The Failure to Fulfill Court-Ordered Reparations for the Victims of Serious Crimes in the Democratic Republic of the Congo," International Center for Transitional Justice, <https://www.ictj.org/sites/default/files/ICTJ-Briefing-DRC-Reparations-2012-ENG.pdf> (last accessed 26 October 2015).

Ransom, Roger L. and Richard Sutch (1990), "Who Pays for Slavery?," in Richard America (ed.), *The Wealth of Races: The Present Value of Benefits from Past Injustices*, New York: Greenwood Press, pp. 31–54.

Rawls, John (1971), *A Theory of Justice*, Cambridge, MA: Harvard University Press.

Rawls, John (1993), *Political Liberalism*, New York: Columbia University Press.

Sen, Amartya (1992), *Inequality Reexamined*, Cambridge, MA: Harvard University Press.

Sen, Amartya (2009), *The Idea of Justice*, Cambridge, MA: Harvard University Press.

Thompson, Janna (2001), "Historical Injustice and Reparation: Justifying Claims of Descendants," *Ethics*, vol. 112, no. 1, pp. 114–35.

United Nations News Centre (2011), "UN Panel Pays Out $880 million in Reparations for Iraq's Invasion of Kuwait," 28 April, <http://www.un.org/apps/news/story.asp?NewsID=38214#.Vi9jAdLhDs0> (last accessed 26 October 2015).

United States Institute of Peace (2011), "Truth Commission: Argentina," <http://www.usip.org/publications/truth-commission-argentina> (last accessed 26 October 2015).

van Hasselt, Ivar (2010), *Access to Justice: Human Rights Abuses Involving Corporations – The Netherlands*, International Commission of Jurists, <http://icj.wpengine.netdna-cdn.com/wp-content/uploads/2012/06/Netherlands-access-justice-publication-2010.pdf> (last accessed 26 October 2015).

Vernon, Richard (2003), "Against Restitution," *Political Studies*, vol. 51, no. 3, pp. 542–57.

Part III

Justice and International Institutions

Chapter 7

NARROW VERSUS COMPREHENSIVE JUSTIFICATION IN HUMANITARIAN AID: A CASE STUDY OF THE CERF

Alexander Brown

INTRODUCTION

Virtually all humanitarian action is constrained either directly or indirectly by the international humanitarian system – a complex web of UN resolutions, international institutions (including funding mechanisms), norms, objectives, rules, regulations, codes of practice and standard operating procedures.[1] This chapter is interested in those who are (partly) morally responsible for this system. That is to say, it is interested in what those who are (partly) morally responsible for this system owe to those who are subject to it.

Putting this issue in terms of 'moral responsibility' has an important implication: that those who are (partly) morally responsible for the international humanitarian system can be legitimately called upon to justify it. Or, to be more precise, contributors to the international humanitarian system can be legitimately called upon to answer for particular parts of the system reflecting the particular contributions they make.

When I say that a justification is owed to all those who are 'subject to' the international humanitarian system I mean all those who find themselves caught up in humanitarian emergencies and who have the vagaries of this system and its constituent parts imposed upon them. I have in mind not only those who actually receive humanitarian relief but also those who do not. The latter group includes, for example, all those who would have benefited from humanitarian projects proposed by United Nations (UN) frontline agencies, but who do not do so because of unsuccessful applications by those agencies for financing from international emergency response funds, or all those who would have benefited from humanitarian projects proposed by non-governmental organisations (NGOs) and international non-governmental organisations (INGOs), but who do not do so as a result of failed or non-existent sub-agreements between those (I)NGOs and UN frontline agencies.

What type of justifications are those responsible for the international humanitarian system obligated to provide? Consider the distinction between *narrow* and *comprehensive* justification. Whereas a narrow justification is one that answers the call for justification in only certain respects whilst leaving one or more ensuing question unanswered, a fully comprehensive justification is one that can answer the call for justification for all ensuing questions.[2] I shall argue that those who are responsible for the international humanitarian system have an obligation to provide an adequately comprehensive justification for it. Part of the significance of this argument rests in the fact that hitherto the justifications offered by domestic politicians, senior figures at the UN and the representatives of major (I)NGOs have tended to be narrow. They have sought to defend international humanitarian funding mechanisms, for example, on the grounds that they improve timeliness and predictability in emergency relief but without justifying the adoption of these objectives. I will argue that *one* way to provide an adequately comprehensive justification for international humanitarian funding mechanisms is to show not only that they support humanitarian objectives viewed as *principles of regulation for the international humanitarian system* but also that these principles of regulation can be justified in terms of *fundamental principles of global morality*.

For the purposes of this chapter a principle of regulation is a principle that actors might choose to adopt (explicitly or implicitly) for the regulation of (parts of) institutional systems, whereas a fundamental principle (of global morality) is a principle that provides a valid reason to adopt a principle of regulation or to adopt some rather than other principles of regulation.[3] Fundamental principles of global morality can be duty-based (duties of justice or of aid), rights-based, consequentialist or even founded upon virtue ethics. They can also be articulated at lower or higher levels of abstraction. A highly abstract fundamental principle might lend support to more than one principle of regulation, but it will only lend support to those principles that can be reasonably interpreted as satisfying its demands.

In order to make my task manageable I shall focus on one particular cog in the international humanitarian system. Although the UN

Central Emergency Response Fund (CERF) only accounts for around 4 per cent of total annual humanitarian funding (Barber et al. 2008: 10), it represents a significant innovation in the way humanitarian aid is financed. The CERF is a standing fund of $500 million[4] annually that can be called upon by UN frontline agencies and partner organisations to tackle humanitarian emergencies. While it is widely agreed that the CERF has made advances toward the objectives of timeliness, predictability and equity in emergency relief, questions remain unanswered about these objectives. This chapter seeks to develop a more comprehensive justification of the CERF by supplementing conventional justifications with one of two fundamental principles of global morality: the Principle of Global Minimal Concern and Respect or the Principle of Global Equal Concern and Respect. I will argue that only the Principle of Global Equal Concern and Respect provides support for all the objectives commonly associated with the CERF. Finally, based on this principle I shall outline some further ways in which the CERF should be reformed to make it more just. The overall strategy is to start with the stated objectives of the CERF (timeliness, predictability and geographical equity), to work backwards to an appropriate fundamental principle of global morality, and then to work forwards to the stated objectives and on to the implementation of those objectives (keeping in mind the appropriate fundamental principle). One of the key results of this process will be a critique of some of the ways in which the CERF is currently operationalised through its two funding windows: Rapid Response Grants and Underfunded Emergencies Grants.

NARROW VERSUS COMPREHENSIVE JUSTIFICATION

Scholars have done much to clarify the many, and sometimes problematic, ways in which humanitarians can be viewed, and sometimes view themselves, as moral agents. Distinctions abound in the literature. Drawing on Weberian theory, Craig Calhoun (2008: 89) suggests that one of the enduring tensions in humanitarian endeavour is whether to pursue value-rational or instrumental-rational courses of action. Jennifer Rubenstein (2008: 219) highlights the dilemma between consequentialist and deontological humanitarian commitments. Stephen Hopgood (2008: 121–2) underscores the distinction between duty-based arguments for humanitarianism and humanitarianism as a form of virtue ethics. Thomas Weiss (1999: 2) contrasts those who believe

that humanitarianism is at its best when it adheres to principles of neutrality and impartiality (thereby insulating itself from political aims and
objectives) with those who believe that any fully justified humanitarian
action could not, and should not, be disassociated from the political.
This chapter takes as its starting point an alternative, deeper distinction
concerning moral agency. It is a distinction between two different ways
in which those responsible for the international humanitarian system
can try to justify that system.

As stated above, a narrow justification is one that answers the call for
justification in only certain respects, but also leaves one or more ensuing
questions unanswered. An ensuing question is one that emerges from
the presentation of a putative justification, and which it is legitimate to
ask. Justifications can be narrow in various different ways. A justification
that takes the form *the ends justify the means* can be narrow *inter alia* if
it does not pause to justify forms of behaviour that are assumed as part
of its factual premises,[5] or if it fails to properly address questions about
the absolute importance of the ends, or if it does not demonstrate that
the means are superior to other possible means, or if it does not explain
whether the ends justify the means in the context of possible negative
secondary consequences of pursuing the means. By way of illustra-
tion, an argument that purports to justify the actions of humanitarians
in a war zone on the grounds that they are helping to save the lives of
refugees or internally displaced persons is rightly considered narrow if it
does not address the issue of whether or not powerful local actors actually exploit humanitarian aid to entrench their control over refugees and
to fund further violent activities (see, for example, Terry 2002).

If a justification takes the form *the proposed institution or practice
adheres to a principle of regulation*, then it too can be a narrow justification for a number of reasons. It can be narrow if it does not properly
address ensuing questions about whether the principle of regulation
is actually being correctly applied to a given situation, for example.
According to Rubenstein (2007), an argument that seeks to justify the
shift of foreign aid away from official development assistance toward
the relief of sudden-onset emergencies on the strength of a principle
of regulation which requires actors to give priority to those who are
worst off measured in terms of unmet needs is a narrow justification
if it neglects to answer the legitimate question of whether or not the
victims of sudden-onset emergencies are in fact systematically worse
off than victims of failed development. This type of justification can

also be narrow if it fails to justify why actors should adopt some rather than other principles of regulation. Thus, it is one thing to declare that a given humanitarian institution or practice adheres to the twelve 'Guiding Principles' of emergency humanitarian assistance set out in the Annex to UN General Assembly Resolution A/RES/46/182 (1991) (including principles of humanity, neutrality and impartiality); it is quite another to justify why it is morally fitting to adopt *that* particular set of principles rather than some alternative set of principles. In addition, there can be instances where adhering to one principle of regulation can involve the violation of another principle of regulation. Here a justification can be narrow if it fails to address why it is right to uphold one principle over another. There can also be instances where a principle of regulation admits of a range of competing interpretations. Under these circumstances a justification can be narrow if it fails to provide reasons to support one or some interpretations over others.

In contrast to this, a fully comprehensive justification is one that answers, or could answer, the call for justification in all significant respects, leaving no ensuing questions unanswered. In the case of a justification that takes the form *the ends justify the means*, it is a fully comprehensive justification only if it can be supplemented with justifications for any forms of behaviour that are assumed as part of its factual premises, and can answer ensuing questions about the absolute importance of the ends, about whether or not the means are superior to other possible means, and about why the ends justify the means despite the secondary consequences of pursuing the means. Likewise, where a justification takes the form *the proposed institution or practice adheres to a principle of regulation,* it is a fully comprehensive justification only if it can provide reasons to believe that the principle of regulation is being correctly applied, reasons to believe that it is morally fitting to adopt the principle of regulation such as reasons based on a fundamental principle of global morality, reasons to accept that the principle of regulation should take priority over other principles in cases of conflict, and some basis on which to support some interpretations of the principle of regulation over others.[6]

The distinction between narrow and comprehensive justifications represents two ends of a spectrum. In practice few justifications are completely narrow, just as few are fully comprehensive. So the real question is what degree of comprehensiveness contributors to the international humanitarian system owe to those who are subject to it.

Whilst there are several points along the continuum that could merit attention, I shall concentrate on just two.

According to what I shall call the Narrow Justification Thesis, an adequate justification for the international humanitarian system (or parts thereof) requires only that it is, or can be, justified to all those who are subject to it in terms of objectives which can be interpreted as principles of regulation. This thesis places the benchmark for adequate justification closer to the narrow end of the spectrum than the comprehensive end. The problem with this thesis, as I see it, is that although a justification which invokes principles of regulation may seem reasonable from the viewpoint of donors and practitioners, it can nevertheless remain inadequate when considered from the perspective of persons who are caught up in humanitarian emergencies. This is for two reasons. First, as the victims of such emergencies their continued existence is dependent on the international humanitarian system. This means that, at least in one sense, the stakes are much higher for them than they are for humanitarian donors and practitioners. Second, those who are ultimately denied access to humanitarian relief (or have a much smaller chance of receiving relief) because a decision is made to adopt one rather than another possible set of objectives/principles of regulation are subject to this system of decision-making without giving direct consent for it and with minimal practical input into the principles adopted by it.[7] For both of these reasons, I affirm the Comprehensive Justification Thesis: an adequate justification for the international humanitarian system (or parts thereof) requires that it is, or can be, justified to all those who are subject to it not merely in terms of objectives which can be interpreted as principles of regulation but also in terms of fundamental principles of global morality that support the adoption of these objectives/principles of regulation, as well as an account of the grounds of the fundamental principles of global morality. This thesis places the benchmark for adequate justification closer to the comprehensive end of the spectrum than the narrow end.

Before turning to consider the case study of the CERF in detail, I need first to address the issue of variable responsibility. As stated at the start of this chapter, the international humanitarian system is a complex web of UN resolutions, international institutions, norms, objectives, rules, regulations, codes of practice and standard operating procedures. Among the many types of contributors to this complex web are national governments, regional and international governmental organisations, most notably the UN and its frontline agencies and partner organisations including (I)NGOs, as well as all those states, private companies and individuals who support the system through donations, and last but not least the community of people who work on the ground as either professional or unpaid humanitarians. In response to this picture I adopt what I shall call the Variable-Responsibility Thesis: the nature and extent of the obligation to justify the international humanitarian system or parts thereof depends on the type of contribution an actor makes to that system. In the case of the CERF this thesis implies that if it is legitimate to claim that the Secretary-General of the UN contributes to the CERF in a different type of way than the Head of the Office for the Coordination of Humanitarian Affairs (OCHA) and the Emergency Relief Coordinator (ERC), that the OCHA contributes to the CERF in a different type of way than donors, that (I)NGOs that interact with UN agencies contribute to the international humanitarian system in a different type of way than UN agencies themselves, then it is also legitimate to claim that the nature and extent of the obligation to justify the CERF is different for each of these actors. In relation to the present chapter, however, the key question is whether any of these actors can legitimately claim that they are obliged to provide only a narrow and not a comprehensive justification of the CERF. Arguably if any of these actors has a case for claiming an obligation to provide only a narrow justification for the CERF it is (I)NGOs: the reason being that they have perhaps the least influence over the creation, maintenance and running of the CERF.[8] This does not apply to the Head of OCHA and probably does not apply to large donors. Nevertheless, putting to one side the complex issue of whether it is possible and appropriate to draw a line between those contributors who do and those who do not have an obligation to provide a comprehensive justification, I shall proceed on the assumption that at least some actors are so obligated.

THE CERF'S INITIAL OBJECTIVES AS NARROW JUSTIFICATIONS

In 2005, Jan Egeland, the UN Under-Secretary-General for Humanitarian Affairs (the Head of the OCHA and the ERC), suggested to Kofi Annan, UN Secretary-General, that the latter include in his reform agenda to the 2005 World Summit a proposal to replace the Central Emergency Revolving Fund (which only provided loans) with a new Central

Emergency Response Fund (CERF) that could disperse a maximum of $500 million per annum, including a grant facility of up to $450 million as well as a loan facility of $50 million (Egeland 2008). The Under-Secretary-General would be responsible for the operational management of the CERF supported by a New York based CERF Secretariat and an Advisory Group selected from across the humanitarian community including donors, UN agencies and partner (I)NGOs. The target ceiling of $500 million would be made up of voluntary contributions from governments, (I)NGOs, companies and individuals. The OCHA would also encourage member states to support the CERF through multi-year commitments. The new CERF would be an international emergency response fund intended for life-saving activities, and the humanitarian services which support those activities, undertaken by the UN's frontline humanitarian agencies, including the World Food Programme (WFP), the Food and Agriculture Organization (FAO), the World Health Organization (WHO), the UN Children Fund (UNICEF), the UN High Commissioner for Refugees (UNHCR), as well as the International Organization for Migration (IOM) and a range of other implementing partners at the country level, not least (I)NGOs. As specified in UN General Assembly Resolution A/RES/60/124 (2006), the enlarged CERF was designed:

> to ensure a more predictable and timely response to humanitarian emergencies, with the objectives of promoting early action and response to reduce loss of life, enhancing response to time-critical requirements and strengthening core elements of humanitarian response in underfunded crises, based on demonstrable needs and on priorities identified in consultation with the affected State as appropriate. (para. 15)

Applications for CERF grants are made through two windows: the first involving applications for Rapid Response Grants, and the second for Underfunded Emergencies Grants. Both grants are designed to fund life-saving activities, but whereas the Rapid Response Grants are intended for rapid responses to sudden-onset emergencies (including natural disasters and complex emergencies such as wars and ethnic violence) or rapidly deteriorating conditions in an existing emergency,[9] the Underfunded Emergencies Grants are intended for any ongoing humanitarian crises 'in which life-saving activities have been and are likely to remain underfunded' (OCHA 2010a). In the case of Rapid

Response Grants allocations can be made at any time. Up until April 2010 agencies had only three months to expend the funds, although they now have six months. Up to two-thirds of the CERF grant facility is earmarked for the Rapid Response window (UN Secretariat 2010). Allocations under the Underfunded Emergencies window are made in two rounds tracking the launch of the annual Consolidated Appeals Process (CAP) and following the mid-year review of those appeals. It is a condition of funding that agencies expend the funds by 31 December of the same calendar year for grants from the first round, and by 30 June of the following calendar year for grants from the second round. Up to one third of the CERF grant facility is earmarked for the Underfunded Emergencies window (UN Secretariat 2010).

Each year the OCHA publishes on its website (www.unocha.org/ cerf/) statistics on the CERF (both donations and allocations of funds) that are presented as part of the justification for its continued operation. The figures from 2006 to 2015 reveal that although the CERF has yet to receive the maximum of $500 million in any one year, its total receipts have been in excess of $400 million in each year since 2010. The OCHA has also been able to allocate close to the available funds each year. In 2010, for example, the CERF received $429 million and the ERC approved the allocation of $406 million to agencies working in forty-five countries, including $25 million to the victims of the earthquake in Haiti and $40 million to the flood response in Pakistan.

Those who are responsible for humanitarian institutions like the CERF have tended to justify those institutions with reference to how well they fulfil their formal purposes or objectives. This, however, fails to address whether these purposes or objectives are themselves justified or justifiable. When the new CERF was launched in 2006 the President of the UN General Assembly heralded it as 'the most important qualitative step forward we have taken since 1991' (Al-Khalifa 2006). Kofi Annan added that 'for the international community, the CERF is not simply a fund; it is a statement of principle' (Annan 2006). Since then the OCHA has been at pains to underscore the success of the CERF in meeting its objectives of improvements in timeliness, predictability and geographical equity in humanitarian assistance. These ways of thinking have also been duplicated by some of the major (I)NGOs in this field. The conventional wisdom of the international humanitarian community, then, is that the adequacy of the justification for the CERF turns on its success in meeting its objectives.

My aim here is to challenge this conventional wisdom. Whilst those who are morally responsible for the CERF have furnished justifications which satisfy an obligation to provide a narrow justification, they have typically failed to present justifications that can satisfy the obligation to provide an adequately comprehensive justification, where the latter depends on answering questions about why certain objectives are the right ones to adopt in the first place.

In what follows I shall focus on the three main objectives of time-liness, predictability and geographical equity.[10] By way of context, in 2005 Egeland and many others believed that the international response to humanitarian emergencies was characterised by sluggish-ness, unpredictability and inequity. First, it was simply taking too long to create and respond to Consolidated Appeals and Flash Appeals under the CAP relative to the urgency of unmet needs on the ground. A standing fund was required in order to create greater continuity between the urgency on the ground and urgency of the humanitarian response. Second, the CAP was susceptible to the vagaries of donor partiality and media interest making the provision of assistance unpre-dictable. Egeland's proposal for an enlarged CERF that could address these problems was given strong backing by the UK's International Development Secretary, Hilary Benn, who would go on to make his country the largest single donor in 2006 ($70 million), a position it has retained in every year from 2006 to 2011. Speaking at the official UN launch of the enlarged CERF, Benn (2006) declared: 'It is simply not good enough that when crisis strikes, UN agencies have had to pass around the begging bowl to help.' He cited the fact that in 2005 the Democratic Republic of Congo (DRC) received $10 per head, while in Darfur the figure was $100 per head, and the victims of the Boxing Day tsunami received $1,000 per head. He also made reference to the fact that all too often, it took a camera crew to prick the conscience of the world before a response was forthcoming – he was not alone in highlighting the 'CNN-effect' (Shah 2005). As Egeland himself put it: 'We must move from lottery to predictability so all those who suffer receive aid' (Egeland 2006). Third, it was pointed out that the CAP system had often produced funding discrepancies among countries, and that over time these discrepancies had produced inequity in the geographical distribution of humanitarian assistance. The following passage from Kofi Annan's 2005 report to the General Assembly is instructive:

A review of contributions made through the Consolidated Appeal Process since 1994 indicates a trend of concentrated giving to a select number of high-profile emergencies such as those in Afghanistan and Iraq or in the countries affected by the Indian Ocean tsunami. Although the analysis does not capture all humanitarian funding, it suggests an uneven distribution of funds in favour of the humanitarian crises that enjoy significant political and media attention. In contrast, the emergencies outside the headlines and with high levels of humanitarian need, particularly those in Africa, are consistently underfunded. [. . .] A source of predictable humanitarian funding is needed to ensure a timely, life-saving response capacity and to provide a minimum level of equity in the geographical distribution of assistance. (Annan 2005)

The objectives of timeliness, predictability and geographical equity have not changed in the intervening period. In respect of timeliness, the *Two Year Evaluation* of the CERF commissioned by the Under-Secretary-General for Humanitarian Affairs concluded that the expanded CERF had in fact enabled the OCHA 'to kick-start the international response to an emergency, to meet time-critical requirements and to intervene quickly in deteriorating situations, by funding essential enabling activities and key sectors' (Barber et al. 2008: 11). Similar conclusions appear in the *5-Year Evaluation* of the CERF which was once again commissioned by the Under-Secretary-General. This evaluation provides detail on how greater timeliness has been achieved. The CERF has enabled much quicker disbursements of money to UN agencies: the process of proposal, decision and disbursement now takes on average four weeks under the CERF mechanism (Channel Research 2011: 5). In the case of the Haiti earthquake in 2010, $10 million was released from the CERF for UN humanitarian aid efforts less than twenty-four hours after the quake. The *5-Year Evaluation* finds that the CERF has had an even greater impact where UN agencies have access either to alternative emergency response funds at the country level or to their own funding reserves. The CERF promotes early action and response to reduce loss of life by serving as a guarantor for UN agencies which can submit proposals through the CERF Rapid Response window (say) and receive Letters of Understanding of funding within a matter of days. UN agencies can then start to use available emergency response funds at the country level or their own funding reserves safe in the knowledge that these funds will be replenished or topped up from the CERF once the process of proposal, decision and disbursement has been completed (ibid.: 5).

On the question of predictability in emergency response funding, the *Two Year Evaluation* defends the impartiality of the CERF's allocation decisions. The argument here is that because these decisions are based on demonstrable needs UN agencies at the country level can predict whether or not they will be successful or not in applying for grants. If decisions were influenced by political considerations or media attention, then this would make the allocation decisions unpredictable. The authors of the *Two Year Evaluation* conclude: 'CERF grants have generally been allocated for activities that are highly relevant in relation to the needs of disaster-affected communities, especially in rapid response. [. . .] In this, the CERF has succeeded in reinforcing the principles of impartiality and needs-based response' (Barber et al. 2008: 17). This picture is complicated, however, by the fact that subsequent evaluations of the CERF have employed importantly different interpretations of the predictability objective. The *5-Year Evaluation* emphasises a lack of 'predictability' surrounding operational aspects of the Underfunded Emergencies window at the country and international levels. It maintains that UN staff working at the country level viewed these grants as being less predictable because decisions about recipient countries were being taken at the CERF headquarters in New York and because they were not kept well informed of those decisions. 'Staff in one country that had received a UFE allocation in 2010 was unaware that they would not receive one in the first round of 2011, even though the allocations had already been decided' (Channel Research 2011: 76).

Nevertheless, the OCHA has also defended its positive contribution to the objective of providing a minimum level of equity in the geographical distribution of assistance. For example, in its *Analysis of CERF Activities in 2009* the OCHA (2010b) claims that the CERF Underfunded Emergencies Grant window has contributed to reducing funding discrepancies between major humanitarian emergencies in different countries. The analysis document contains a graph depicting a steep curve in the funding that major humanitarian emergencies in different countries received under the CAP system in 2007 and 2008, but a much shallower curve for 2009. A second graph highlights the CERF contribution to the total CAP funding in 2009. 'It shows that the funding discrepancies between major humanitarian crises would have been even greater if not for the CERF grants. By targeting resources to key humanitarian emergencies which were underfunded, the CERF improved the relative allocation of resources worldwide' (OCHA 2010b: 3).

Reflecting on these three main justifications it is evident that they are not always as rigorously defined or distinguished as they could be. Nevertheless, it is possible to reinterpret them in terms of a set of principles of regulation that are quite familiar to moral and political philosophers. Starting with the Rapid Response Grants, the justification from timeliness can be interpreted as an instance of, or being derived from, the Principle of Aid.[11] According to this principle, those actors who can respond to humanitarian emergencies have a duty to do so. If the Principle of Aid is interpreted to imply a duty to engage in emergency life-saving activities, and emergency life-saving activities are in turn defined as activities that are required to be undertaken within a very short period of time in order to reduce loss of life caused by lack of adequate food, clean water, shelter, medical care, acts of violence, and so on, then it seems safe to say that the Principle of Aid demands timeliness.

Sticking with the Rapid Response window, the objective of increasing predictability is designed to counteract a defining feature of the Principle of Aid that is often viewed negatively. If the duty to aid is an imperfect duty, then fulfilling this duty is left to the discretion of agents, concerning what, when, how and on whom to focus aid. The objective of increasing predictability works instead to squeeze the space normally given over to donor discretion. However, the use of 'predictability' to justify the CERF conflates two separate principles of regulation. The first is made explicit in the 2007 Oxfam Briefing Paper on the CERF. 'When supporting the CERF, donors relinquish control over their contributions to the ERC [Emergency Relief Coordinator] and HCs [UN Humanitarian Coordinators]. In theory, this increases impartiality on the basis of funding criteria' (Oxfam 2007: 18). Following this line of thought it might be argued that the CERF Rapid Response window adheres to the Principle of Impartiality. According to this principle, decisions on the allocation of emergency response funds should be guided by relevant criteria, where such criteria exclude media attention and political interests. A second principle adds positive substance to the term 'relevant criteria'. According to the Principle of Needs, decisions on the allocation of emergency response funds should be guided by assessments of demonstrable needs. Of course, humanitarians typically operate under the condition that it is impossible to meet all unmet needs at the same time and the Principle of Needs is silent on the question of what to do when not all unmet needs can be met. A third principle makes this explicit. According to the Principle of Unmet Needs, decisions on the allocation of emergency response funds should be guided by demonstrable needs and by other considerations appropriate to when it is impossible to meet all unmet needs at the same time. Once again, further principles are required in order to give content to the concept of appropriate considerations. According to the Principle of Prioritisation, the response to humanitarian emergencies should be guided by an agreed scheme of prioritisation among unmet needs based on a set of prioritisation factors. Among the prioritisation factors that might figure in an agreed scheme of prioritisation are: the aim of getting people to a sufficient level of met needs, the relative level of unmet needs prior to assistance, the numbers of people that are likely to be helped by the humanitarian project, and the relative cost of the humanitarian project (see Pogge 2007: 222–8). So, for example, it might be determined on the basis of the agreed prioritisation factors that one country is a greater priority than another, that one area within the country has greater priority than elsewhere, that in this area the sick, the elderly and young children are a greater priority than other people, or even that clean drinking water is a higher priority than tents.

Turning to the Underfunded Emergencies window, its attention is fixed on something like the Principle of Equity in the Geographical Distribution of Humanitarian Assistance (the Principle of Equity). According to this principle, emergency response funds should be allocated in such a way as to provide a minimum level of equity in the geographical distribution of assistance. This principle is ambiguous, however, between a naïve reading and a more sophisticated reading. On a naïve reading, the Principle of Equity demands *equality* in the geographical distribution of humanitarian funding regardless of the requirements of other principles. It is not difficult to think of counter-examples to the Principle of Equity under such a reading. Consider examples where insisting on equality of funding across countries would mean a failure to distribute humanitarian relief according to the Principle of Prioritisation.[12] On a more sophisticated reading, the Principle of Equity demands an *equitable* distribution of total annual humanitarian funding. On this reading, an unequal distribution of funding across countries is acceptable provided that it is equitable (just, fair, impartial, and so on). Now it might be asked whether, on the sophisticated reading, the Principle of Equity is doing any genuine work above and beyond the conjunction of the Principle of Impartiality, the Principle of Needs, the Principle of Unmet Needs and the Principle of Prioritisation. The short answer is that it depends on the circumstances. If the distribution of total annual humanitarian funding *did* adhere to all of these other principles, then the further requirement of equity would be redundant. However, that is not the situation in which the CERF operates. It operates in the context of the CAP, a much larger distribution of international humanitarian funding that does not live up to these other principles. Therefore, the purpose of allocating the Underfunded Emergencies Grants in accordance with the Principle of Equity is to counteract inequities in the distribution of total annual humanitarian funding.[13] Somalia is a case in point. In 2009 it received $50.5 million through the Rapid Response Grant window, but in terms of total CAP funding it would have lagged behind countries with similar humanitarian needs, most notably Chad, Sudan and Kenya, had it not received an additional $10 million via the Underfunded Emergencies window (OCHA 2010b: 2–3).

Whilst the above reference to 'a minimum level of equity in the geographical distribution of assistance' reflects the aim of using the CERF's Underfunded Emergencies window to counteract inequities in the distribution of total annual humanitarian funding, the word 'minimum' indicates that the aim is not to eradicate all inequity in the total amount of humanitarian funding allocated across countries but to ensure that there is not *too much* inequity. On the surface, this appears to be a statement of principle about how much inequity is acceptable. At first glance, this might seem strange, since surely no amount of inequity should be acceptable. However, on closer inspection this argument is more likely to reflect the practical limitation of what can be achieved by the CERF. Because the CERF's grant facility accounts for only 4 per cent of total annual humanitarian funding, and the Underfunded Emergencies Grants window comprises only a third of that facility, it would be impossible to use Underfunded Emergencies Grants to eradicate all inequity associated with the humanitarian system as a whole. Hence, the CERF is justified by the Principle of Equity when the former advances as far as it can be reasonably expected to advance the goal of equity in the distribution of total annual humanitarian funding. I shall return to the question of what is reasonable below.

Armed with these principles of regulation we are now in a position to consider whether any of the main justifications for the CERF are adequately comprehensive. The short answer is that they are not. Before explaining why these justifications are not adequately comprehensive, I should first make it clear that even when justifications are facially made by the CERF organisation to the CERF's donors and to the relevant INGOs or even indigenous NGOs, the most important addressees of moral justifications are those who are ultimately subject to the international humanitarian system. That is to say, following on from the previous section, I assume that comprehensive justification is the right of the potential recipients of humanitarian aid, and I evaluate the justifications accordingly.

The justification from timeliness is narrow in at least the following respect. The argument that the CERF increases the speed of humanitarian funding is silent on an important question relating to the secondary consequences of the CERF on (I)NGOs. Since (I)NGOs cannot apply to the CERF directly they must go through the process of approaching UN agencies to become partners. According to the *5-Year Evaluation*, only around 25 per cent of the CERF grant facility is passed through to operating partners including (I)NGOs, and the timeframe for money from the CERF grants to be passed on to these partners is on average two to three months (Channel Research 2011: 7, 70). This would be less of a problem if (I)NGOs were able to attract funds from donors outside of the CERF mechanism as they did before 2006. However, the *Two Year Evaluation* found that despite a sustained increase in donations by the seven highest CERF donors to (I)NGOs,[14] in many countries and for the particular (I)NGOs who work in those countries many CERF donors have reduced their funding. 'NGOs reported [. . .] reductions in funding in different countries as some donors now often direct them to pooled funds and CERF whenever approached with a funding request' (Barber et al. 2008: 82). This was a particular problem in DRC and Sudan where some (I)NGOs 'argued that since they cannot apply for CERF funds and are relatively minor players in the CHF allocations in DRC and Sudan, their direct access to funds in those countries [. . .] has therefore declined' (ibid.: 82).

The justification from predictability also stands in need of further support. To give a concrete example, in August 2010 a memo was leaked to a left-wing political blog in the UK in which DFID's Director of Policy recommended that the new Conservative–Liberal Democrat government drop, amongst other things, its commitments to the CERF (Straw 2010). A further leaked email suggested that Andrew Mitchell, Benn's successor as International Development Secretary, was minded to follow the recommendation (Asthana and Gallagher 2010). However, reacting to what he described as the world's 'woefully inadequate' humanitarian response to the flooding in Pakistan (Mitchell 2010a), he ultimately decided to provide the CERF with £40 million in 2010 and pledged to provide the same again in 2011 (Mitchell 2010b). Mitchell faced public criticism over his decision with a number of UK opinion polls suggesting that most people were in favour of cutting foreign aid for the sake of maintaining important domestic welfare services.[15] Why should the UK government allocate large sums of taxpayers' money to foreign aid in the context of significant cuts to domestic welfare services? The point here is that in order to justify the UK's donation to the CERF in 2010 and 2011 it was not sufficient to appeal to the Principle of Aid since the Principle of Aid might conceivably have been used to justify the UK's non-donation to the CERF (on grounds of unmet need at home). In addition to this, some people in the UK were uneasy concerning the donation of money to an international relief fund that had allocated $85 million to Pakistan between 2006 and 2010 (making it the sixth-ranked recipient). The case of Pakistan had particular significance because the London 7/7 bombers had attended training camps in Pakistan. Of course, many people in the international humanitarian community would justify the CERF on the grounds that it increases impartiality and prevents precisely these sorts of political considerations from colouring decisions regarding the allocation of emergency relief. However, to say that the CERF increases impartiality avoids the more fundamental question of whether or not it is actually unjust for humanitarian donors to engage in partial giving of the sort condemned. The proposition that it is unjust for states to prefer to make humanitarian funding decisions on the basis of political considerations cannot be taken as given. Comprehensive justification requires reasons to believe that the Principle of Impartiality should be adopted.

The same problem applies to the justification from equity. To justify the CERF on the grounds that it adheres to the Principle of Equity is to fail to provide an adequately comprehensive justification for the CERF so long as ensuing questions about why the Principle of Equity should be adopted remain unanswered. To the extent that inequities in the distribution of total annual humanitarian funding reflect the discretion of donors concerning where to send their money, the deeper question is once again whether or not it is appropriate to counteract this discretion.

Let me be clear about the purpose of this section. My intention is not to press for the exclusion or retraction of the stated objectives of the CERF: timeliness, predictability and geographical equity. Rather, it is to point out that considered from the perspective of the moral rights of those subject to the international humanitarian system these objectives are not adequately comprehensive justifications as they stand. In order to place them within more complex webs of justificatory arguments that are adequately comprehensive it is necessary to supplement them by calling on fundamental principles of global morality.

TOWARDS A COMPREHENSIVE JUSTIFICATION OF THE CERF

Although there are numerous fundamental principles to which one might try to appeal in trying to comprehensively justify key aspects of the CERF,[16] for the purposes of this chapter I shall focus on two. According to what I shall call the Principle of Global Minimal Concern and Respect, actors involved in creating and maintaining the international system have an obligation to treat those subject to that system with a minimal level of concern and respect. Of course, this principle is highly abstract and to have any purchase must be further interpreted at the level of application, not least around the meaning of 'minimal'. Nevertheless, by drawing on plausible interpretations of the Principle of Global Minimal Concern and Respect it is possible to justify the Principle of Aid and in that way provide a more comprehensive justification for parts of the CERF Rapid Response window.[17] The justification might be that providing a timely response to humanitarian emergencies, with the objectives of promoting early action and response to reduce loss of life, is a way of meeting the duty to aid, and more fundamentally, of showing a minimal level of concern and respect. Presumably saying to someone, 'We see that you are in desperately urgent need, but we have elected to adopt principles of regulation that do not emphasise the importance of early action and response to reduce loss of life,' fails to show a minimal level of concern and respect to that person on the most reasonable interpretation of what that means.

Turning to the CERF's second main objective of ensuring a more predictable response to humanitarian emergencies, it is no longer obvious that the Principle of Global Minimal Concern and Respect can provide the requisite fundamental justification. One characteristic feature of the Principle of Global Minimal Concern and Respect is that it only requires actors involved in the international humanitarian system to treat the objects of that system with an absolute rather than relative level of concern and respect, where the requisite level of concern and respect is low rather than high. One implication is that actors are permitted to show partiality towards some victims of humanitarian emergencies on the basis of criteria other than demonstrable need or fair priority. Saying to someone, 'We can see that you are in great need, but we have more in common with some other people who are also in great need, so we are going to help them first,' is not incompatible with showing a minimal level of concern and respect to the person who is put to the back of the queue. The requirement to pay attention to the Principle of Impartiality would seem to depend on a different fundamental principle of global morality, one that demanded both high and equal concern and respect.

Much the same can be said for the Underfunded Emergencies window and the Principle of Equity. Under a sophisticated reading, this principle demands that the CERF does its bit to counteract inequity in the distribution of total annual humanitarian funding – for example, by devoting a proportion of the CERF to underfunded crises in the Horn of Africa. It is difficult to motivate this principle of regulation on the basis of a fundamental principle according to which actors are only required to show a minimal degree of concern and respect for persons caught up in humanitarian emergencies. Those seeking to defend the Principle of Equity, and therefore the aim of tackling some of the inequities produced by the CAP, must appeal to a more demanding fundamental principle of global morality.

I believe that the Principle of Global Equal Concern and Respect is just such a principle. According to this principle, actors involved in creating and maintaining the international system have an obligation to treat the objects of that system with equal concern and respect. This obligation is special because it requires concern and respect of a high order, and because it binds persons together with obligations of equal concern and respect who do not share membership of the same communities. This principle applies to international humanitarian funding mechanisms like the CERF and to the objectives and principles of regulation adopted by its organisational bodies. I have argued that the CERF's main objectives can be interpreted in terms of the Principle of Impartiality, the Principle of Needs, the Principle of Unmet Needs, the Principle of Prioritisation and the Principle of Equity. I believe that each of these principles can be plausibly construed as an attempt to treat the objects of life-saving activities with equal concern and respect. For, they each emphasise the importance of ensuring that other things remaining equal the victims of humanitarian emergencies receive the relief they need no matter where they happen to be located in the world and what communities they belong to, which in turn reflects a deep commitment to the equal concern and respect owed to all human beings caught up in international systems.

Notwithstanding all of this, it is right to ask whether the appeal to principles of global morality is enough. For, the appeal to one or other fundamental principle of global morality to justify principles of regulation leaves unanswered ensuing questions about why it is appropriate to apply that principle (or what triggers that principle). I accept the force of this point, namely, that adequately comprehensive justification may depend on an account of the grounds of fundamental principles, that is, an account of why fundamental principles are applicable. Fortunately, there are numerous such accounts available in the literature.[18] Some writers have sought to ground the appropriateness of asking questions of global justice in the existence of international schemes of cooperation for mutual benefit.[19] Cooperation can be deeper or shallower, which has implications for the content of the principles of justice (see Wolff 2009). Other writers (Nagel 2005: 125) maintain that requirements of (egalitarian) justice depend on the existence of the kinds of conditions of associative responsibility that can only be found among citizens of a state. Neither of these theories provides a sound basis for applying principles of global justice to the CERF, however, since it is difficult to characterise the CERF as a scheme of cooperation for mutual benefit or as exemplifying conditions of associative responsibility.[20] Yet they do not exhaust the possibilities. Still other writers (Tan 2004: 174) ground principles of global justice in the 'grave implications' that the international system can have for the lives of people worldwide.[21] Drawing on these ways of thinking, Rubenstein argues that the very existence of the international humanitarian system qua an 'institutional social structure' can be sufficient to ground principles of global morality, and that '[t]his responsibility is heightened by the fact that aid recipients are profoundly affected by this system, but at present they have little capacity to influence it' (Rubenstein 2009: 525).

I introduce these theories in order to make it clear what a comprehensive justification would need to include in order to be considered adequate. Since I intend in the next section to flesh out further implications of the Principle of Global Equal Concern and Respect for future reforms to the CERF, I shall now say something briefly about the possible grounds of *this* principle.

I propose that what makes it appropriate to speak of *justice* in relation to the CERF is not merely the fact that it has institutional norms, objectives, rules, regulations, codes of practice and standard operating procedures but also the particular quality of what it does. It is the fact that the CERF is a system for the distribution of goods which helps to generate a requirement that it be just. Thus, according to what Joshua Cohen and Charles Sabel call Weak Institutionalism:

> the existence of an institution with responsibilities for distributing a particular good (education, or health, or decent wages and working conditions, for example) is necessary and sufficient to require that institution to meet the obligation of equal concern in fulfilling its responsibility. (Cohen and Sabel 2006: 153)[22]

Even so, one drawback with Weak Institutionalism is that it is not obvious that merely by assuming distributive responsibilities for a particular good an agent becomes bound by the demands of equal concern and respect for the objects of those responsibilities. For this reason I propose to combine Weak Institutionalism with the above-mentioned grave implications view in order to produce the following hybrid theory, which I shall call Strong Institutionalism. On this view, the existence of an institution with responsibilities for distributing a particular good is sufficient to generate a requirement on the part of that institution to treat persons with equal concern and respect in fulfilling its responsibilities provided that access (or lack thereof) to the good in question has grave implications for the lives of the individuals concerned.[23]

According to Strong Institutionalism, the existence of the international humanitarian system and its serious impact on recipients' lives can create duties of egalitarian justice between the affluent governments/peoples and the recipients of humanitarian aid. Now this may seem to imply that if this scheme *was* put in place, then it must be because of some prior recognition by the affluent governments/ peoples of higher-level cosmopolitan duties. The further implication being that the relevant comprehensive justification must rely on an even more fundamental principle of morality that generates duties to create an international humanitarian system. This is, however, not necessarily the case. For, Strong Institutionalism is consistent with the realist explanation that affluent governments/peoples create a system of humanitarian aid as an instrument of foreign policy (to cultivate a climate conducive to worldwide private investment, to maintain international peace and security, to promote democracy and other liberal institutions and values, and so on). What matters in terms of triggering duties of global equal concern and respect is that these institutions exist and that they have grave implications for people's lives.

To recap, the point of this section has been not only to explain how the Principle of Impartiality, the Principle of Needs, the Principle of Unmet Needs, the Principle of Prioritisation and the Principle of Equity can be justified in terms of the Principle of Global Equal Concern and Respect but also to tell a plausible story about how the adoption of that principle itself can be motivated by a particular hybrid theory of the grounds of global justice, Strong Institutionalism.[24]

Assuming that it is possible to ground the Principle of Global Equal Concern and Respect using the hybrid theory of Strong Institutionalism, and that this can be done in the context of developing an adequately comprehensive justification of the CERF (including an adequately comprehensive justification of its three main objectives), it is now appropriate to consider some of the implications of this scheme of comprehensive justification for future reforms of the CERF. The motivation for seeking a comprehensive justification for the CERF is not merely for the sake of honouring the Comprehensive Justification Thesis (because people affected are owed such a justification in a general sense), it is also that such justifications can shed light on whether, and how, the CERF mechanism could be made more just.

IMPLICATIONS

Having adopted the more demanding of two fundamental principles of global morality we cannot afford to be sanguine about the current practices and operating procedures of the CERF. Thus I propose three reforms to the CERF. These reforms leave largely intact the stated objectives of the CERF but raise serious concerns over how those objectives are operationalised under the current arrangements of the CERF, and they do so by calling upon the Principe of Global Equal Concern and Respect.

The first reform relates to the way in which the CERF funding mechanism is split into two windows: the Rapid Response window and the Underfunded Emergencies window. What implications does a commitment to the Principle of Global Equal Concern and Respect have for this separation? At one level these two windows are intended to reflect an underlying distinction between sudden-onset emergencies and rapidly deteriorating conditions in existing emergencies, on the one hand, and slow-onset and ongoing humanitarian crises, on the other hand. Arguably, however, this distinction stands in tension with a commitment to the idea that we should treat all persons who are subject to the aid system with equal concern and respect irrespective of which types of humanitarian emergencies they are caught up in.

The fact that there is an uneven split of funds between the Rapid Response window (two thirds) and the Underfunded Emergencies window (one third) creates two further unwelcome consequences from the perspective of equal concern and respect. First, it creates a perverse incentive on the part of UN agencies to hope that there is a rapid deterioration of the situation they are dealing with on the ground so that they are more likely to be able to access funds. Second, it provides UN agencies with a reason to present situations as rapid deteriorations of events rather than ongoing crises even if they are not; to spin the nature and causes of actual emergencies. This means that projects are supported by Rapid Response grants which are in reality a response to ongoing crises that have been underfunded. It is difficult to square these sorts of distortions with a principle that demands equal concern and respect for people who are subject to the international humanitarian system. Not merely does the distortion of humanitarian emergencies show a lack of respect for those caught up in those emergencies, where respect means amongst other things recognising the right to a fair and accurate representation of one's predicament, but it also shows a lack of concern, since it exposes them to the risk that if this distortion is later brought out into the open it could have a negative impact on public opinion towards the funding of humanitarian aid.[25]

Of course, if it were demonstrated that sudden-onset and rapidly deteriorating emergencies on average produce greater unmet needs than slow-onset and ongoing crises, then this would help to make the case for the uneven split. But little or no evidence for this generalisation has been presented. For example, amid public criticism of his backing of the CERF in 2010 Mitchell fought back declaring that '2010 will be remembered as a dreadful year for humanitarian disasters.' He went on to argue: 'Even in difficult economic times, Britain can be proud that it stood by people in their hour of need. [. . .] It is vital that countries back the [CERF] and make sure we are ready to help when it will be needed most' (Mitchell 2010c). Yet Mitchell's justification fails to recognise the truism that today's sudden-onset emergency can very easily become tomorrows ongoing humanitarian crisis. When the CERF is used to fund humanitarian projects in the same countries year after year, to respond to situations that have imperceptibly shifted from sudden-onset emergencies to ongoing humanitarian crises, what is the special significance of the concept of 'hour of need'? Moreover, many humanitarian projects target situations that are a complex mixture of a sudden-onset disaster, a rapid deterioration of events and an ongoing humanitarian crisis. The 2011 emergency in Somalia, for example, resulted from long-term poverty caused by state failure, conflict and multi-year drought, which together caused a rapid deterioration of events.

For all of these reasons, the Principle of Global Equal Concern and Respect points in the direction of getting rid of the separation between the CERF windows altogether, and using other principles to allocate resources across this divide.

Nonetheless, it might be insisted that the true point of maintaining a separation between the Rapid Response window and the Underfunded Emergencies window is to ensure that *some* CERF funds are used to address inequity in the distribution of total annual humanitarian funding. What matters is not the type of emergency but the fact that the humanitarian system tends to produce inequity in funding, something the CERF can be used to counteract. However, this justification still leaves unanswered ensuing questions about the current practice of devoting only a third of the CERF grant facility to the Underfunded Emergencies window. For, if it is appropriate to use some of the CERF to counteract inequity in the distribution of total annual humanitarian funding, then why limit the proportion of funds given over to this task to a third of the CERF? No doubt it is important to strike a reasonable balance between using the CERF to address humanitarian emergencies and using the CERF to counteract inequity in the distribution of total annual humanitarian funding. But what reasons are there for thinking that a two thirds/one third split strikes such a balance? In the absence of such reasons perhaps the default situation should be an even split between the two.

My second proposed reform has to do with the rules concerning the time span for expending CERF funds. Under the present rules UN agencies are required to expend Rapid Response Grants within six months, whereas they have up to twelve months to expend Underfunded Emergencies Grants. Assuming that the victims of sudden-onset or rapidly deteriorating humanitarian emergencies have a right to the same equal concern and respect as the victims of ongoing humanitarian crises that are likely to remain underfunded, the difference in timing stands in need of justification. It might be argued that there is a practical reason to provide a twelve-month period for expending Underfunded Emergencies Grants. It is that UN agencies need extra time to form agreements with partner organisations. The *5-Year Evaluation* estimates that it takes on average two months for UN agencies to make agreements with and disperse funds to (I)NGOs in the case of Rapid Response Grants but three months in the case of Underfunded Emergencies Grants (Channel Research 2011: 71). What is not clear, however, is whether the difference in time is intrinsic to the different types of emergencies for which the grants are being used or rather a reflection of the fact that UN agencies are permitted by the system to take longer in expending Underfunded Emergencies Grants than Rapid Response Grants. If the agreements and dispersals are taking longer in the case of Underfunded Emergencies Grants simply because UN agencies are given more time to play with, this constitutes a sound practical explanation for what is happening on the ground but it is certainly not a principled explanation that could answer a demand for comprehensive justification from those who are adversely affected by what is happening.

My third reform focuses on the related issue of to whom CERF grants can be allocated. Under the current arrangements only UN agencies can make applications for funding directly to the CERF. Even though (I) NGOs provide a good deal of the implementation capacity in humanitarian relief, they must wait for funds to be allocated to UN agencies and then try to develop sub-agreements with those agencies. Part of the rationale here is the perceived added complexity of allocating funds directly to (I)NGOs.[26] Yet it remains the case that often (I)NGOs can provide human resources, expertise and local knowledge in response to humanitarian emergencies that UN agencies find difficult to match. This is especially true where (I)NGOs already have programmes running in countries hit by disasters, or where they have practical experience in working with particular representatives of local and national organisations. Faith-based (I)NGOs can sometimes have more access to those who are most vulnerable within local communities than workers from UN frontline agencies, for instance. Therefore, excluding (I)NGOs from being able to apply directly for CERF grants runs the risk that those who are particularly dependent on their work are put at a disadvantage compared with those who are not. (Global equal concern and respect means *inter alia* ensuring that everything that should be done for people is being done for everyone regardless of where they happen to be located and that what is being done for people is equally sensitive to the values and belief systems of local communities.[27]) It is especially difficult to justify the present rules to the family who is caught up in a humanitarian crisis but has to wait additional weeks for life-saving aid from the only humanitarians operating in the area, an (I)NGO, simply because of the rules surrounding to whom CERF financing can be directly allocated. For this reason I propose that the CERF should no longer be the special reserve of UN agencies.

Notes

1. I am very grateful to Jennifer Rubenstein and Adriana Sinclair whose penetrating comments on a previous draft of this chapter compelled me in a number of instances to clarify arguments and correct mistakes. I would also like to thank the two editors, whose various careful observations helped me enormously.
2. The distinction between narrow and comprehensive justification is inspired by G. A. Cohen's (1992) concept of comprehensive justification.
3. According to Cohen (2003), a fundamental principle is 'fact-insensitive', which is to say that it does not depend on any facts. Contrary to Cohen, in this chapter I shall adopt the position that fundamental principles are fact-sensitive in the sense that facts must form at least part of the grounds for applying them. Thus, in 'Towards a Comprehensive Justification of the CERF' below I discuss different theories of the grounds of global justice.
4. All figures represent millions of US dollars.

5. For an analysis of narrow justifications in connection with distributive justice and economic incentives for the talented, see Cohen (1992).

6. I do not suppose that a justification is comprehensive only if it provides determinate reasons to favour a single interpretation. Comprehensiveness is consistent with a degree of indeterminacy. Hence the requirement is for reasons to believe that some interpretations are better than others.

7. One ought to recognise, of course, that the creation of an international humanitarian funding mechanism like the CERF is difficult to achieve without a resolution by the General Assembly, the main representative, deliberative and policymaking organ of the UN, and one that comprises all Members. It is also true that the governing organisation of the CERF incorporates advisory groups with members selected from across the humanitarian community, and that there is a well-established system of transnational political movements and organisations that try to monitor and hold to account the CERF's activities and decision-making. However, this does not mean that the victims of humanitarian emergencies are in any meaningful sense the *joint authors* of the norms, objectives, rules, regulations, codes of practice and standard operating procedures of the international humanitarian system including the CERF. For this to be the case might require the sort of informal and open-ended consultative pro-cesses, equal ability to set the agenda and to choose between alternatives, and systematic chances to become active participants in decision-making that is currently only seen in national or even sub-national democratic systems.

8. For a discussion of the degree to which NGOs do in fact help to create and sustain the institution of international humanitarian aid, see Rubenstein (2009).

9. Information available at <http://ochaonline.un.org/cerf/WhatistheCERF/RapidResponseGrants/tabid/2841/language/en-US/Default.aspx>   (last accessed 16 September 2011).

10. I do not claim that these are the only justifications, merely that they have a prominent place in UN resolutions, OCHA documents and various evaluations of the CERF, some of which were commissioned by OCHA and some undertaken by (I)NGOs. Beyond these justifications, the issue of value for money has been a particular preoccupation of donors since the global financial crises. In March 2011, for example, the Department for International Development (DFID) published its *Multilateral Aid Review* evaluating the value for money of various humanitarian and development institutions from the perspective of UK taxpayers. Value for money was based on two clusters of criteria: first, contribution to UK and international development objectives, including but not limited to whether or not the institution has the objective of responding to humanitarian emergencies

by ensuring that the basic needs of those affected are met, and the extent to which it demonstrates delivery against objectives and contributes to humanitarian results; second, organisational strengths, including but not limited to whether or not the institution is cost and value conscious, its degree of transparency and accountability, and the extent to which it fosters partnership behaviour. Institutions receive a score of between 0 and 4 for each criterion. The review determined the overall value for money provided by the CERF as 'good', scoring it an average of 3.5 for contribution to UK and international development objectives and 2.4 for organisational strengths.

11. Some writers refer to this instead as the Principle of Rescue. See, for example, Nagel (2005: 130–2).

12. The following example is due to Thomas Pogge. '[I]magine an INGO that, with its limited resources, can either build two wells in Ethiopia, providing safe drinking water to 5,000, or else build one well in Chad, providing safe drinking water to 1,000. The former project would protect many more people, but the latter would achieve a fairer distribution of INGO resources across countries because other funds have already been allocated to projects in Ethiopia. If we choose the former project, we can justify to the 1,000 Chadians our neglect of their plight: "We do not have the resources to protect all those as badly off as you are. We must choose where to concentrate our efforts. We have chosen to focus on Ethiopia, because we can protect the most persons there. Had we chosen to protect you instead, we would have protected a much smaller number." But how could we justify to the 5,000 Ethiopians our neglect of their plight, if we choose the latter project? How could we explain to them that we find protecting them less important than protecting 1,000 Chadians who are no worse off than they are?' (Pogge 2007: 232).

13. The key difference here is between ensuring that all marginal funding provided by the CERF is equitable and using available CERF financing in whichever way is necessary in order to address inequity in the distribution of total annual humanitarian funding.

14. Not including the UK.

15. A poll conducted by MoneySavingExpert.com (2010) asked respondents what they would cut if they were chancellor, and 67 per cent of respondents answered that they would cut overseas aid, the highest percentage of nine areas of government spending.

16. For a good introduction to principles of global distributive justice, see Caney (2005).

17. I do not propose that the Principle of Aid is the only principle supported by the Principle of Global Minimal Concern and Respect. Another relevant principle not mentioned so far is the Principle of Harm Avoidance.

According to this principle, actors who intend to provide emergency humanitarian relief around the world should first and foremost do no harm to recipients. See, for example, Anderson (1999) and Barnett and Snyder (2008).

18. For an overview of recent developments, see Abizadeh (2007) and Risse (2012).
19. This idea can also be found in the work of John Rawls, who seeks principles of justice for what he calls 'a cooperative venture for mutual advantage' (1999: 2; 2001: 10).
20. It is far from clear that people who contribute to the CERF are taking part in a scheme of cooperation for mutual benefit, for instance. Some countries are highly unlikely ever to avail of aid, whereas they do regularly give large amounts of money. Other countries give little or nothing but regularly receive aid.
21. Some of these writers point to Rawls's idea of 'profound and pervasive' (1999: 82; 2001: 10) impacts as the source of this theory.
22. This view has some traction in the literature. For example, Norman Daniels (2008: 352) argues that organisations such as the WHO must show equal concern in the distribution of public health expertise and technology by virtue of assuming these distributive responsibilities.
23. Strong Institutionalism sets out only a sufficient condition for triggering principles of global egalitarian justice. It recognises the possibility of other grounds of justice, and so does not stipulate a necessary condition. See also Brown (2009: ch. 5).
24. In other words, the argument is intended to show how the scheme of comprehensive justification could work for those who accept Strong Institutionalism. Of course, those who reject Strong Institutionalism might not accept the Principle of Global Equal Concern and Respect, and consequently may reject the Principle of Impartiality, preferring instead the view that it is not unjust for humanitarian aid to be heavily influenced by political considerations.
25. Whilst I claim that an uneven split of resources between the two funding windows constitutes an unwelcome incentive for dramatising situations to get access to more funds, I do not mean to claim that this incentive would be *eliminated entirely* if the uneven split were abolished. Rather, the suggestion is merely that the incentive to distort would be *lessened* if the share of resources available for ongoing crises were on a par with the share of resources available for sudden-onset emergencies.
26. The OCHA is not alone in its ambivalence towards dealing directly with (I)NGOs. A UK review of humanitarian emergency response commissioned by Andrew Mitchell refers to 'the chaos of coordination of NGOs' (Ashdown 2011: 35).

27. I do not intend to imply here that being equally sensitive to the values
and belief systems of local communities involves permitting local values
and belief systems to trump international humanitarian aims, so that if a
local community happens to care more about saving camels than elders,
then humanitarian agencies are not permitted to save elders rather than
camels. Rather, my claim is that showing equal respect means being duly
sensitive to the values and belief systems of local communities and in ways
that do not unfairly discriminate between communities.

References

Abizadeh, Arash (2007), 'Cooperation, Pervasive Impact, and Coercion: On
the Scope (Not Site) of Distributive Justice', *Philosophy and Public Affairs*,
vol. 35, no. 4, pp. 318–58.

Al-Khalifa, Sheikha (2006), *Comments Made at the UN Launch of the CERF*, New
York, 9 March, quoted by the UN News Centre, 'UN Launches Landmark
Disaster Relief Fund to Speed Up Emergency Assistance', <http://www.
un.org/apps/news/story.asp?NewsID=17748&Cr=disaster&Cr1>   (last
accessed 26 October 2015).

Anderson, Mary (1999), *Do No Harm: How Aid Can Support Peace – Or War*,
Boulder, CO: Lynne Rienner.

Annan, Kofi (2005), *Improvement of the Central Emergency Revolving Fund: Report
of the Secretary-General (A/60/432)*, 20 October, <http://www.iom.int/jahia/
webdav/shared/shared/mainsite/policy_and_research/un/60/A_60_432_
en.pdf> (last accessed 26 October 2015).

Annan, Kofi (2006), *Comments Made at the UN Launch of the CERF*, New York, 9
March, quoted by the UN News Centre, 'UN Launches Landmark Disaster
Relief Fund to Speed Up Emergency Assistance', <http://www.un.org/
apps/news/story.asp?NewsID=17748&Cr=disaster&Cr1> (last accessed 26
October 2015).

Ashdown, Paddy (2011), *Humanitarian Emergency Response Review*, DFID
Publications,   <http://www.dfid.gov.uk/Documents/publications1/HERR.
pdf> (last accessed 26 October 2015).

Asthana, Anushka and Paul Gallagher (2010), 'Department for International
Development Slashes Aid Commitments', *The Observer*, 15 August, <http://
www.guardian.co.uk/society/2010/aug/15/government-slashes-interna-
tional-development-pledges> (last accessed 26 October 2015).

Barber, Martin, Abhijit Bhattacharjee, Roberta M. Lossio and Lewis Sida
(2008), *The Central Emergency Response Fund: Two Year Evaluation (Final
Report)*, <https://docs.unocha.org/sites/dms/Documents/CERF_Two-Year_
Evaluation.pdf> (last accessed 26 October 2015).

Barnett, Michael and Jack Snyder (2008), 'The Grand Strategies of

Humanitarianism', in M. Barnett and T. Weiss (eds), *Humanitarianism in Question*, Ithaca, NY: Cornell University Press, pp. 143–71.

Benn, Hilary (2006), 'Comments at the UN Launch of the CERF', *IRIN News*, 10 March, <http://www.irinnews.org/Report.aspx?ReportId=58395> (last accessed 26 October 2015).

Brown, Alexander (2009), *Ronald Dworkin's Theory of Equality: Domestic and Global Perspectives*, Basingstoke: Palgrave Macmillan.

Calhoun, Craig (2008), 'The Imperative to Reduce Suffering: Charity, Progress, and Emergencies in the Field of Humanitarian Action', in M. Barnett and T. Weiss (eds), *Humanitarianism in Question*, Ithaca, NY: Cornell University Press, pp. 73–97.

Caney, Simon (2005), *Justice Beyond Borders: A Global Political Theory*, Oxford: Oxford University Press.

Channel Research (2011), *5-Year Evaluation of the Central Emergency Response Fund: Synthesis Report (Final Draft)*, <http://www.unicef.org/evaluation/files/5yr-SynthesisFinal-USA-2011-009-1.pdf> (last accessed 26 October 2015).

Cohen, G. A. (1992), 'Incentives, Inequality, and Community', in G. B. Petersen (ed.), *The Tanner Lectures on Human Values: Volume Thirteen*, Salt Lake City: University of Utah Press, pp. 262–329.

Cohen, G. A. (2003), 'Facts and Principles', *Philosophy and Public Affairs*, vol. 31, pp. 211–45.

Cohen, Joshua and Charles Sabel (2006), 'Extra Rempublicam Nulla Justitia?', *Philosophy and Public Affairs*, vol. 34, no. 2, pp. 147–75.

Daniels, Norman (2008), *Just Health: Meeting Health Needs Fairly*, New York: Cambridge University Press.

Department for International Development (2011), *Multilateral Aid Review*, March 2011, <https://www.gov.uk/government/uploads/system/uploads/attachment_data/file/67583/multilateral_aid_review.pdf> (last accessed 27 October 2015).

Egeland, Jan (2006), *Comments Made at the UN Launch of the CERF*, New York, 9 March, quoted by the UN News Centre, 'UN Launches Landmark Disaster Relief Fund to Speed Up Emergency Assistance', <http://www.un.org/apps/news/story.asp?NewsID=17748&Cr=disaster&Cr1> (last accessed 26 October 2015).

Egeland, Jan (2008), 'Progress on the Front Lines', in S. Hidalgo and A. López-Claros (eds), *The Humanitarian Response Index 2007: Measuring Commitment to Best Practice*, Basingstoke: Palgrave Macmillan.

Hopgood, Stephen (2008), 'Saying "No" to Wal-Mart? Money and Morality in Professional Humanitarianism', in M. Barnett and T. Weiss (eds), *Humanitarianism in Question*, Ithaca, NY: Cornell University Press, pp. 98–123.

Mitchell, Andrew (2010a), *Address to the General Assembly of the United Nations*,

20 August, <http://www.un.org/News/Press/docs/2010/ga10969.doc.htm> (last accessed 27 October 2015).

Mitchell, Andrew (2010b), *UN Central Emergency Relief Fund, United Kingdom Parliament Written Answers and Statements,* 16 December, <http://www. theyworkforyou.com/wrans/?id=2010-12-16b.27704.h> (last accessed 27 October 2015).

Mitchell, Andrew (2010c), *Comments Made at the Department for International Development,* London, 29 December, quoted in, 'Britain Accuses G20 Countries of Failing to Contribute to Disaster Relief Fund', *The Observer,* <http://www.theguardian.com/global-development/2010/dec/26/britain-accuses-g20-disaster-relief> (last accessed 26 October 2015).

MoneySavingExpert.com (2010), *If You Were Chancellor What Would You Cut?,* online poll, <http://www.moneysavingexpert.com/poll/19-10-2010/if-you-were-chancellor-whatd-you-cut> (last accessed 27 October 2015).

Nagel, Thomas (2005), 'The Problem of Global Justice', *Philosophy and Public Affairs,* vol. 33, no. 2, pp. 113–47.

Oxfam (2007), *The UN Central Emergency Response Fund One Year On,* Oxfam Briefing Paper no. 100, <https://www.oxfam.org/sites/www.oxfam.org/files/The%20UN%20Central%20%20Emergency%20Fund%20One%20Year%20On.pdf> (last accessed 27 October 2015).

Pogge, Thomas (2007), 'Moral Priorities for International Human Rights NGOs', in D. Bell and J. Coicaud (eds), *Ethics in Action: The Ethical Challenges of International Human Rights Nongovernmental Organizations,* Cambridge: Cambridge University Press, pp. 218–56.

Rawls, John [1971] (1999), *A Theory of Justice: Revised Edition,* Oxford: Oxford University Press.

Rawls, John (2001), *Justice as Fairness: A Restatement,* Cambridge, MA: Harvard University Press.

Risse, Mathias (2012), *The Grounds of Justice: An Inquiry About the State in Global Perspective,* Princeton, NJ: Princeton University Press.

Rubenstein, Jennifer (2007), 'Distribution and Emergency', *The Journal of Political Philosophy,* vol. 15, no. 3, pp. 296–320.

Rubenstein, Jennifer (2008), 'The Distributive Commitments of International NGOs', in M. Barnett and T. Weiss (eds), *Humanitarianism in Question,* Ithaca, NY: Cornell University Press, pp. 215–34.

Rubenstein, Jennifer (2009), 'Humanitarian NGOs' Duties of Justice', *Journal of Social Philosophy,* vol. 40, no. 4, pp. 524–41.

Shah, Anup (2005), 'Media and Natural Disasters', *Global Issues,* 23 October, <http://www.globalissues.org/article/568/media-and-natural-disasters> (last accessed 27 October 2015).

Straw, Will (2010), 'DFID Recommend Slashing 100 Projects to Help the World's Poor', *Left Foot Forward,* 12 August, <http://www.leftfootforward.

org/2010/08/dfid-recommend-slashing-100-projects-to-help-the-worlds-poor> (last accessed 27 October 2015).

Tan, Kok-Chor (2004), *Justice without Borders*, Cambridge: Cambridge University Press.

Terry, Fiona (2002), *Condemned to Repeat? The Paradox of Humanitarian Action*, Ithaca, NY: Cornell University Press.

United Nations General Assembly (1991), Resolution A/RES/46/182, <http://www.un.org/documents/ga/res/46/a46r182.htm> (last accessed 27 October 2015).

United Nations General Assembly (2006), Resolution A/RES/60/124, <http://www.unicef.org/emerg/files/Res_60_124.pdf> (last accessed 27 October 2015).

United Nations Office for the Coordination of Humanitarian Affairs (OCHA) (2010a), *CERF Underfunded Emergencies Window: Procedures and Criteria*, March, <https://docs.unocha.org/sites/dms/CERF/UFE_Guidelines_March_2010_Review_June_2011.pdf> (last accessed 27 October 2015).

United Nations Office for the Coordination of Humanitarian Affairs (OCHA) (2010b), *Analysis of CERF Activities in 2009*, <https://docs.unocha.org/sites/dms/CERF/Analysis_of_CERF_2009_revised.pdf> (last accessed 27 October 2015).

United Nations Secretariat (2010), *Secretary-General's Bulletin: Establishment and Operation of the Central Emergency Response Fund*, ST/SGB/2010/5, New York, 23 April, <http://daccess-dds-ny.un.org/doc/UNDOC/GEN/N10/327/44/PDF/N1032744.pdf?OpenElement> (last accessed 27 October 2015).

Weiss, Thomas (1999), 'Principles, Politics, and Humanitarian Action', *Ethics and International Affairs*, vol. 13, no. 1, pp. 1–22.

Wolff, Jonathan (2009), 'Global Justice and Norms of Co-operation: The "Layers of Justice" View', in S. de Wijze, M. Kramer and I. Carter (eds), *Hillel Steiner and the Anatomy of Justice*, New York: Routledge, pp. 34–53.

Chapter 8

GLOBAL JUSTICE AND THE MISSION OF THE EUROPEAN UNION

Philippe Van Parijs

UNPRECEDENTED ACHIEVEMENT, UNPRECEDENTED CHALLENGES

When we are thinking about how the European Union should evolve, what competences it should be given, what direction it should take, what is the ultimate objective?[1] The answer is simple: justice. But what is justice? Any conception of justice relevant for our times must combine two elements, both strongly rooted in our European traditions, but neither of them exclusive to them: equal respect for the diversity of conceptions of the good life that characterises our pluralist societies and equal concern for the interests of all members, present and yet to come, of the society concerned. This concern, moreover, must be responsibility-sensitive – distributive justice is not a matter of outcomes but of opportunities – and it must be efficiency-sensitive – a fair distribution need not be a strictly equal distribution, but rather one that sustainably maximises the condition of the worst off. Justice, in brief, means real freedom for all, the greatest real freedom for those with least of it.[2]

But who are the 'all' among whom distributive justice requires that real freedom should be distributed fairly? All citizens of our nation-state? All citizens of the European Union? All members of mankind? My answer, here again, is quite simple: 'all' means 'all', 'justice' means 'global justice'. As regards the fair distribution of resources, any distinction made between human beings in terms of which nation they belong to is as ethically unsustainable as are distinctions made in terms of gender or race. This is not to say, however, that nation-states should vanish. But they are sheer tools to be used, not moral entities to be honoured.[3]

It is against this normative background that we need to appreciate both the mind-boggling, unprecedented achievement constituted by this weird political entity now called the European Union, and the frightening, unprecedented challenges it now faces. To appreciate the magnitude of the achievement, just remember John Stuart Mill's persuasive indictment of multinational and especially multilingual democracy. A multinational political entity can live together forever under a despotic regime, Mill wrote. But make it democratic, and it will fall apart, with political borders soon tending to coincide with national borders.[4] And yet we have the European Union, indeed even one that grew much faster than some said it should have done, through the voluntary *Anschluß* of one country after another. True, the process of European integration is imperfect, messy, chaotic, tortuous, frustrating and, many would say, profoundly undemocratic. But once aware of the obstacles, how can you expect the road to be straight? The task of combining respect for our national and linguistic diversity with effective democratic decision-making in the service of justice is daunting. But there is no alternative to getting it done: because it is needed to avoid dramatic social regression for our own people, but also because the European Union offers the closest approximation in the history of the world to the sort of institutional framework we increasingly need at the global level.[5]

WHY INTER-PERSONAL SOLIDARITY NEEDS TO BE EUROPEANISED

Among the many components of this task, none matters more to the sustainable achievement of social justice than the reshaping of the relationship between welfare state institutions and the single European market. The core of the challenge can be outlined as follows.

When discussing the role of the EU in social policy as in any other domain, it makes sense to appeal to the principle of subsidiarity, understood as a rule for ascribing the burden of proof: when there is a choice between two levels of democratic government for the allocation of a particular competence, always start with a presumption in favour of the lower, more decentralised level. Why? For four general reasons. First, opting for the lower level leaves more room for diversity, for experimentation and hence for mutual learning. Second, it makes it possible to have policies more responsive to local objective circumstances.

Third, it makes it possible to have policies more responsive to local preferences, as shaped by the local public debate. Fourth, it makes it possible to make decision-makers more accountable to those who are supposed to benefit from the policies and to pay for them.

In addition, there is a fifth reason that applies specifically to social policy, insofar as it is genuinely redistributive: the lower the level, the more homogeneous the population involved, the greater the political viability of generous redistribution, as a result of greater trust, of greater mutual identification, of greater 'fellow-feeling'. This specific reason but also the last two general reasons are particularly strong when opting for the lower level enables one to function at the level of linguistically more homogeneous populations. This is obviously the case if social policy competences are located at the level of the member states rather than at the level of the EU.[6]

So is the matter settled? Not at all. Because the subsidiarity principle states no more than a presumption, and one that happens to be vulnerable, in this particular case, to a number of considerations which, taken together, call for direct EU involvement in social policy of an unprecedented nature and magnitude. The first of these considerations can be expressed by means of a paradox.[7] What should the EU do in matters of social policy in order to have a maximal impact on the member states' social policies? Just do nothing. Just let the four freedoms – the free movement of labour, capital, goods and services – do their job. Let them make their powerful pressure fully felt through the mutual adjustment of self-interested mobile economic agents and competitiveness-concerned member state governments, helped by a few ruthless decisions by the European Court of Justice.

The same underlying consideration can also be expressed as follows. True, owing to some of the reasons adduced above in support of the subsidiarity principle, the member states constitute a more suitable level than the EU as regards the *political* feasibility of strongly redistributive social policies. But with the four freedoms strongly entrenched and their potential gradually perceived throughout the EU, the *economic* feasibility of generous social policies at that level decreases day by day.[8] This is no doubt something we could and should have anticipated from a brief glance at the United States. The bulk of whatever redistribution there is in the US happens at the federal level, mainly today in the form of solidarity with the elderly (through Social Security and Medicare) and with the working poor (through the Earned Income Tax Credit).

The fact that so little inter-personal redistribution is happening in the US at the level of individual states can safely be attributed, more than to any other factor, to the 'four freedoms' US residents have long enjoyed across states. This strongly suggests that it is high time to question the subsidiarity-based presumption in favour of organising inter-personal solidarity at the national level. Failing to do so may not just drive the generosity of our welfare states down to the American level, which we are so keen to stigmatise. It seems bound to drive us even lower.

THREE MORE REASONS FOR SYSTEMATIC TRANSNATIONAL TRANSFERS

Transnational redistribution is not only needed as a result of intra-national redistribution becoming economically less sustainable. It is also needed as such for three additional reasons, logically independent but mutually reinforcing. First, we need transnational redistribution as an insurance device against the asymmetric shocks and diverging trends to which the member states are subjected in a context in which the single market favours greater sectoral specialisation while globalisation creates permanent uncertainty. Especially in the Eurozone, where the instrument of currency adjustment is no longer available, an automatic stabiliser in the form of transfers from the areas that are more competitive and gain more from globalisation and the single market to the other areas constitutes an intelligent way of buffering risks and thereby enabling member states to take fuller advantage of more integrated markets.[9]

Second, transnational transfers operate as population stabilisers. In the linguistically and culturally more diverse context of the EU, labour migration to the more affluent member states is far more disruptive than it is across state borders in the United States. Therefore, it happens less often and hence fails to play the adjustment role it plays in the US. Therefore too, it should not happen as often. The greater negative externalities of migration in linguistically more diverse Europe make the stabilising role of transnational transfers all the more important.

Third and most fundamentally, EU-wide transnational transfers are increasingly felt to be required directly by social justice. In a context of ever growing transnational trade and mobility, communication and debate, it is becoming increasingly surrealistic to assume that issues of distributive justice can arise only between citizens of the same member state. On the one hand, we are becoming aware of how the EU's very existence, institutional framework and policies affect the material prospects of the citizens of all member states. In addition, Europe's citizens are increasingly involved, individually or through an ever wider range of associations, in an EU-wide conversation, an EU-wide forum of argumentation, contestation and justification, which is less and less reducible to bargaining for mutual benefit among the representatives of the member states to which they belong. It will still take a while before social justice will be self-evidently identified with global justice. But the realisation that it needs to be conceived and pursued at EU level is around the corner.

MINIMUM STANDARDS?

In order to take proper account of these two considerations, I have no doubt that we shall have to go further than the imposition of common minimum standards of social policy to all member states. This is trivially the case for the last three considerations – minimum standards entail no transnational transfers. But it is also the case for the first one – the need to step in for failing intra-national solidarity – because of two difficulties intrinsic to the minimum standards strategy. One goes, in the US discussion, under the label 'unfunded mandates': a higher unit of government cannot legitimately impose a costly duty on lower units, especially the poorer among them, unless it is willing to cover at least part of the cost.

The other difficulty takes the form of a dilemma. Either the standards are quite detailed and therefore in sharp tension with the principle of subsidiarity. Or they remain quite vague, typically in the form of a minimal share of social expenditure in GDP, but they then raise intractable problems once it is realised how important it is that they should capture the 'hidden welfare state' (the implicit transfers embedded in the tax system), disentangle sheer insurance (which involves no ex ante redistribution) from solidarity proper, and address the impact of social policy on the pre-tax-pre-transfer distribution of income.[10]

Against this background, direct involvement of the European Union in the organisation and funding of the most redistributive components of social policy is no longer just a distant dream but an urgent necessity. The necessity may remain a dream, however, if we cannot come up with any practical way of making it happen. Three models are worth thinking about.

MEANS-TESTED EURO-STIPENDIUM?

First, there is the model neatly illustrated by Philippe Schmitter and Michael Bauer's 'Euro-Stipendium' proposal. What they propose, is 'the payment each month of a stipulated amount of Euros to all citizens or legal permanent residents living within the EU whose total earnings amount to less than a third of the average income of everyone living within its borders' (Schmitter and Bauer 2001: 56). Such a proposal amounts to a massive means-tested transfer to all European house-holds below some poverty line. It sounds consonant with the sub-sidiarity principle, at least understood this time as 'Let the lower level try first, and only intervene at the higher level if it fails.' And it clearly addresses head on the need for direct EU involvement stemming from all four considerations spelled out above.

However, leaving out some correctable defects, the Euro-Stipendium proposal suffers from two major flaws. First, its implementation requires a standardised, uniformly implemented notion of income: for example, how is household composition taken into account? Who counts as a member of the household? How is the income of the self-employed assessed? What about income in kind? Should home owner-ship be counted as an implicit income? How vigorously must income from informal economic activity be tracked? The harmonisation of the relevant income notion and its firm and uniform implementation are essential to the legitimacy and hence to the sustainability of the scheme. But they would raise in each member state such sensitive issues that any EU scheme that relies on such a notion is a pipe dream.

Second, it is easy to understand that the design of such a means-tested transnational scheme is intrinsically perverse. Just think of two countries with the same GDP per capita, and suppose that one has a more unequal distribution of disposable income and hence a greater proportion of poor people, say owing to lousy educational and social policies. It is intrinsic to any such scheme that this country will be rewarded for the lousiness of its anti-poverty policies, and the other country punished for its good performance. A scheme that makes net transnational transfers a positive function of the poverty gap is bound to provide both perverse rewards and perverse incentives and hence to be both very unfair and very inefficient.[11]

EU CO-PAYMENT?

One obvious and more familiar alternative is co-payment. It is quite commonly used in countries in which the administration of social assistance is a decentralised – typically municipal – competence, while part of the funding is centralised, precisely to avoid the 'unfunded mandate' problem mentioned above.

This works fine when the more centralised level is firmly in control of most of the other instruments of social policy. But if the co-payment of social assistance is envisaged between the European Union and the member states, very strong, unnecessary and undesirable constraints on the member states' autonomy in designing their own social policies are bound to emerge.

This is the case, first of all, because the European Union will understandably want to have a say on the benefit levels and eligibility conditions of the programmes it co-funds. This is also the case, with far broader implications, because the EU will need to block the member states' understandable temptation to dump onto the co-funded social assistance scheme people who would more usefully be covered by other branches of their transfer system (disability allowances, old age pensions, child support, student grants, employment subsidies, and so on). From the member states' standpoint, these other schemes have the disadvantage of having to be funded exclusively out of their own resources, and shifting some of the cost to the EU level by reducing eligibility to these schemes will be hard to resist. To keep such moral hazard under check, active EU regulation throughout the social policy realm will be required, at the expense of the considerations that support the subsidiarity principle.

UNIVERSAL EURO-DIVIDEND?

Is there an alternative? Yes, there is: what could be called a *Euro-dividend*, a modest universal basic income paid to all legal residents of the European Union and entirely funded at EU level, which can be topped up at will at a national or sub-national level by other universal benefits, by a means-tested and conditional social assistance scheme and of course by a social insurance system.[12]

The level need not be uniform across the Union. It can reflect differences in purchasing power (not in GDP per capita, which would amount to cancelling the transnational redistributive effect). The funding must be centralised, but it should definitely not consist, for the reasons hinted at above, in an EU-wide personal income tax. VAT is a more appropriate instrument or, more innovatively, a 'super-Tobin' tax on *all* electronic transactions. Moreover, an energy or carbon tax could provide part of the funding, as could the phasing out of agricultural policy transfers, possibly also of social and structural funds, for which the Euro-dividend would provide a partial substitute.[13] A gradual introduction is conceivable, but the steps should not consist in income categories, regions or sectors, but in age groups. One could envisage a universal basic pension, as already exists in some member states, or perhaps more sensibly given the demographic situation of the EU, in the form of an EU-wide child benefit.[14]

No need here to find a uniform definition of disposable or taxable income. No perverse incentives for the nation-states' anti-poverty programmes. And no unnecessary restriction of the member states' room for innovation or adjustment to local conditions and preferences. Far from imposing top-down a mega welfare state, a firm common floor for the most redistributive dimension of social policy keeps fiscal competition and social dumping under check and thereby allows each member state to maintain and improve its own preferred version of the welfare state. As an antidote to the race to the bottom, this bottom-up conception of an active social Europe is fully compatible with subsidiarity properly understood.

Far more would need to be said about how much readjustment in the other components of the welfare state this third model of direct EU involvement would require; about how it would handle migration, legal and illegal, from outside the EU; about how a universal basic income approach can be viewed as a central component of the so-called active welfare state in its emancipatory (as opposed to repressive) version; and about how it fits into a conception of distributive justice as real freedom for all.[15] My point here is only to explain why the basic income proposal is so important if one is to meet the need for an inter-personal transfer system at a supra-national level. However urgent this need and however neatly a universal Euro-dividend would meet it, however, the latter may still make little sense because of being politically out of reach.

POLITICAL FEASIBILITY

Is such an ambitious model of EU-level social policy politically feasible? Definitely not now. But this is not the end of the story. It is a call for sharp thinking and resolute action in order to make possible what is indispensable. First of all, we need a thicker European civil society. There are already far more people active in Brussels because of the presence of the EU's institutions without working for them than there are Eurocrats in the strict sense. We need more of them. We need stronger EU-wide social partners, more and stronger EU-wide associations and lobbies of all sorts which weave together all layers of EU society, not just the economic, political and cultural elite, and enable people across Europe to understand each other, identify with each other and mobilise together. An active social Europe will only come about if it can be 'bottom-up' in this sense, too.

Next, we need electoral institutions at EU level that make it rewarding to construct and publicly defend the general interest of the European population as a whole.[16] We might think, as some have proposed, of a direct election of the President of the European Commission or of the European Council. But there is no need to ape the United States. With our national cleavages and parliamentary traditions, a different option is preferable: the election of some small percentage of the members of the European Parliament in a single EU-wide constituency, combined with an increase in the specifically European stakes of the EU parliamentary elections, for example by making the choice of the President of the European Commission depend on the electoral scores in this constituency.[17]

Third, we need a thorough democratisation of competence in one single lingua franca, which will – need I say – be English. One of the key conditions for a viable generous social policy beyond the level of a nation-state is a lively democratic forum, and hence an ability to communicate conveniently and mobilise effectively across borders. This ability must be widely shared by all classes of citizens, not only the rich and powerful who can afford the wonderful but expensive help of interpreters and translators. Only the learning of a common language can achieve this. If we want to circumvent Mill's indictment of multinational and especially multilingual democracy, if we want to enable the EU to do what it needs to do, we need to accelerate the acquisition and appropriation of English as a second language throughout the European continent. The satisfaction of this third condition is essential for the first two to produce their full impact. It is bound to produce some undesirable side effects, which need to be identified and addressed. But the ability to communicate cheaply and effectively through a shared language will be as essential to the mobilization that will produce EU-wide institutionalised solidarity as it was to the mobilisation that produced our national welfare states.[18]

All this makes for many tasks ahead, both intellectual and political. Too many, some may feel inclined to say, and too tough. Yet, there is no option but to take them on. There will be hesitations, standstills, probably even serious regressions owing to the conditions just mentioned not being sufficiently met. But the direction should be clear, in the general interest of all us Europeans, but also as an essential step in the learning process that will yield the institutions we need on the world level: in order to make minimally fair and efficient collective decisions, in order to forestall deadly wars for increasingly scarce resources, indeed in order to make human life on earth sustainable. This is the immodest mission of the EU's unprecedented experiment. There is no time to waste. *Avanti!*

Notes

1. Early versions of the core ideas of this text were presented under the title 'Bottom-up Social Europe' at the Conference on The Future of European Social Policy organised by the Finnish Presidency of the European Union (Helsinki, 10 November 2006) and at the seminar on 'Basic Income: A Concept for Decent Living and Working Conditions for Everyone' organised by the green group in the European Parliament (Brussels, 3 July 2007).
2. The conception of justice expounded and defended in my book *Real Freedom for All* (1995) corresponds to just one way of satisfying these desiderata. Other 'liberal egalitarian' conceptions of justice include those proposed by John Rawls (1971), Ronald Dworkin (2000) and Amartya Sen (2009).
3. I spell this out in Van Parijs (2007) and chapter 1 of Van Parijs (2011b).
4. See the famous chapter 16 ('On Nationality') of his 'Considerations on Representative Government' (Mill [1861] 1991).
5. For this reason, the most important and most specific contribution the European Union can make to global justice is not through its development aid programme, nor even through its contribution to fair deals in matters of climate change or international trade, but by gradually constructing the

socio-economic and political institutions which are required by the pursuit of social justice on a scale that does not match that of a nation-state.

6. See the essays collected in Van Parijs (2004).

7. See Välimäki (2006: 275): 'The following of the subsidiarity principle has also implied that the member states have not actively promoted the social dimension of the Union. This has created a paradox. The EU influences member states' policies more through the internal market than expected. If the member states were interested in strengthening EU social policy, the EU's impact on the member states' systems would be less.'

8. The fact that no race to the bottom is detectable so far when looking at shares of social expenditure in GDP should not mislead us. There is no reason to expect the bulky and swelling mass of earnings-related old age pensions to be under strong pressure. But the genuinely redistributive part of the welfare states is, as shown for example in falling ratios of benefits to earnings (Obinger 2005).

9. Since I first wrote this passage, as part of my 2006 keynote lecture in Helsinki, its relevance has been made considerably more salient by the 'Greek crisis' and the subsequent crisis of the euro. The fifty US states have been able to cope happily with huge divergences for decennia despite their inability to adjust through the devaluation of distinct currencies. The fundamental reason is that the impacts of these divergences on the states' per capita incomes and public budgets are systematically buffered by two mechanisms: inter-state migration and the massive tax-and-transfer system practically entirely organised, as mentioned before, at the federal level. As the first of these mechanisms is bound to remain more modest and/or more problematic in the EU context (for reasons explained in the next paragraph), there is no way in which the Eurozone can avoid permanent havoc without a transnational transfer system even more developed (though far simpler) than what exists at the federal level in the US.

10. Standards of this sort have been proposed for example by Fritz Scharpf. See the discussion in Scharpf (2000) and Van Parijs (2000).

11. For discussion, see Schmitter and Bauer (2001), Van Parijs and Vanderborght (2001), Matsaganis (2001), Bauer and Schmitter (2001) and Howard (2006).

12. See Genet and Van Parijs (1992), Van Parijs (1996), Van Parijs (2013) and Vanderborght and Van Paris (2001). The oldest known formulation of such a proposal at EU level can be found in a 1975 report to the European Parliament's Economic and Monetary Affairs Committee by the British MEP Sir Brandon Rhys Williams. One key component of the 'European social contract' he there proposes would consist in bringing into line all the basic welfare systems of the community, as a way of removing one

powerful barrier to the free movement of workers and their families. A first step could be made with a unified community-wide child benefit system (which individual countries would be free to top up). 'A further step forward would include a full-scale tax-credit system incorporating a structure of positive personal allowances as a feature of the community tax system.' Such a basic income system, in his view, has two advantages that are particularly relevant in the European context. First, it would 'provide an opportunity to carry through a regional policy at personal level, since it would [. . .] carry purchasing power outwards from the centres of wealth to the districts and even into the houses where incomes are below the average'. Second, 'it would help to raise the incomes of farmers with low earnings without interfering with the prices of their products', and thus provide a partial alternative to the Common Agricultural Policy. He concludes: 'The European Social Contract must combine the benefits of security and unity afforded to the citizens of communist societies with the personal freedom and self-respect which are the best characteristics of the property-owning democracies' (quoted in *Basic Income*, no. 4, Spring 1989, available at <http://www.basicincome.org/bien/pdf/BI4.pdf>, last accessed 27 February 2016).

13. Along these lines, see Genet and Van Parijs (1992) and Schmitter and Bauer (2001), respectively.

14. A warm supporter of moves towards a basic income in national contexts, Anthony Atkinson (1996) has been arguing that basic income 'has particular salience in the European Union, where it can provide a secure foundation for a Europe-wide minimum income', beginning with a basic income for children pitched at a level related to the general income level of each country. See his restatement of this proposal of an 'EU-wide child basic income' in Atkinson (2015: 222–3).

15. See Van Parijs and Vanderborght (2017) for a comprehensive treatment.

16. These points are further developed in Van Parijs (2015) and Van Paris (2016).

17. More generally, having part of the Parliament's seats allocated on a polity-wide constituency is arguably a necessary condition for the smooth running of a parliamentary democracy in a polity deeply divided along territorial lines. See Deschouwer and Van Parijs (2010) and Van Parijs (2011a: esp. chs 5, 9, 10).

18. In chapter 1 of Van Parijs (2011b), I make the case of a single lingua franca, and in the subsequent chapters I discuss at length the issues of justice its adoption gives rise to.

References

Atkinson, Anthony B. (1996), 'The Distribution of Income: Evidence, Theories and Policy', *De Economist*, vol. 144, no. 1, pp. 1–21.

Atkinson, Anthony B. (2015), *Inequality: What Can Be Done?*, Cambridge, MA: Harvard University Press.

Bauer, Michael W. and Philippe Schmitter (2001), 'Dividend, Birth-Grant or Stipendium?', *Journal of European Social Policy*, vol. 11, no. 4, pp. 348–52.

Deschouwer, Kris and Philippe Van Parijs (2010), *Electoral Engineering for a Stalled Federation*, Re-Bel e-book no. 5, Brussels: The Re-Bel initiative, <http://www.rethinkingbelgium.eu/rebel-initiative-files/ebooks/ebook-4/Re-Bel-e-book-4.pdf> (last accessed 26 October 2015).

Dworkin, Ronald (2000), *Sovereign Virtue: The Theory and Practice of Equality*, Cambridge, MA: Harvard University Press.

Genet, Michel and Philippe Van Parijs (1992), 'Eurogrant', *Basic Income Research Group Bulletin*, no. 15, pp. 4–7.

Howard, Michael (2006), 'A NAFTA Dividend: A Proposal for a Guaranteed Minimum Income for North America', *Basic Income Studies*, vol. 2, no. 1, pp. 1–23.

Matsaganis, Manos (2001), 'The Trouble with the Euro-Stipendium', *Journal of European Social Policy*, vol. 11, no. 4, pp. 346–8.

Mill, John Stuart [1861] (1991), 'Considerations on Representative Government', in *On Liberty and Other Essays*, ed. J. Gray, Oxford: Oxford University Press, pp. 203–467.

Obinger, Herbert (2005), 'The Dual Convergence of Welfare States', paper presented at the Center for European Studies, Harvard University, 9 February.

Rawls, John (1971), *A Theory of Justice*, Cambridge, MA: Harvard University Press.

Scharpf, Fritz (2000), 'Basic Income and Social Europe', in R. J. van der Veen and L. Groot (eds), *Basic Income on the Agenda*, Amsterdam: Amsterdam University Press, pp. 154–60.

Schmitter, Philippe and Michael W. Bauer (2001), 'A (Modest) Proposal for Expanding Social Citizenship in the European Union', *Journal of European Social Policy*, vol. 11, no. 1, pp. 55–65.

Sen, Amartya (2009), *The Idea of Justice*, Cambridge, MA: Harvard University Press.

Välimäki, Kari (2006), 'Seeking a New Balance', in J. Saari (ed.), *The Europeanization of Social Protection: The Political Responses of Eleven Member States*, Helsinki: Ministry of Social Affairs and Health, pp. 261–77.

Van Parijs, Philippe (1995), *Real Freedom for All: What (If Anything) Can Justify Capitalism?*, Oxford: Oxford University Press.

Van Parijs, Philippe (1996), 'Basic Income and the Two Dilemmas of the Welfare State', *The Political Quarterly*, vol. 67, no. 1, pp. 63–6.

Van Parijs, Philippe (2000), 'Basic Income at the Heart of Social Europe? Reply to Fritz Scharpf', in R. J. van der Veen and L. Groot (eds), *Basic Income on the Agenda*, Amsterdam: Amsterdam University Press, pp. 161–9.

Van Parijs, Philippe (ed.) (2004), *Cultural Diversity versus Economic Solidarity*, Brussels: De Boeck, <http://www.uclouvain.be/en-12569> (last accessed 26 October 2015).

Van Parijs, Philippe (2007), 'International Distributive Justice', in R. Goodin, P. Pettit and T. Pogge (eds), *The Blackwell's Companion to Contemporary Political Philosophy*, vol. II, Oxford: Blackwell, pp. 638–52.

Van Parijs, Philippe (2011a), *Just Democracy: The Rawls-Machiavelli Programme*, Colchester: ECPR Press.

Van Parijs, Philippe (2011b), *Linguistic Justice for Europe and for the World*, Oxford: Oxford University Press.

Van Parijs, Philippe (2013), 'The Euro-Dividend', in R. Bellamy and U. Staiger (eds), *The Eurozone Crisis and the Democratic Deficit*, London: University College London European Institute, pp. 16–17; also in *Roadmap to a Social Europe*, Brussels: European Trade Union Confederation (2013), pp. 44–6.

Van Parijs, Philippe (2015), 'Epilogue: Justifying Europe', in L. van Middelaar and P. Van Parijs (eds), *After the Storm. How to Save Democracy in Europe*, Tielt: Lannoo, 247–61.

Van Parijs, Philippe (2016), 'Demos-cracy for the European Union. Why and How', in L. Cabrera and T. Pogge (eds), *Institutional Cosmopolitanism*, Oxford: Oxford University Press.

Van Parijs, Philippe and Yannick Vanderborght (2001), 'From Euro-stipendium to Euro-dividend', *Journal of European Social Policy*, vol. 11, no. 4, pp. 342–6.

Van Parijs, Philippe and Yannick Vanderborght (2017), *Basic Income. A Radical Proposal for a Free Society and a Sane Economy*, Cambridge, MA: Harvard University Press.

INDEX

210

EU representative:
Easy Access System Europe
Mustamäe tee 50, 10621 Tallinn, Estonia
Gpsr.requests@easproject.com

www.ingramcontent.com/pod-product-compliance
Lightning Source LLC
Chambersburg PA
CBHW070415270326
41926CB00014B/2815